THE *unofficial* GUIDE®
ᴛᴏDisneyland®
2006

THE *unofficial* GUIDE®
to Disneyland*

2006

BOB SEHLINGER

* Disneyland® is officially known as the Disneyland Resort®

WILEY

Please note that prices fluctuate in the course of time, and travel information changes under the impact of many factors that influence the travel industry. We therefore suggest that you write or call ahead for confirmation when making your travel plans. Every effort has been made to ensure the accuracy of information throughout this book, and the contents of this publication are believed correct at the time of printing. Nevertheless, the publishers cannot accept responsibility for errors or omissions or for changes in details given in this guide or for the consequences of any reliance on the information provided by the same. Assessments of attractions and so forth are based upon the author's own experience, and, therefore, descriptions given in this guide necessarily contain an element of subjective opinion, which may not reflect the publisher's opinion or dictate a reader's own experience on another occasion. Readers are invited to write the publisher with ideas, comments, and suggestions for future editions.

Published by:
John Wiley & Sons, Inc.
111 River Street
Hoboken, NJ 07030

Produced by Menasha Ridge Press

Cover design by Michael J. Freeland

Interior design by Vertigo Design

Photo credit: Disneyland® Resort

For information on our other products and services or to obtain technical support please contact our Customer Care Department within the U.S. at ☎ 800-762-2974, outside the United States at ☎ 317-572-3993, or fax 317-572-4002.

Wiley also publishes its books in a variety of electronic formats. Some content that appears in print may not be available in electronic formats.

ISBN 0-7645-8342-5

Manufactured in the United States of America
    5 4 3 2

CONTENTS

LIST *of* MAPS *and* ILLUSTRATIONS

ACKNOWLEDGMENTS

SPECIAL THANKS TO OUR FIELD RESEARCH TEAM who rendered a Herculean effort in what must have seemed like a fantasy version of Sartre's No Exit to the tune of "It's a Small World." We hope you all recover to tour another day.

Peals of laughter and much appreciation to nationally renowned cartoonist Tami Knight for her brilliant and insightful work.

Gabriela Oates, Molly Merkle, Steve Jones, Annie Long, Marie Hillin, and Christina Crowe all energetically contributed to shaping this latest edition. Betsy Amster provided invaluable counsel regarding the organization of the guide. Psychologists Dr. Karen Turnbow, Dr. Gayle Janzen, and Dr. Joan Burns provided much insight concerning the experiences of young children at Disneyland.

Many thanks also to Carla Stec for editorial work on this book. Cartography was provided by Steve Jones, and the index was prepared by Ann Cassar.

—Bob Sehlinger

INTRODUCTION

WHY "UNOFFICIAL"?

DECLARATION OF INDEPENDENCE

THE AUTHOR AND RESEARCHERS of this guide specifically and categorically declare that they are and always have been totally independent of the Walt Disney Company, Inc., of Disneyland, Inc., of Walt Disney World, Inc., and of any and all other members of the Disney corporate family.

The material in this guide originated with the authors and researchers and has not been reviewed, edited, or in any way approved by the Walt Disney Company, Inc., Disneyland, Inc., or Walt Disney World, Inc.

This guidebook represents the first comprehensive *critical* appraisal of Disneyland. Its purpose is to provide the reader with the information necessary to tour the theme parks with the greatest efficiency and economy and with the least amount of hassle and standing in line. The researchers of this guide believe in the wondrous variety, joy, and excitement of the Disney attractions. At the same time, we realistically recognize that Disneyland is a business, with the same profit motivations as businesses all over the world.

In this, the "unofficial," guide, we have elected to represent and serve you, the reader. The contents were researched and compiled by a team of evaluators who were, and are, completely independent of the Walt Disney Company, Inc. If a restaurant serves bad food, if a gift item is overpriced, or if a certain ride isn't worth the wait, we can say so; in the process, we hope we can make your visit more fun, efficient, and economical.

DANCE TO THE MUSIC

A DANCE HAS A BEGINNING and an end. But when you're dancing you're not concerned about getting to the end or where on the dance floor you might wind up. In other words, you're totally in the moment. That's the way you should be on your Disneyland vacation.

You may feel a bit of pressure concerning your vacation. Vacations, after all, are very special events, and expensive ones to boot. So you work hard to make your vacation the best that it can be. Planning and organizing are essential to a successful Disneyland vacation, but if they become your focus, you won't be able to hear the music and enjoy the dance.

So think of us as your dancing coach. We'll teach you the steps to the dance in advance so that when you're on vacation and the music plays, you will dance with effortless grace and ease.

THE IMPORTANCE OF BEING GOOFY

THE DISNEY PR DIRECTOR LOOKED UP from a report about Villains smoking on the character bus to find Peter Waters nervously standing in his office.

"Peter, what's wrong?"

"Well, sir, it's Mickey. We have a situation . . . It's bad."

"What? Another situation? I haven't gotten over Grumpy's identity crisis. Remember? He ate some mushrooms and thought he was Tinkerbell . . . tried to put the moves on Hercules. They're both still in therapy."

"Actually sir, this could be worse. Our biggest fear about Mickey Mouse after he turned 70 was that he'd begin showing signs of old age. Children might not respond well to a giant balding mouse with thick-rimmed glasses yelling at everyone because he's hard of hearing."

The director had a bad feeling about what was coming next. Images of leaky Depends, hair-plug surgeries gone astray, and dentures falling into the buffet at Chef Mickey's flashed through his mind. Peter had his full attention.

"We were thinking the complete opposite of what's happened. It turns out that mice age very differently. At the ripe old age of 70, Mickey has just hit puberty."

The director leaped up, knocking his chair over. "What? You're kidding? That's wonderful news! This means Mickey will outlive us all. So what's the crisis?"

"Umm . . ., sir, Mickey's voice is changing. His trademark eerily high voice is dissolving into a deep baritone. Yesterday at the character breakfast, his deep, booming voice made the children cry. A preacher among the guests thought he was possessed!"

Panic, then determination, swept over the director. "What are you doing about this?" he asked.

"We've already tried several things but nothing's worked. We're about out of ideas."

"Well, Peter, tell me what you've tried?"

"The first plan was to hire someone to do a voice-over. After an exhaustive search, we found the perfect match. We hired Mike Tyson."

"Are you kidding? The boxer? Surely he doesn't possess a voice like Mickey's."

"Please sir, don't say 'possess'. Tyson may be violent and look pumped up on steroids, but when he opens that mouth, his voice is like Tweety Bird . . . high-pitched and sweet. Things were actually going pretty well with Mike until we had this little incident."

"Explain yourself."

"Sir, the first practice session went perfectly; Mike sounded just like Mickey. However, during the lunch break at the second practice things got ugly. An assistant poured Tyson a double espresso. He got all jumpy and wound up and bit Pluto's ear. When Pluto threatened legal action, corporate counsel decided that it's just too much of a risk to bring in an outsider. So we've had to drop the voice-over idea."

"Our next strategy involved the tech team creating a device that Mickey talked through, which transformed his baritone back to the familiar high-pitched chirp. However, there were complications."

"Uh huh, I'll bet there were. Like what, pray tell."

"Unfortunately, the team could not isolate the right pitch frequency to filter Mickey's voice. When they tried the device at a press conference yesterday, Mickey's voice came through so high that it shattered six windows and the Wicked Witch's mirror. Flying glass nicked Michael Eisner's furrowed brow and Arial took a direct hit to her dorsal fin. When the team attempted to adjust the device, Mickey sounded like Darth Vader on helium. But sir, we haven't given up. We've got one idea left. We call it our 'nuclear option,' but it's pretty much a sure thing."

"Peter, I'm afraid to ask."

"Well, sir, tomorrow we're taking Mickey to the Urologist . . ."

And so it goes . . .

What really makes writing about Disneyland fun is that the Disney people take everything so seriously. Day to day, they debate momentous decisions with far-ranging consequences: Will Goofy look swishy in a silver cape? Have we gone too far with the Little Mermaid's cleavage? At a time when the nation is concerned about the drug problem, should we have a dwarf named "Dopey"?

Unofficially, we think having a sense of humor is important. This guidebook has one, and it's probably necessary that you do, too—not to use this book, but to have fun at Disneyland. Disneyland is among tourist destinations what New York is among cities: big, complex, and intimidating. A certain amount of levity is required simply to survive. Think of the Unofficial Guide as a private trainer to help get your sense of humor in shape. It will help you understand the importance of being Goofy.

The Death of Spontaneity

One of our all-time favorite letters is from a man in Chapel Hill, North Carolina. He writes:

> *Your book reads like the operations plan for an amphibious landing . . . Go here, do this, proceed to Step 15. . . . You must think that everyone [who visits Disneyland] is a hyperactive, type-A, theme-park commando. What happened to the satisfaction of self-discovery or the joy of spontaneity? Next you will be telling us when to empty our bladders.*

As it happens, we at the *Unofficial Guide* are a pretty existential crew. We are big on self-discovery when walking in the woods or watching birds. Some of us are able to improvise jazz without reading music, while others can whip up a mean pot of chili without a recipe. When it comes to Disneyland, however, we all agree that you either need a good plan or a frontal lobotomy. The operational definition of self-discovery and spontaneity at Disneyland is the "pleasure" of heat prostration and the "joy" of standing in line.

It's easy to spot the free spirits at Disneyland Park and Disney's California Adventure, particularly at opening time. While everybody else is stampeding to Splash Mountain or Indiana Jones, they are the ones standing in a cloud of dust puzzling over the park map. Later, they are the people running around like chickens in a thunderstorm trying to find an attraction with less than a 40-minute wait. Face it, Disneyland Resort is not a very existential place. In many ways it's the quintessential system, the ultimate in mass-produced entertainment, the most planned and programmed environment imaginable. Spontaneity and self-discovery work about as well at Disneyland as they do on your tax return.

We're not saying you can't have a great time at Disneyland. Bowling isn't very spontaneous either, but lots of people love it. What we *are* saying is that you need a plan. You don't have to be compulsive or inflexible about it, just think about what you want to do before you go. Don't delude yourself by rationalizing that the information in this modest tome is only for the pathological and superorganized. Ask not for whom the tome tells, Bubba; it tells for thee.

HOW *this* GUIDE WAS RESEARCHED *and* WRITTEN

WHILE MUCH HAS BEEN WRITTEN concerning Disneyland Resort, very little has been comparative or evaluative. In preparing this guide, nothing was taken for granted. The theme parks were visited at different times throughout the year by a team of trained observers who conducted detailed evaluations, rating the theme parks along with all of their component rides, shows, exhibits, services, and concessions according to a formal, pretested rating criteria. Interviews with attraction patrons were conducted to determine what tourists of all age groups enjoyed most and least during their Disneyland visit.

Although our observers are independent and impartial, we do not claim special expertise or scientific background relative to the types of exhibits, performances, or attractions viewed. Like you, we visit the Disneyland Parks as tourists, noting our satisfaction or dissatisfaction. Disneyland offerings are marketed to the touring public, and it is as the public that we have experienced them.

The primary difference between the average tourist and the trained evaluator is that the latter approaches attractions equipped with professional skills in organization, preparation, and observation. The trained evaluator is responsible for much more than simply observing and cataloging. While the tourist is being entertained and delighted by the *Enchanted Tiki Room,* the professional evaluator seated nearby is rating the performance in terms of theme, pace, continuity, and originality. The evaluator is also checking out the physical arrangements: Is the sound system clear and audible without being overpowering; is the audience shielded from the sun or rain; is seating adequate; can everyone in the audience clearly see the stage? Similarly, detailed and relevant checklists are prepared by observer teams and applied to rides, exhibits, concessions, and to the theme park in general. Finally, observations and evaluator ratings are integrated with audience reactions and the opinions of patrons, to compile a comprehensive quality profile of each feature and service.

In compiling this guide, we recognize the fact that a tourist's age, gender, background, and interests will strongly influence his or her taste in Disneyland offerings and will account for his or her preference of one ride or feature over another. Given this fact, we make no attempt at comparing apples with oranges. How, indeed, could a meaningful comparison be made between the serenity and beauty of the Storybook Land Canal Boats and the wild roller coaster ride of California Screamin'? Instead, our objective is to provide the reader with a critical evaluation and enough pertinent data to make knowledgeable decisions according to individual tastes.

The essence of this guide, then, consists of individual critiques and descriptions of each feature of the Disneyland parks, supplemented with some maps to help you get around and several detailed touring plans to help you avoid bottlenecks and crowds. Because so many Disneyland guests also visit Universal Studios Hollywood, we have included comprehensive coverage and a touring plan for that park as well.

A WORD TO OUR READERS ABOUT ANNUAL REVISIONS

SOME OF YOU WHO purchase each new edition of the *Unofficial Guide* have chastised us for retaining examples, comments, and descriptions from previous years' editions. This letter from a Grand Rapids, Michigan, reader is typical:

> *Your guidebook still has the same little example stories. When I got my [new] book I expected a true update and new stuff, not the same-old, same-old!*

First, the *Unofficial Guide* is a reference work. Though we are flattered that some readers read the guide from cover to cover, and that some of you find it entertaining, our objective is fairly straightforward: to provide information that enables you to have the best-possible Disneyland vacation.

Each year during our revision research, we check every attraction, restaurant, hotel, shop, and entertainment offering. Although there are many changes, much remains the same from year to year. When we profile and critique an attraction, we try to provide the reader with the most insightful, relevant, and useful information, written in the clearest possible language. It is our opinion that if an attraction does not change, then it makes little sense to risk clarity and content for the sake of freshening up the prose. Disneyland guests who try the Mad Tea Party, the Haunted Mansion, or the Matterhorn Bobsleds today, for example, experience the same presentation as guests who visited Disneyland in 2002, 1990, or 1986. Moreover, according to our extensive patron surveys (about 1,000 each year), today's guests still respond to these attractions in the same way as prior-year patrons.

The bottom line: we believe that our readers are better served if we devote our time to that which is changing and new as opposed to that which remains the same. The success or failure of this *Unofficial Guide* is determined not by the style of the writing but by the accuracy of the information and, ultimately, whether you have a positive experience at Disneyland. Every change to the guide we make (or don't make) is evaluated in this context.

WE GOT ATTITUDE

SOME READERS DISAGREE about our attitude toward Disney. One, a 30-something woman from Golden, Colorado, lambasted us, writing:

> *I read your book cover to cover and felt you were way too hard on Disney. It's disappointing, when you're all enthused about going, to be slammed with all these criticisms and possible pitfalls.*

A reader from Little Rock, Arkansas, also took us to task, commenting:

> *Your book was quite complimentary of Disney, perhaps too complimentary. Maybe the free trips you travel writers get at Disney World are chipping away at your objectivity.*

And from a Williamsport, Pennsylvania, mother of three:

> *Reading your book irritated me before we went because of all the warnings and cautions. I guess I'm used to having guidebooks pump*

me up about where I'm going. But once I arrived I found I was fully prepared and we had a great time. In retrospect, I have to admit you were right on the money. What I regarded as you being negative was just a good dose of reality.

A Vienna, Virginia, family chimed in with this:

After being at Disney for three days at the height of tourist season, I laughed out loud at your "The Death of Spontaneity" section. We are definitely free-spirit types who don't like to plan our days when we are on vacation. A friend warned us, and we got your guidebook. After skimming through it before we left, I was terrified that we had made a terrible mistake booking this vacation. Thanks to your book, we had a wonderful time. If it had not been for the book, we definitely would have been trampled by all the people stampeding to Space Mountain while we were standing there with our maps.

Finally, a reader from Phoenixville, Pennsylvania, prefers no opinions at all, writing:

Although each person has the right to his or her own opinion, I did not purchase the book for an opinion.

For the record, we've always paid our own way at Disneyland Resort: hotels, admissions, meals, the works. We don't dislike Disney, and we most definitely don't have an ax to grind. We're positive by nature and much prefer to praise than to criticize. Personally, we have enjoyed the Disney parks immensely over the years, both experiencing them and writing about them. Disney, however, as with all corporations (and all people, for that matter), is better at some things than others. Because our readers shell out big bucks to go to Disneyland, we believe they have the right to know in advance what's good and what's not. For those who think we're overly positive, please understand that *The Unofficial Guide to Disneyland* is a guidebook, not an exposé. Our overriding objective is for you to enjoy your visit. To that end we try to report fairly and objectively. When readers disagree with our opinions, we, in the interest of fairness and balance, publish their point of view right alongside ours. To the best of our knowledge, the *Unofficial Guides* are the only travel guides in print that do this.

The Sum of All Fears

Every writer who expresses an opinion is quite accustomed to readers who strongly agree or disagree. It comes with the territory. Troubling in the extreme, however, is the possibility that our efforts to be objective have frightened some readers away from Disneyland, or stimulated in others a state of apprehension. For the record, if you enjoy theme parks, Disneyland and Walt Disney World are as good as it gets: absolute nirvana. They're upbeat, safe, fun, eye-popping, happy, and exciting. Even if you arrive knowing nothing about the place and make every possible touring mistake, chances are about 90% that you'll have a wonderful time anyway. In the end, guidebooks don't make or break great destinations. They are simply tools to help you enhance your experience and get the most vacation for your money.

As wonderful as Disneyland is, however, it is nevertheless a complex destination. Even so, it's certainly not nearly as challenging or difficult as visiting New York, San Francisco, Paris, Acapulco, or any other large city or destination. And, happily, there are numerous ways, if forewarned, to save money, minimize hassle, and make the most of your time. In large measure, that's what this guide is about: giving you a heads-up regarding potential problems or opportunities. Unfortunately, some folks reading the *Unofficial Guide* unconsciously add up the various warnings and critical advice and conclude that Disneyland is altogether too intimidating or, alternatively, too expensive or too much work. They lose track of the wonder of Disneyland and become focused instead on what might go wrong.

Our philosophy is that knowledge is power (and time, and money, too). You're free to follow our advice or not at your sole discretion. But you'd be denied the opportunity to exercise that discretion if we failed to fairly present the issues.

With or without a guidebook, you'll have a great time at Disneyland. If you let us, we'll help you smooth the potential bumps. We are certain that we can help you turn a great vacation into an absolutely superb one. Either way, once there, you'll get the feel of the place and quickly reach a comfort level that will allay your apprehensions and allow you to have a great experience.

The Unofficial Guide Publishing Year

We receive many queries each year asking when the next edition of the *Unofficial Guide* will be available. Usually our new editions are published and available in the stores by late August or early September. Thus the 2007 edition will be on the shelves in the autumn of 2006.

LETTERS, COMMENTS, AND QUESTIONS FROM READERS

MANY OF THOSE who use *The Unofficial Guide to Disneyland* write to us asking questions, making comments, or sharing their own strategies for visiting Disneyland. We appreciate all such input, both positive and critical, and encourage our readers to continue writing. Readers' comments and observations are frequently used in revised editions of this *Unofficial Guide,* and have contributed immeasurably to its improvement.

Reader Questionnaire

At the back of this guide is a short questionnaire you can use to express opinions about your Disneyland Resort visit. The questionnaire is designed to allow every member of your party, regardless of age, to tell us what he or she thinks. Clip the questionnaire on the dotted lines and mail it to:

Reader Survey
The Unofficial Guide to Disneyland
P.O. Box 43673
Birmingham, AL 35243

If you write us or return our reader-survey form, you can rest assured that we won't release your name and address to any mailing-list companies, direct-mail advertisers, or other third party. Unless you instruct us otherwise, we will assume that you do not object to being quoted in a future edition.

How to Contact the Author

Write to Bob Sehlinger, care of *The Unofficial Guide to Disneyland* at the above address, or e-mail **UnofficialGuides@menasharidge.com.**

When you write, put your address on both your letter and envelope; sometimes the two get separated. It is also a good idea to include your phone number and e-mail address. If you e-mail us, please tell us where you're from. Remember, as travel writers, we're often out of the office for long periods of time, so forgive us if our response is slow. *Unofficial Guide* e-mail is not forwarded to us when we're traveling, but we will respond as soon as possible when we return.

Questions from Readers

Questions frequently asked by readers are answered in an appendix at the end of this *Unofficial Guide.*

DISNEYLAND RESORT: *an* OVERVIEW

IF YOU'VE NOT BEEN TO DISNEYLAND for a while, you'll hardly know the place.

First, of course, there is the Disneyland Park, the original Disney theme park and the only park that Walt Disney saw completed in his lifetime. Much more than the Magic Kingdom at Walt Disney World, Disneyland Park embodies the quiet, charming spirit of nostalgia that so characterized Walt Disney himself. Disneyland Park is vast, yet intimate, etched in the tradition of its creator, yet continually changing.

Disneyland was opened in 1955 on a 107-acre tract surrounded almost exclusively by orange groves, just west of the sleepy and little-known Southern California community of Anaheim. Constrained by finances and ultimately enveloped by the city it helped create, Disneyland operated on that same modest parcel of land until just recently.

Disneyland Park is a collection of adventures, rides, and shows symbolized by the Disney characters and the Sleeping Beauty Castle.

Disneyland Park is divided into eight sub-areas or "lands" arranged around a central hub. First encountered is **Main Street, U.S.A.,** which connects the Disneyland entrance with the central hub. Moving clockwise around the hub, the other lands are **Adventureland, Frontierland, Fantasyland,** and **Tomorrowland.** Two major lands, **Critter Country** and **New Orleans Square,** are accessible via Adventureland and Frontierland but do not connect directly with the central hub. A newer land, **Mickey's Toontown,** connects to Fantasyland. All eight lands will be described in detail later.

Growth and change at Disneyland (until 1996) had been internal, in marked contrast to the ever-enlarging development of spacious Walt Disney World near Orlando, Florida. Until recently, when something new was added at Disneyland, something old had to go. The Disney engineers, to their credit, however, have never been shy about disturbing the status quo. Patrons of the park's earlier, modest years are amazed by the transformation. Gone are the days of the "magical little park" with the Monsanto House of the Future, flying saucer–style bumper cars, and Captain Hook's Pirate Ship. Substituted in a process of continuous evolution and modernization are state-of-the-art fourth-, fifth-, and sixth-generation attractions and entertainment. To paraphrase Walt Disney, Disneyland will never stop changing as long as there are new ideas to explore.

Disneyland Park was arguably Walt Disney's riskiest venture. It was developed on a shoestring budget and made possible only through Disney's relationship with ABC Television and a handful of brave corporate sponsors. The capital available was barely sufficient to acquire the property and build the park; there was nothing left over for the development of hotels or the acquisition and improvement of property adjoining the park. Even the Disneyland Hotel, connected to the theme park by monorail, was owned and operated by a third party until less than a decade ago.

Disneyland's success spawned a wave of development that rapidly surrounded the theme park with mom-and-pop motels, souvenir stands, and fast-food restaurants. Disney, still deep in debt, looked on in abject shock, powerless to intervene. In fact, the Disneyland experience was etched so deeply into the Disney corporate consciousness that Walt purchased 27,500 acres and established his own autonomous development district in Florida (unaccountable to any local or county authority) when he was ready to launch Walt Disney World.

Though the Florida project gave Disney the opportunity to develop a destination resort in a totally controlled environment, the steady decline of the area encircling Disneyland continued to rankle him. After tolerating the blight for 30 years, the Walt Disney Company (finally flush with funds and ready for a good fight) set about putting Disneyland Park right. Quietly at first, then aggressively, Disney began buying up the mom-and-pop motels, as well as the few remaining orange and vegetable groves near the park.

In June 1993, the City of Anaheim adopted a Disney plan that called for the development of a new Disney destination resort, including a second theme park situated in what was once the Disneyland parking lot; a Disney-owned hotel district with 4,600 hotel rooms; two new parking facilities; and improvements, including extensive landscaping of the streets that provide access to the complex. City of Anaheim, Orange County, and State of California infrastructure changes required to support the expanded Disney presence included widening Interstate 5, building new interchanges, moving a major power line, adding new sewer systems, and expanding utilities capacity.

By the end of 2000, all of the changes, modifications, and additions were finished, and Disneyland began the new century as a complete, multi–theme park resort destination. The second and newest park, Disney's California Adventure, celebrated its grand opening on February 8, 2001.

Disney's California Adventure is an odd-shaped park built around a lagoon on one side and the Grand Californian Hotel on the other, with one of Disney's trademark mountains, Grizzly Peak, plopped down in the middle. An abbreviated entranceway leads to three "lands"or districts. Inside the front gate and to the left is the Hollywood Studios Backlot, a very diminutive version of the Disney-MGM Studios theme park. Then there's Golden State, a catch-all district that combines California's industry, cuisine, natural resources, people, and history. Next is A Bug's Land, with characters and attractions based on the Disney/Pixar film *A Bug's Life*. Finally, Paradise Pier recalls the grand old seaside amusement parks of the early twentieth century. Disney's California Adventure (or "DCA" to the initiated) is described in detail later in the guide.

The entrances of Disneyland Park and Disney's California Adventure face each other across a palm-studded pedestrian plaza called the Esplanade. The Esplanade begins at Harbor Boulevard and runs west, between the parks, passing into Downtown Disney—a dining, shopping, entertainment, and nightlife venue. From Downtown Disney the Esplanade continues via an overpass across West Street/Disneyland Drive, past the new monorail station, to the Disneyland and Paradise Pier Hotels.

Sandwiched between the Esplanade and Downtown Disney on the north and Disney's California Adventure on the south is the 750-room Disney Grand Californian Hotel. Designed in the image of rustic national park lodges, the Grand Californian supplants the Disneyland Hotel as Disneyland's prestigious lodging property.

North of the hotels and across West Street from Disneyland Park is a huge multistory parking garage that can be accessed directly from I-5. This is where most Disneyland guests park. Tram transport is provided from the parking garage, adjacent oversized-vehicle lot, and outlying lots to the Esplanade. Kennels are located by the parking garage. Ticket booths are situated along the Esplanade.

HAPPY ANNIVERSARY, DISNEYLAND!

ON MAY 5, 2005, Disneyland kicked off its 50th Anniversary with an 18-month celebration involving Disney theme parks worldwide. At Disneyland, new attractions, parades, shows, and special events mark the occasion. The Disney Cruise line is even operating cruises from the port of Los Angeles.

SHOULD I GO TO DISNEYLAND PARK IF I'VE SEEN WALT DISNEY WORLD?

DISNEYLAND PARK IS ROUGHLY comparable to the Magic Kingdom theme park at Walt Disney World near Orlando, Florida. Both are arranged by "lands" accessible from a central hub and connected to the entrance by a Main Street. Both parks feature many rides and attractions of the same name: Space Mountain, Jungle Cruise, Pirates of the Caribbean, It's a Small World, and Dumbo the Flying Elephant, to name a few. Interestingly, however, the same name does not necessarily connote the same experience. Pirates of the Caribbean at Disneyland Park is much longer and more elaborate than its Walt Disney World counterpart. Big Thunder Mountain is more elaborate in Florida, and Dumbo is about the same in both places.

Disneyland Park is more intimate than the Magic Kingdom, not having the room for expansion enjoyed by the Florida park. Pedestrian thoroughfares are narrower, and everything from Big Thunder Mountain to the Castle is scaled down somewhat. Large crowds are

Attractions Found Only at Disneyland Park	
Adventureland	Indiana Jones Adventure
	"Tarzan Treehouse, Climb to Adventure"
Fantasyland	Pinocchio's Daring Journey
	Casey Jr. Circus Train
	Storybook Land Canal Boats
	Alice in Wonderland
	Mr. Toad's Wild Ride
	Matterhorn Bobsleds
Frontierland	Sailing Ship *Columbia*
	Fantasmic!
	(also at Disney-MGM Studios) (seasonal)
Main Street	*Disneyland: The First 50 Years*
Mickey's Toontown	Roger Rabbit's Car Toon Spin
	Goofy's Bounce House
	Chip 'n' Dale's Treehouse
New Orleans Square	The Disney Gallery

Critical Comparison of Attractions Found at Both Parks *

ADVENTURELAND

Enchanted Tiki Birds   Both versions were recently upgraded

Jungle Cruise   More realistic audio-animatronic (robotic) animals and longer ride at Walt Disney World

CRITTER COUNTRY

Splash Mountain   Slower loading at Disneyland

FANTASYLAND

Carousels   About the same at both parks

Castles   Far larger and more beautiful at the Magic Kingdom

Dumbo, the Flying Elephant   About the same at both parks

It's a Small World   About the same at both parks

Mad Tea Party   The same at both parks

Peter Pan's Flight   Better at Disneyland

Snow White's Scary Adventures   Magic Kingdom version is better

FRONTIERLAND

Big Thunder Mountain Railroad   About the same; sights and special effects are better at the Magic Kingdom

Tom Sawyer Island   Comparable, but a little more elaborate and with food service at the Magic Kingdom

Various river cruises (canoes, boats, etc.)   More interesting sights at the Magic Kingdom, but only Disneyland offers canoes.

MAIN STREET

WDW/Disneyland Railroad   The Disneyland Railroad is far more entertaining by virtue of the Grand Canyon Diorama and the Primeval World components not found at the Magic Kingdom

NEW ORLEANS SQUARE

Haunted Mansion   Slight edge to the Magic Kingdom version

Pirates of the Caribbean   Far superior and more politically correct at Disneyland

TOMORROWLAND

Astro Orbiter   About the same at both parks

Buzz Lightyear   About the same at both parks

Autopia/Tomorrowland Speedway   Disneyland version is superior

Space Mountain   Better at Disneyland

---

*It should be noted that several of the attractions at Disney's California Adventure Park (DCA), such as the *Twilight Zone* Tower of Terror, *Playhouse Disney*, *It's Tough to Be A Bug*, and *Muppet Vision 3-D*, appeared first at one of the Walt Disney World theme parks. A version of Soarin' over California is the first DCA attraction exported to Walt Disney World. None of the remaining DCA attractions are found at Walt Disney World.

more taxing at Disneyland Park because there is less room for them to disperse. At Disneyland Park, however, there are dozens of little surprises, small unheralded attractions tucked away in crooks and corners of the park, which give Disneyland Park a special charm and variety that the Magic Kingdom lacks. And, of course, Disneyland Park has the stamp of Walt Disney's personal touch.

To allow for a meaningful comparison, we have provided a summary of those features found only at Disneyland Park (listed alphabetically), followed by a critical look at the attractions found at both parks (on page 13).

PART ONE

PLANNING *before* YOU LEAVE HOME

GATHERING INFORMATION

IN ADDITION TO THIS GUIDE, we recommend that you obtain copies of the following publications:

I. THE DISNEY TRAVEL SALES CENTER CALIFORNIA BROCHURE This full-color booklet describes Disneyland in its entirety and lists rates for the Disneyland Hotel. Also described are Disneyland package vacations with lodging options at more than 25 nearby hotels. The brochure is available from most full-service travel agents, or it can be obtained by calling the Walt Disney Travel Sales Center at ☎ 714-520-7070. If you are in a hurry, a two-page faxed brochure is also available.

2. DISNEYLAND GUIDEBOOK FOR GUESTS WITH DISABILITIES If members of your party are sight- or hearing-impaired, or partially or wholly non-ambulatory, you will find this small guide very helpful. Disney does not mail them, but copies are readily available at the park.

3. THE DISNEY CRUISE LINE BROCHURE AND DVD As part of the Disneyland anniversary celebration, the Disney Cruise Line operates seven-day cruises to the Mexican Riviera on the Disney Magic out of the port of Los Angeles. The brochure provides details on the cruises and on vacation packages that combine a cruise on the Disney Cruise Line with a stay at Disneyland Resort. Disney Cruise Line also offers a free planning DVD that tells all you'd need to know about Disney cruises and then some. To obtain a copy call ☎ 888-DCL-2500 or order online at **www.disneycruise.com.**

4. CALIFORNIA TRAVELER DISCOUNT GUIDE Another good source of lodging, restaurant, and attraction discounts throughout the state of California, the California Traveler Discount Guide, can be obtained by calling ☎ 352-371-3948, Monday through Friday, 8 a.m. to 5 p.m., EST. Published by Exit Information Guide, the Discount Guide is free, but you will be charged $3 for postage and handling. Similar guides to other states are available at the same number. You can also order online at **www.travelersdiscountguide.com,** or by mail at 4205 NW 6th Street, Gainesville, FL, 32609. Or go to **www.travelersdiscountguide.com** to order online.

Disneyland Main Information Address and Phone

The following address and phone numbers provide general information. Inquiries may be expedited by using addresses and phone numbers specific to the nature of the inquiry (other addresses and phone numbers are listed elsewhere in this chapter, under their relevant topics).

Disneyland Guest Relations
P.O. Box 3232
1313 South Harbor Boulevard
Anaheim, CA 92803-3232
☎ 714-781-4565 for recorded information
☎ 714-781-7290 for live information

The Phone from Hell

Sometimes it is virtually impossible to get through on the Disneyland information numbers listed above. When you get through, you will get a recording that offers various information options. If none of the recorded options answer your question, you will have to hold for a live person. Eat before you call—you may have a long wait. If, after repeated attempts, you get tired of a busy signal in your ear or, worse, 20 minutes' worth of mice singing "Cindarellie" in an alto falsetto while you wait on hold, call the Disneyland Hotel at ☎ 714-956-6425.

Cyber Disney

There are a number of good, independent Disneyland information sources on the Internet. The following are brief profiles of our favorites:

ANAHEIMOC.ORG is the official Web site of the Anaheim/Orange County Visitors and Convention Authority. You'll find everything from hotels and restaurants to weather and driving instructions on this site.

INTERCOTWEST.COM The Internet Community of Tomorrow—West is an active and friendly Web site filled with detailed information on every corner of the Disneyland Resort. Featured are frequent news updates and descriptions, reviews, and ratings of every attraction, restaurant, and shop at the resort. The site is also host to the largest Disney-related multimedia gallery on the Web, with thousands of photos chronicling the parks' recent history. Intercot West taps into the Internet's spirit of community via its interactive moderated discussion boards, a place where Disney fans convene to gain insightful trip planning tips and make new friends. Intercot West is a part of

Intercot (**www.intercot.com**), which features vacation planning information for Walt Disney World.

MOUSEPLANET.COM Mouse Planet is a comprehensive resource for Disneyland data, offering features and reviews by guest writers, information on the Disney theme parks, discussion groups, and news. The site includes an interactive Disney restaurant and hotel review page where users can voice opinions on their Disney dining and lodging experiences. Also available are trip reports by site contributors and users.

LAUGHINGPLACE.COM This site features daily updated headlines and columns on all things Disney, including theme parks, films, TV, stage, merchandise, collectibles, and more. The free site specializes in current news on the Disney theme parks and resorts, with information such as hours, show times, events, and highlights of specific attractions. LaughingPlace offers interactive, user-rated attraction guides, lively discussion boards, and a customizable home page with a unique trip countdown feature and park info. The Web site, which distributes an informative daily newsletter via e-mail, is also the home of LaughingPlace Radio and The LaughingPlace Store.

YESTERLAND.COM You can visit the Disneyland of the past at Yesterland, where retired Disneyland attractions are brought back to life through vivid descriptions and historic photographs. Yesterland attraction descriptions relate what it was once like to experience the Flying Saucers, the Mine Train through Nature's Wonderland, the Tahitian Terrace and dozens of other rides, shows, parades, and restaurants.

MOUSESAVERS.COM This site specializes in finding you the deepest discounts on hotels, park admissions, and rental cars. Mousesavers does not actually sell travel, but rather unearths and publishes special discount codes that you can use to obtain the discounts. It's the first place we look for deals when we travel to Disneyland Resort.

In addition to the foregoing information, Disneyland operates an official Web site, **www.disneyland.com.** Universal Studios Hollywood can be found online at **www.universalstudios.com.**

ADMISSION OPTIONS

SINCE THE OPENING OF DISNEY'S California Adventure (DCA) park, Disneyland Resort has revamped its admission options. Although additional changes are expected, you can currently purchase a One-Day, One-Park Ticket, a Two-Day Park Hopper Passport, a Three-Day Park Hopper Passport, a Four-Day Park Hopper Passport, a Five-Day Park Hopper Bonus Passport, or an Annual Passport. These admissions can be purchased at the park entrance,

unofficial **TIP**
The money you can save makes researching Disney's dizzying array of ticket options worthwhile.

at the Disneyland Resort hotels, from the Walt Disney Travel Sales Center, from Disneyland Ticket Mail Order, on the Disneyland Internet site, and at most Disney stores in the western United States. Some passes are available at a discounted rate for children between three and nine years of age; one- and two-year-olds are exempt from admission fees. More information on ordering tickets follows.

Admission prices, not unexpectedly, increase from time to time. For planning your budget, however, the following provides a fair estimate:

	ADULT (10 & up)	CHILD (3–9)
One-Day, One-Park Ticket with Tax	$56	$46
One-Day Park Hopper	$76	$66
Two-Day Park Hopper	$106	$86
Three-Day Park Hopper	$159	$129
Four-Day Park Hopper	$189	$159
Five-Day Park Hopper	$209	$179
Deluxe Annual Pass **(some blackout dates)**	$209	$209
Premium Annual Pass **(no blackout dates)**	$329	$329

One-Day, One-Park Ticket

This pass is good for one day's admission at your choice of Disneyland Park or Disney's California Adventure. As the name implies, you cannot "hop" from park to park.

When can a One-Day, One-Park ticket become a Park Hopper Pass?

If you purchase a One-Day, One-Park ticket, you can use it as a Park Hopper Pass if the park you're touring closes before the other park. Let's say you used your One-Day, One-Park ticket to visit DCA, which closes on that day at 6 p.m. If, when you leave DCA, Disneyland Park is still open, you can use your One-Day, One-Park ticket to gain admission. Remember, this works only after the park in question, DCA in this example, has closed.

Park Hopper Passports

Park Hopper Passes are good for one, two, three, four, or five days, respectively, and allow you to visit both parks on the same day. These multiday passes do not have to be used on consecutive days, but expire 13 days after their first use.

The 13-day expiration is in marked contrast to similar passes sold at Walt Disney World for which you can purchase a No Expiration option. If you mistakenly bought multiday passes because you were not aware of the 13-day expiration, call ☎ 714-781-7290 and ask to be connected to Guest Communications. Guest Communications has the authority to issue you a voucher for the unused days on your pass. It is required, however, that you return your expired passes.

Anytime before a pass expires, you can apply the value of unused days toward the cost of a higher-priced pass. If you buy a Four-Day Park Hopper Pass, for example, and then decide you'd rather have an annual pass, you can apply the value of unused days on the Park Hopper toward the purchase of the annual pass.

If you've been to Walt Disney World in Florida and brought home some partially used Park Hopper Passes, you can use them at Disneyland. It's a one-way street though: Disneyland Park Hopper Passes are not accepted at Walt Disney World.

Annual Passports

The Disneyland Resorts offer several annual passes. The Premium Annual Passport is good for an entire year with no blackout dates. The pass costs $329 and is good for admission to both parks (excluding arcades). Southern California Annual Passports, priced at $149, provide admission to both parks for a year excluding 160 preselected blackout dates. These are available to residents in zip codes 90000–93599, and to Baja, California, residents in zip codes 21000–22999. Prices for children are the same as those for adults on all annual passes. Annual passes are a good idea if you plan to visit Disneyland parks five or more days in a year. If you purchase your annual pass in July of this year and schedule your visit next year for June, you'll cover two years' vacations with a single annual pass.

unofficial **TIP**
If you visit Disneyland three or more days each summer, an annual pass is a potential money saver.

Admission passes can be ordered through the mail by writing:

Disneyland Ticket Mail Order
P.O. Box 61061
Anaheim, CA 92803-6161

Disneyland Ticket Mail Order accepts personal checks and money orders. Mail orders take three to four weeks to process. To order tickets by telephone, call ☎ 714-781-4400.

In addition to Disneyland Ticket Mail Order, Disneyland admissions can be purchased in advance from Disneyland Resort hotels; the Disneyland Web site, **www.disneyland.com;** Disney Stores in the Western United States; and the Walt Disney Travel Sales Center, ☎ 800-854-3104.

Admission and Disneyland Hotel Discounts

For specials and time-limited discounts on Disneyland Resort admissions, visit **www.mousesavers.com.**

Rides and Shows Closed for Repairs or Maintenance

Rides and shows at Disneyland parks are sometimes closed for maintenance or repairs. If there is a certain attraction that is important to you, call ☎ 714-781-7290 before your visit to make sure it will be operating. A mother from Dover, Massachusetts, wrote us, lamenting:

> We were disappointed to find Space Mountain, Swiss Family Treehouse, and the Riverboat closed for repairs. We felt that a large chunk of the [park] was not working, yet the tickets were still full price and expensive!

HOW MUCH DOES IT COST TO GO TO DISNEYLAND FOR A DAY?

LET'S SAY WE HAVE A FAMILY OF FOUR—Mom and Dad, Tim (age 12) and Tami (age 8)—driving their own car. Since they plan to be in the area for a few days, they intend to buy the Three-Day Park Hopper Passes. A typical day would cost $351, excluding souvenirs, lodging, and transportation. See the following chart for a breakdown of expenses.

How Much Does a Day Cost?

Breakfast for four **at Denny's with tax and tip**	$28.00
Disneyland parking fee	9.00
One day's admission on a Three-Day Park Hopper Passport	
Dad: Adult, Three-Day with tax = $159 divided by 3 (days)	53.00
Mom: Adult, Three-Day with tax = $159 divided by 3 (days)	53.00
Tim: Adult, Three-Day with tax = $159 divided by 3 (days)	53.00
Tami: Child, Three-Day with tax = $129 divided by 3 (days)	43.00
Morning break **(soda or coffee)**	14.00

Fast-food lunch (burger, fries, soda), no tip	36.00
Afternoon break (soda and popcorn)	20.50
Dinner in park at counter-service restaurant with tax	41.50
Souvenirs (Mickey T-shirts for Tim and Tami) with tax*	38.00
One-day total (not including lodging and travel)	$389.00

Cheer up, you won't have to buy souvenirs every day.

TIMING YOUR VISIT

SELECTING THE TIME OF YEAR FOR YOUR VISIT

CROWDS ARE LARGEST AT DISNEYLAND DURING THE SUMMER (Memorial Day through Labor Day) and during specific holiday periods during the rest of the year. The busiest time of all is Christmas Day through New Year's Day. Thanksgiving weekend, the week of Washington's Birthday, spring break for schools and colleges, and the two weeks around Easter are also extremely busy. To give you some idea of what *busy* means at Disneyland, more than 77,000 people have toured Disneyland Park on a single day! While this level of attendance is far from typical, the possibility of its occurrence should prevent all but the ignorant and the foolish from challenging this mega-attraction at its busiest periods. For the record, attendance at Disney's California Adventure Park runs about one-third that of Disneyland Park.

The least-busy time of all is from after Thanksgiving weekend until the week before Christmas. The next slowest times are September through the weekend preceding Thanksgiving, January 4 through the first week of March, and the week following Easter up to Memorial Day weekend. At the risk of being blasphemous, our research team was so impressed with the relative ease of touring in the fall and other "off" periods that we would rather take our children out of school for a few days than do battle with the summer crowds. Though we strongly recommend going to Disneyland in the fall or in the spring, it should be noted that there are certain trade-offs. The parks often close earlier on fall and spring days, sometimes early enough to eliminate evening parades and other live entertainment offerings. Also, because these are slow times of the year at Disneyland, you can anticipate that some rides and attractions may be closed for maintenance or renovation. Finally, if the parks open late and close early, it's tough to see everything, even if the crowds are light.

unofficial **TIP**
You can't pick a less crowded time to visit Disneyland than the period following Thanksgiving weekend and leading up to Christmas.

Most readers who have tried Disney theme parks at varying times during the year agree. A gentleman from Ottawa, Ontario, who toured in early December, wrote:

It was the most enjoyable trip I have ever had, and I can't imagine going [back to Disneyland] when it is crowded. Even without the crowds we were still very tired by afternoon. Fighting crowds certainly would have made a hellish trip. We will never go again at any other time.

unofficial TIP
In our opinion, the risk of encountering colder weather and closed attractions during an off-season visit to Disneyland is worth it.

Not to overstate the case: We want to emphasize that you can have a great time at the Disneyland parks regardless of the time of year or crowd level. In fact, a primary objective of this guide is to make the parks fun and manageable for those readers who visit during the busier times of year.

SELECTING THE DAY OF THE WEEK FOR YOUR VISIT

THE CROWDS AT WALT DISNEY WORLD in Florida are comprised mostly of out-of-state visitors. Not necessarily so at Disneyland, which, along with Six Flags Magic Mountain, serves as an often-frequented recreational resource for the greater Los Angeles and San Diego communities. To many Southern Californians, Disneyland Park and Disney's California Adventure are their private theme parks. Yearly passes are available at less cost than a year's membership to the YMCA, and the Disney management has intensified its efforts to appeal to the local market.

What all this means is that weekends are usually packed. Saturday is the busiest day of the week. Sunday, particularly Sunday morning, is the best bet if you have to go on a weekend, but it is also extremely busy.

During the summer, Monday and Friday are very busy; Tuesday and Wednesday are usually less so; and Thursday is normally the slowest day of all. During the "off-season" (September through May, holiday periods excepted) Thursday is usually the least crowded day, followed by Tuesday.

At Walt Disney World in Florida, there are four theme parks with a substantial daily variance in attendance from park to park. At Disneyland Resort, Disneyland Park usually hosts crowds three times larger than those at Disney's California Adventure, but because DCA is smaller, crowd conditions are comparable. Expressed differently, the most crowded and least crowded days are essentially the same for both Disneyland parks.

TOP TEN AMERICAN THEME PARKS

Compared with 2003 figures, 2004 theme-park attendance was up at all of the parks, with Universal Studios Orlando posting the largest gain at 14%.

THEME PARK	ANNUAL ATTENDANCE	AVERAGE DAILY ATTENDANCE
Magic Kingdom	15.2 million	41,644
Disneyland	13.4 million	36,712

THEME PARK	ANNUAL ATTENDANCE	AVERAGE DAILY ATTENDANCE
Epcot	9.4 million	25,753
Disney-MGM Studios	8.3 million	22,740
Animal Kingdom	7.8 million	21,370
Universal Studios Orlando	6.7 million	18,356
Islands of Adventure	6.3 million	17,260
Disney's California Adventure	5.6 million	15,342
SeaWorld	5.6 million	15,310
Universal Studios Hollywood	5.0 million	13,699

2004 attendance figures. Source: *Amusement Business* magazine.

Early Entry Is Back! (sort of)

Talk about indecision, Disney can't quite decide whether to offer early entry or not. One year it's available, the next it's gone. After being abandoned (again) in 2004, early entry was resurrected in 2005, but only in limited form. Four days each week, usually Monday, Tuesday, Thursday, and Saturday mornings, Disneyland resort guests who purchased travel packages from the Walt Disney Travel Company are admitted to Fantasyland only in Disneyland Park one hour before the park opens to the general public. Qualifying travel packages must include Three- to Five-Day Park Hopper admissions. For additional information call ☎ 714-520-7070.

OPERATING HOURS

IT CANNOT BE SAID THAT THE DISNEY FOLKS are not flexible when it comes to hours of operation for the parks. They run a dozen or more different operating schedules during the year, making it advisable to call ☎ 714-781-4565 the day before you arrive for the exact hours of operation.

PACKED PARK COMPENSATION PLAN

THE THOUGHT OF TEEMING, JOSTLING THRONGS jockeying for position in endless lines under the baking Fourth-of-July sun is enough to wilt the will and ears of the most ardent Mouseketeer. Why would anyone go to Disneyland on a summer Saturday or during a major holiday period? Indeed, if you have never been to Disneyland, and you thought you would just drop in for a few rides and a little look-see on such a day, you might be better off shooting yourself in the foot. The Disney folks, however, being Disney folks, feel kind of bad about those interminably long lines and the basically impossible touring conditions on packed days and compensate their patrons with a no-less-than-incredible array of first-rate live entertainment and happenings.

Throughout the day the party goes on with shows, parades, concerts, and pageantry. In the evening, there is so much going on that you have to make some tough choices. Big-name music groups perform on the River Stage in Frontierland and at the Fantasyland Theatre. Other concerts are produced concurrently at the Hyperion Theater in Disney's California Adventure. There are always parades, fireworks, and the Disney characters make frequent appearances. No question about it, you can go to the Disneyland parks on the Fourth of July (or any other extended-hours, crowded day), never get on a ride, and still get your money's worth. Admittedly, it's not the ideal situation for a firsttimer who really wants to see the parks, but for anyone else it's one heck of a good party.

unofficial **TIP**
If it's not your first trip to Disneyland and you must go during a crowded holiday weekend, you may have just as much fun enjoying Disney's fantastic array of shows, parades, fireworks, and more as you would riding the rides.

If you decide to go on one of the parks' "big" days, we suggest that you arrive an hour and 20 minutes before the stated opening time. Use the touring plan of your choice until about 1 p.m. and then take the monorail to Downtown Disney for lunch and relaxation. Southern Californian visitors often chip in and rent a room for the group (make reservations well in advance) at the Disneyland or Grand Californian Hotels, thus affording a place to meet, relax, have a drink, or change clothes before enjoying the pools at the hotel. A comparable arrangement can be made at other nearby hotels as long as they furnish a shuttle service to and from the park. After an early dinner, return to the park for the evening's festivities, which really get cranked up at about 8 p.m.

GETTING THERE

INTERSTATE 5 (I-5) HAS BEEN WIDENED, and improved interchanges allow Disney patrons to drive directly into and out of parking facilities without becoming enmeshed in surface street traffic.

To avoid traffic problems, we make the following recommendations:

1. Stay as close to Disneyland as possible. If you are within walking distance, leave your car at the hotel and walk to the park. If your hotel provides efficient shuttle service (that is, will get you to the parks at least a half hour before opening), use the shuttle.

2. If your hotel is more than five miles from Disneyland and you intend to drive your car, leave for the park extra early, say an hour or more. If you get lucky and don't encounter too many problems, you can relax over breakfast at a restaurant near Disneyland while you wait for the parks to open.

3. If you must use the Santa Ana Freeway (I-5), give yourself lots of extra time.

southern california at a glance

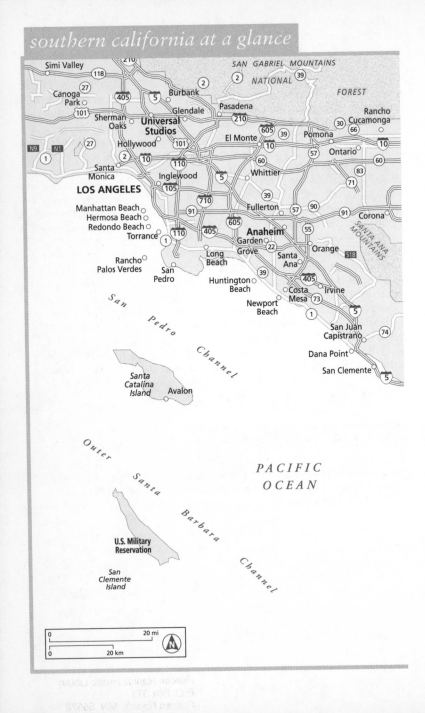

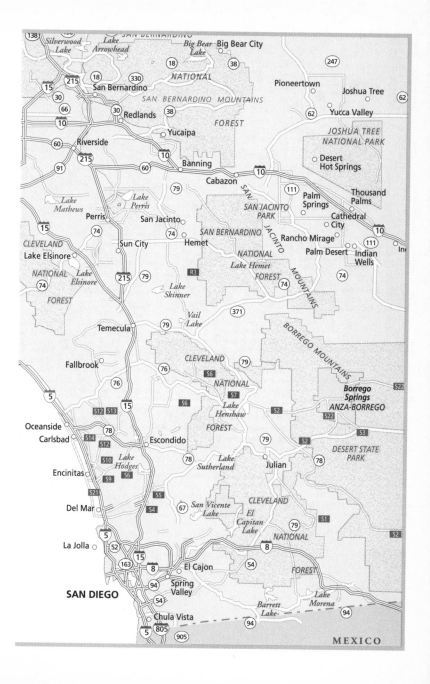

getting around the disneyland resort

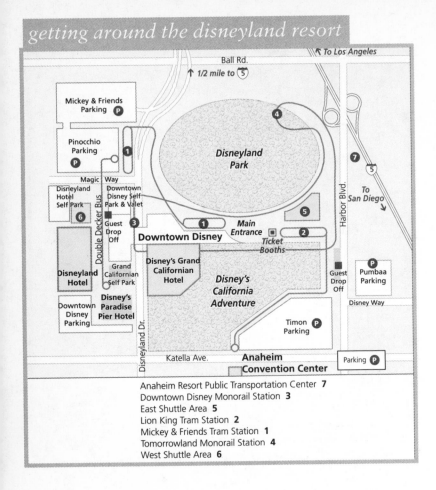

Anaheim Resort Public Transportation Center **7**
Downtown Disney Monorail Station **3**
East Shuttle Area **5**
Lion King Tram Station **2**
Mickey & Friends Tram Station **1**
Tomorrowland Monorail Station **4**
West Shuttle Area **6**

4. Any time you leave the park just before, at, or just after closing time, you can expect considerable congestion in the parking lots and in the loading area for hotel shuttles. The easiest way to return to your hotel (if you do not have a car in Disneyland Resort parking lot) is to take the monorail to the Disneyland Hotel, or walk to the Grand Californian Hotel, then take a cab to your own hotel. While cabs in Anaheim are a little pricey, they are usually available in ample numbers at the Disneyland hotels and at the pedestrian entrance on Harbor Boulevard. When you consider the alternatives of fighting your way onto a hotel shuttle or trudging back to your hotel on worn-out feet, spending a couple of bucks for a cab often sounds pretty reasonable.

5. If you walk or use a hotel shuttle to get to the parks and are then caught in a monsoon, the best way to return to your hotel without getting soaked is to take the monorail to the Disneyland Hotel and catch a taxi from there.

6. Finally, the Orange County Transit District provides very efficient bus service to Disneyland with three different long-distance lines. Running approximately every 30 minutes during the day and evening, service begins at 5 a.m. and concludes between 6:30 and 10:55 p.m., depending on the season and your location. Buses drop off and pick up passengers at the Disneyland Hotel. From there, guests can take a Disney tram to the park entrance. Trams run approximately every six minutes. Bus fare is about $1.25 and the tram is free. For additional information, call ☎ 714-636-7433 or look up **www.octa.net.** For public transportation in the immediate area surrounding Disneyland, see our discussion of the Anaheim Resort Transit (ART) system below.

TAKING A TRAM OR SHUTTLE BUS FROM YOUR HOTEL

TRAMS AND SHUTTLE BUSES ARE PROVIDED by many hotels and motels in the vicinity of Disneyland. Usually without charge, they represent a fairly carefree means of getting to and from the theme parks, letting you off near the entrances and saving you the cost of parking. The rub is that they might not get you there as early as you desire (a critical point if you take our touring advice) or be available at the time you wish to return to your lodging. Also, some shuttles are direct to Disneyland, while others make stops at other motels and hotels in the vicinity. Each shuttle service is a little bit different, so check out the particulars before you book your hotel. If the shuttle provided by your hotel runs regularly throughout the day to and from Disneyland and if you have the flexibility to tour the parks over two or three days, the shuttle provides a wonderful opportunity to tour in the morning and return to your lodging for lunch, a swim, or perhaps a nap; then you can head back to Disneyland refreshed in the early evening for a little more fun.

Be forewarned that most hotel shuttle services do not add additional vehicles at the parks' opening or closing times. In the mornings, your biggest problem is that you might not get a seat on the first shuttle. This occurs most frequently if your hotel is the last stop for a shuttle that serves several hotels. Because hotels that share a shuttle service are usually located close together, you can improve your chances of getting a seat by simply walking to the hotel preceding yours on the pick-up route. At closing time, and sometimes following a hard rain, you can expect a mass exodus from the parks. The worst-case scenario in this event is that more people will be waiting for the shuttle to your hotel than the bus will hold and that some will be left. While most (but not all) hotel shuttles return for stranded guests, you may suffer a wait of 15 minutes to an hour. Our suggestion, if you are depending on hotel shuttles, is to exit the park at least 45 minutes before closing. If you stay in a park until closing and lack the energy to deal with the shuttle or hike back to your hotel, go to the Disneyland Hotel and catch a cab from there. There is also a cab stand adjacent to the Harbor Boulevard pedestrian entrance and another at the Grand Californian Hotel.

unofficial **TIP**
Warning: Most shuttles don't add vehicles at park opening or closing times. In the mornings, you may not get a seat.

The shuttle loading area is located on the Harbor Boulevard side of the Disneyland Park's main entrances. The loading area connects to a pedestrian corridor that leads to the park entrances. Each hotel's shuttle bus is color-coded yellow, blue, red, silver, or white. Signs of like color designate where the shuttles load and unload.

Anaheim Resort Transit

Anaheim has undergone a renaissance, establishing the 1,100-acre area that surrounds Disneyland and the Anaheim Convention Center as a world-class destination known as The Anaheim Resort. Streets have been widened and attractively landscaped with towering palms as well as ornamental trees and plants. A score of new hotels and restaurants have opened and many of the older hotels have expanded or remodeled.

To complete the Anaheim Resort package, a transit service was added to provide shuttle service to the Disneyland Parks, Downtown Disney, and the convention center. Called Anaheim Resort Transit (ART), the service operates nine routes designated A—H plus J and K. There are just four to six well-marked stops on each route, so a complete circuit on any given route only takes about 20 minutes. All of the routes terminate at Disneyland. To continue on to the convention center, you must transfer at Disneyland to Route C or E.

The shuttle vehicles themselves are little red trolleys similar to the trolleys in San Francisco (except on wheels) and are wheelchair accessible. They run every ten minutes on peak days during morning and evening periods, every 20 minutes during the less busy middle part of the day, and every 20 minutes all day long on non-peak days. Service begins one hour before park opening and ends one hour after park closing. If you commute to Disneyland on ART and then head to Downtown Disney after the parks close, you'll have to find your own way home if you stay at Downtown Disney more than an hour. All shuttle vehicles and the respective stops are clearly marked with the route designation (A–H and J and K).

Hotels served by ART sell one-day, two-day, and five-day passes for $3, $6, and $12, respectively. Children nine years and under ride free with a paying adult. Passes cannot be purchased from the driver. For more information call ☎ 888-364-ARTS or check **www.rideart.org.** Passes are also available in advance or on ART's Web site.

WALKING TO DISNEYLAND FROM NEARBY HOTELS

WHILE IT IS TRUE THAT MOST DISNEYLAND AREA hotels provide shuttle service, or are on the ART routes, it is equally true that an ever-increasing number of guests walk to the parks from their hotels. Shuttles are not always available when needed, and parking in the Disneyland lot has become pretty expensive. There is a pedestrian walkway from Harbor Boulevard that provides safe access to Disneyland for guests on foot. This pedestrian corridor extends from Harbor Boulevard all the way to the Disneyland Hotel, connecting Disneyland Park, Disney's California Adventure, and all of the Disney entertainment and shopping venues.

■ A WORD *about* LODGING

WHILE THIS GUIDE IS NOT ABOUT LODGING, we have found lodging to be a primary concern of those visiting Disneyland. Traffic around Disneyland, and in the Anaheim/Los Angeles area in general, is so terrible that we advocate staying in accommodations within two or three miles of the park. Included in this radius are many expensive hotels as well as a considerable number of moderately priced establishments and a small number of bargain motels.

DISNEYLAND RESORT HOTELS

Disney offers three on-site hotels, the **Grand Californian,** the **Disneyland Hotel,** and the **Paradise Pier Hotel.** The Grand Californian, built in the rustic stone-and-timber style of the grand national park lodges, is the flagship property. Newer, more elaborately themed, and closest to the theme parks and Downtown Disney, the Grand Californian is without a doubt the best place to stay…if you can afford it. Rooms at the Grand Californian start at about $265 and range up to $440 per night.

Next most convenient is the sprawling Disneyland Hotel, the oldest of the three. The Disneyland Hotel, consisting of three guestroom towers, has no theme, but is lushly landscaped and offers large, luxurious guest rooms. Walking from the hotel to the park entrances takes about 7 to 12 minutes. Walking time to the monorail station, with transportation to Disneyland Park, is about three to six minutes. Rates at the Disneyland Hotel run from $205 to $345 per night depending on the season.

The east side of the third Disney hotel overlooks the Paradise Pier section of Disney's California Adventure theme park, hence the name Paradise Pier Hotel. Although there is a South Seas–island flavor, both in the guest rooms and in the public areas, the hotel is not themed. Guest rooms here are large and recently renovated. Walking to the theme-park entrances takes about 10 to 16 minutes, and to the monorail station and Downtown Disney about 5 to 10 minutes. Depending on season, room rates range from $160 to $320 per night.

All three of the Disney hotels offer on-site dining and are within easy walking distance of the restaurants at Downtown Disney. The nicest swimming area can be found at the Grand Californian, where a High Sierras theme is realized in a mountain stream, boulders, and evergreens. The Disneyland Hotel also offers an elaborate, though themeless, pool complex.

HOW TO GET DISCOUNTS ON LODGING AT DISNEYLAND RESORT HOTELS

THERE ARE SO MANY GUEST ROOMS in and around Disneyland Resort that competition is brisk, and everyone, including Disney, wheels and deals to keep them filled. This has led to a more flexible discount policy for Disneyland Resort hotels. Here are tips for getting price breaks:

1. SEASONAL SAVINGS You can save from $15 to $60 per night on a Disneyland Resort hotel room by scheduling your visit during the slower times of the year. Disney uses so many adjectives (regular, holiday, peak, value, etc.) to describe its seasonal calendar, however, that it's hard to keep up without a scorecard. To confuse matters more, the dates for each season vary from hotel to hotel. Our advice: if you're set on staying at a Disney hotel, obtain a copy of the Walt Disney Travel Sales Center Disneyland Resort Vacations Brochure, described on page 15.

If you have a hard time getting a copy of the brochure, forget trying to find the various seasonal dates on the Disneyland Resort Web site. Easier by far is to check them out on the independent-of-Disney **www.mousesavers.com** site described in tip number 3 on the following page.

Understand that Disney seasonal dates are not sequential like spring, summer, fall, and winter. That would be way too simple. For any specific resort, there are sometimes several seasonal changes in a month. This is important because your room rate per night will be determined by the season prevailing when you check in. Let's say that you checked into the Disneyland Hotel on April 19 for a five-night stay. April 19 is in the more expensive peak season that ends on April 20, followed by the less pricey regular season beginning on April 21. Because you arrived during peak season, the peak season rate will be applied during your entire stay, even though more than half of your stay will be in regular season. Your strategy, therefore, is to shift your dates (if possible) to arrive during a less expensive season.

2. ASK ABOUT SPECIALS When you talk to Disney reservationists, inquire specifically about special deals. Ask, for example, "What special rates or discounts are available at Disney hotels during the time of our visit?" Being specific and assertive paid off for an Illinois reader:

> I called Disney's reservations number and asked for availability and rates... [Because] of the Unofficial Guide warning about Disney reservationists answering only the questions posed, I specifically asked, "Are there any special rates or discounts for that room during the month of October?" She replied, "Yes, we have that room available at a special price..." [For] the price of one phone call, I saved $440.

Along similar lines, a Warren, New Jersey, dad chimed in with this:

> Your tip about asking Disney employees about discounts was invaluable. They will not volunteer this information, but by asking we saved almost $500 on our hotel room using a AAA discount. Also, by asking, we got to ride in the front of the monorail, which thrilled our ten-year-old son (and his dad).

3. LEARN ABOUT DEALS OFFERED TO SPECIFIC MARKETS The folks at **www.mousesavers.com** keep an updated list of discounts and reservation codes for use at Disney resorts. The codes are separated into categories such as "for anyone," "for residents of certain states," "for Annual Passport holders," and so on. For example, the site listed a deal targeted to residents of the San Diego area published in an ad in a San Diego newspaper. Dozens of discounts are usually listed on the site, covering almost all Disneyland Resort hotels. Usually anyone calling the Disneyland Central Reservations Office (call ☎ 714-956-6425 and press 3 on the menu) can cite the referenced ad and get the discounted rate.

unofficial **TIP**
To enhance your chances of receiving a pin-code offer, you need to get your name and street or e-mail address into the Disney system.

You should be aware that Disney is tending away from room discount codes that anyone can use. Instead, Disney is targeting people with pin codes in e-mails and direct mailings. Pin-code discounts are offered to specific individuals and are correlated with that person's name and address. Pin-code offers are nontransferable. When you try to make a reservation using the code, Disney will verify that the street or e-mail address to which the pin code was sent is yours.

To enhance your chances of receiving a pin-code offer, you need to get your name and street or e-mail address into the Disney system. One way is to call the Walt Disney Travel Company/Disneyland Reservation Center at ☎ 714-520-7070 and request that written info be sent to you. If you've been to Disneyland previously, your name and address will already be on record, but you won't be as likely to receive a pin-code offer as you would by calling and requesting to be sent information. The latter is regarded as new business. Or expressed differently, if Disney smells blood they're more likely to come after you. On the Web, go to **www.disneyland.com** and sign up to be sent offers and news automatically at your e-mail address.

Mousesavers.com also features a great links page with short descriptions and URLs of the best Disney-related Web sites, and a current-year seasonal rates calendar.

4. EXPEDIA.COM Online travel seller Expedia has established an active market in discounting Disney hotels. Most discounts are in the 4 to 15% range but can go as deep as 25%.

5. DISNEYLAND RESORT WEB SITE Disney has become more aggressive about offering deals on its Web site. Go to **www.disneyland. disney.go.com** and check the page for "Special Offers." When booking rooms on Disney's or any other site, be sure to click on "Terms and Conditions" and read the fine print *before* making reservations.

6. ANNUAL PASS-HOLDER DISCOUNTS Annual pass holders are eligible for a broad range of discounts on dining, shopping, and lodging. If you visit Disneyland Resort once a year or more, of if you plan on a visit of five or more days, you might save money overall by purchasing annual passes. During 2005, we saw resort discounts as deep as 35% offered to annual pass holders. It doesn't take long to recoup the extra bucks you spent on an annual pass when you're saving that kind of money on lodging. Discounts in the 10 to 15% range are more the norm.

7. TRAVEL AGENTS Travel agents are active players in the market and particularly good sources of information on time-limited special programs and discounts. In our opinion, a good travel agent is the best friend a traveler can have. And though we at the *Unofficial Guide* know a thing or two about the travel industry, we always give our agent a chance to beat any deal we find. If our agent can't beat the deal, we let her book it if it's commissionable. In other words, we create a relationship that gives her plenty of incentive to really roll up her sleeves and work on our behalf.

As you might expect, there are travel agents and agencies that specialize, sometimes exclusively, in selling Disneyland and Walt Disney World. These agents have spent an incredible amount of time at both resorts and have completed extensive Disney education programs. They are usually the most Disney-knowledgeable agents in the travel industry.

Most of these specialists and their agencies display the "Earmarked" logo stating that they are an authorized Disney vacation planner.

8. ORGANIZATIONS AND AUTO CLUBS Eager to sell rooms, Disney has developed time-limited programs with some auto clubs and other organizations. Recently, for example, AAA members were offered 10 to 20% savings on Disney hotels and discounts on Disney package vacations. Such deals come and go, but the market suggests there will be more in the future. If you're a member of AARP, AAA, or any travel or auto club, ask whether the group has a program before shopping elsewhere.

9. ROOM UPGRADES Sometimes a room upgrade is as good as a discount. If you're visiting Disneyland Resort during a slower time, book the least expensive room your discounts will allow. Checking in, ask very politely about being upgraded to a "theme-park" or "pool-view" room. A fair percentage of the time, you'll get one at no additional charge.

Non-Disney Hotels

When Walt Disney built Disneyland, he did not have the funding to include hotels or to purchase the property surrounding his theme park. Even the Disneyland Hotel was owned by outside interests until a few years ago. Consequently, the area around the park developed in an essentially uncontrolled manner. Many of the hotels and motels near Disneyland were built in the early 1960s, and they are small and sometimes unattractive by today's standards. Quite a few motels adopted adventure or fantasy themes in emulation of Disneyland. As you might imagine, these themes from three decades ago seem hokey and irrelevant today. There is a disquieting (though rapidly diminishing) number of seedy hotels near Disneyland, and even some of the chain properties fail to live up to their national standards.

If you consider a non-Disney-owned hotel in Anaheim, check its quality as reported by a reliable independent rating system such as those offered by the *Unofficial Guide,* AAA Directories, Mobil Guides, or Frommer's. Checking two or three independent sources is better than depending on one. Also, before you book, ask how old the hotel is and when the guest rooms were last refurbished. Be aware that almost any hotel can be made to look good on a Web site, so don't depend on Web sites alone. Locate the hotel on our street map (pages 36–37) to verify its proximity to Disneyland. If you will not have a car, make sure the hotel has a shuttle service that will satisfy your needs.

GETTING A GOOD DEAL AT NON-DISNEY HOTELS

BELOW ARE SOME TIPS AND STRATEGIES for getting a good deal on a hotel room near Disneyland. Though the following list may seem a bit intimidating and may refer to players in the travel market that are

disneyland hotels

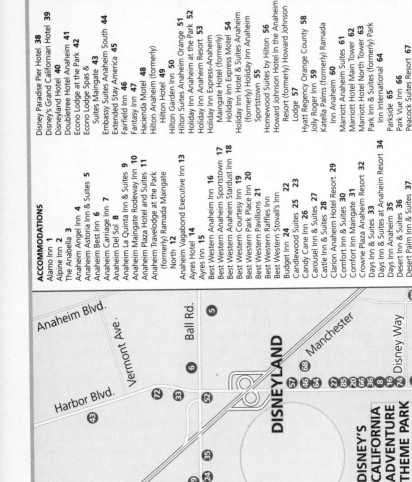

ACCOMMODATIONS

Alamo Inn **1**
Alpine Inn **2**
The Anabella **3**
Anaheim Angel Inn **4**
Anaheim Astoria Inn & Suites **5**
Anaheim Best Inn **6**
Anaheim Carriage Inn **7**
Anaheim Del Sol **8**
Anaheim La Quinta Inn & Suites **9**
Anaheim Maingate Rodeway Inn **10**
Anaheim Plaza Hotel and Suites **11**
Anaheim Travelodge at the Park (formerly) Ramada Maingate North **12**
Anaheim Vagabond Executive Inn **13**
Ayres Hotel **14**
Ayres Inn **15**
Best Western Anaheim Inn **16**
Best Western Anaheim Sportstown **17**
Best Western Anaheim Stardust Inn **18**
Best Western Courtesy Inn **19**
Best Western Park Place Inn **20**
Best Western Pavillions **21**
Best Western Raffles Inn **22**
Best Western Stovall's Inn **23**
Budget Inn **24**
Candlewood Suites **25**
Candy Cane Inn **26**
Carousel Inn & Suites **27**
Castle Inn & Suites **28**
Clarion Anaheim Hotel Resort **29**
Comfort Inn & Suites **30**
Comfort Inn Maingate **31**
Crowne Plaza Anaheim Resort **32**
Days Inn & Suites **33**
Days Inn & Suites at Anaheim Resort **34**
Days Inn Anaheim **35**
Desert Inn & Suites **36**
Desert Palm Inn & Suites **37**

Disney Paradise Pier Hotel **38**
Disney's Grand Californian Hotel **39**
Disneyland Hotel **40**
Doubletree Hotel Anaheim **41**
Econo Lodge at the Park **42**
Econo Lodge Spas & Suites Maingate **43**
Embassy Suites Anaheim South **44**
Extended Stay America **45**
Fairfield Inn **46**
Fantasy Inn **47**
Hacienda Motel **48**
Hilton Anaheim (formerly) Hilton Hotel **49**
Hilton Garden Inn **50**
Hilton Suites Anaheim Orange **51**
Holiday Inn Anaheim at the Park **52**
Holiday Inn Anaheim Resort **53**
Holiday Inn Express-Anaheim Maingate Hotel (formerly) **54**
Holiday Inn Express Motel (formerly) Holiday Inn Anaheim Sportstown **55**
Homewood Suites by Hilton **56**
Howard Johnson Hotel In the Anaheim Resort (formerly) Howard Johnson Lodge **57**
Hyatt Regency Orange County **58**
Jolly Roger Inn **59**
Katella Palms (formerly) Ramada Inn Anaheim **60**
Marriott Anaheim Suites **61**
Marriott Hotel Main Tower **62**
Marriott Hotel North Tower **63**
Park Inn & Suites (formerly) Park Inn International **64**
Parkside **65**
Park Vue Inn **66**
Peacock Suites Resort **67**

Anaheim Blvd.
Vermont Ave.
Ball Rd.
Harbor Blvd.
Manchester
Disney Way
DISNEYLAND
DISNEY'S CALIFORNIA ADVENTURE THEME PARK
Disneyland Dr.
Disneyland Dr.
Manchester Ave.
Magic Way
Disneyland Parking Deck
Walnut St.

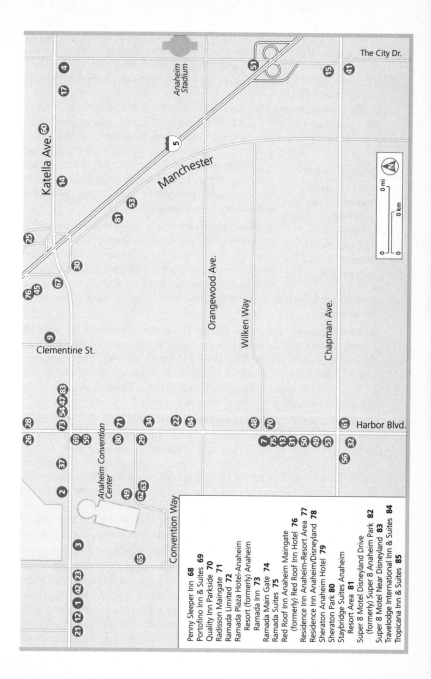

The City Dr.

Anaheim Stadium

Katella Ave.

Manchester

Orangewood Ave.

Wilken Way

Chapman Ave.

Clementine St.

Harbor Blvd.

Anaheim Convention Center

Convention Way

Penny Sleeper Inn **68**
Portofino Inn & Suites **69**
Quality Inn Parkside **70**
Radisson Maingate **71**
Ramada Limited **72**
Ramada Plaza Hotel-Anaheim
  Resort (formerly) Anaheim
  Ramada Inn **73**
Ramada Main Gate **74**
Ramada Suites **75**
Red Roof Inn Anaheim Maingate
  (formerly) Red Roof Inn Hotel **76**
Residence Inn Anaheim-Resort Area **77**
Residence Inn Anaheim/Disneyland **78**
Sheraton Anaheim Hotel **79**
Sheraton Park **80**
Staybridge Suites Anaheim
  Resort Area **81**
Super 8 Motel Disneyland Drive
  (formerly) Super 8 Anaheim Park **82**
Super 8 Motel Near Disneyland **83**
Travelodge International Inn & Suites **84**
Tropicana Inn & Suites **85**

unfamiliar to you, acquainting yourself with the concepts and strategies will serve you well in the long run. Simply put, the tips we provide for getting a good deal near Disneyland will work equally well at just about any other place where you need a hotel. Once you have invested a little time and have experimented with these strategies, you will be able to routinely obtain rooms at the best hotels and at the lowest possible rates.

Be forewarned that Disneyland Resort is right across the street from the Anaheim/Orange County Convention Center, one of the largest and busiest convention centers in the country. Room availability, as well as rates, are affected significantly by trade shows and other events at the convention center. To determine whether such an event will be ongoing during your projected dates, visit **www.ana-heimoc.org/convcalendar.**

unofficial **TIP**
For the best rates and least crowded conditions, try to avoid visiting Disneyland Resort when a major convention or trade show is in progress.

1. Mousesavers.com is a site dedicated to finding great deals on hotels, admissions, and more at Disneyland Resort and Walt Disney World. The site covers discounts on both Disney and non-Disney hotels and is especially effective at keeping track of time-limited deals and discounts offered in a select market, San Diego for example.

2. Travelaxe.com offers free software you can download on your PC (sorry, no Macs) that will scan the better hotel discount sites and find the cheapest rate on the Internet for each of over 80 Disneyland area hotels. The site offers various filters such as price, quality rating, and proximity to a specific location (Disneyland, Convention Center, airport, etc.) that allow you to tailor your search.

3. Expedia.com and **Travelocity.com** These two Web sites sometimes offer good discounts on area hotels. We find that Expedia offers the best deals if you're booking within two weeks of your visit. In fact, some of Expedia's last-minute deals are amazing, really rock-bottom rates. Travelocity frequently beats Expedia, however, if you reserve two weeks to three months out. Neither site offers anything to get excited about if you book more than three months from the time of your visit. If you use either site, be sure to take into consideration the demand for rooms during the season of your visit, and check to see if any big conventions or trade shows are scheduled for the convention center.

4. Priceline.com At Priceline you can tender a bid for a room. You can't bid on a specific hotel but you can specify location ("Disneyland Vicinity") and the quality rating expressed in stars. If your bid is accepted, you will be assigned to a hotel consistent with your location and quality requirements, and your credit card will be charged in a nonrefundable transaction for your entire stay. Notification of acceptance usually takes less than an hour. We recommend bidding $25 to $45 per night for a three-star hotel and $45 to $70 per night for a four-star property. To gauge your chances of success, check to see if any major conventions or trade shows are scheduled for the convention center during your preferred dates.

5. ENTERTAINMENT BOOKS These are area-specific books with discount coupons for hotels, restaurants, entertainment, shopping, and even car washes. The Anaheim version sells for about $45 at the beginning of the year, but is discounted if you buy with only part of the year remaining. Sometimes the books sell out before summer. Unless you live in Orange County, you won't be able to use a lot of the coupons, but sometimes the savings on your hotel and dining will more than justify the purchase. To buy, or for additional information, visit **www.entertainment.com** online.

6. EXIT INFORMATION GUIDE A company called EIG (Exit Information Guide) publishes a book of discount coupons for bargain rates at hotels throughout California. These books are available free of charge at many restaurants and motels along the main interstate highways in and leading to California. However, since most folks make reservations before leaving home, picking up the coupon book en route does not help much. But, for $3 ($5 Canadian) EIG will mail you a copy, allowing you to examine the discounts offered before you make your reservations. You can use a credit card or send a money order or check. The guide is free; the charge is for the postage. Write or call, or order online at **www.travelersdiscountguide.com:**

Exit Information Guide
4205 N.W. 6th Street
Gainesville, FL 32609
☎ 352-371-3948

7. SPECIAL WEEKEND RATES If you are not averse to about an hour's drive to Disneyland, you can get a great weekend rate on rooms in downtown Los Angeles. Most hotels that cater to business, government, and convention travelers offer special weekend discounts that range from 15 to 40% below normal weekday rates. You can find out about weekend specials by calling the hotel or by consulting your travel agent.

8. WHOLESALERS, CONSOLIDATORS, AND RESERVATION SERVICES Wholesalers and consolidators buy rooms, or options on rooms (room blocks), from hotels at a low negotiated rate. They then resell the rooms at a profit through travel agents, through tour packagers, or directly to the public. Most wholesalers and consolidators have a provision for returning unsold rooms to participating hotels, but they are disinclined to do so. The wholesaler's or consolidator's relationship with any hotel is predicated on volume. If they return rooms unsold, the hotel might not make as many rooms available to them the next time around. Thus, wholesalers and consolidators often offer rooms at bargain rates, anywhere from 15 to 50% off rack, occasionally sacrificing their profit margin in the process, to avoid returning the rooms to the hotel unsold.

When wholesalers and consolidators deal directly with the public, they frequently represent themselves as "reservation services." When you call, you can ask for a rate quote for a particular hotel or, alternatively, ask for their best available deal in the area where you prefer to stay. If there is a maximum amount you are willing to pay, say so. Chances are the service will find something that will work for you, even if they have to shave a dollar or two off their own profit. Sometimes you will have to prepay for your room with your credit card when you make your reservation. Most often, you will pay when you check out. Listed below are two services that frequently offer substantial discounts in the Anaheim area.

Anaheim Area Wholesalers and Consolidators

California Reservations   ☎ 800-576-0003   **www.hotellocators.com**

Hotel Reservations Network   ☎ 800-715-7666   **www.hoteldiscounts.com**

10. CLUBS AND ORGANIZATIONS If you belong to AAA, AARP, or a number of other organizations or clubs, you can obtain discounts on lodging. Usually the discounts are modest, in the 5 to 15% range, but occasionally higher.

11. IF YOU MAKE YOUR OWN RESERVATION As you poke around trying to find a good deal, there are several things you should know. First, always call the hotel in question as opposed to the hotel chain's national toll-free number. Quite often, the reservationists at the national numbers are unaware of local specials. Always ask about specials before you inquire about corporate rates. Do not be reluctant to bargain. If you are buying a hotel's weekend package, for example, and want to extend your stay into the following week, you can often obtain at least the corporate rate for the extra days. Do your bargaining before you check in, however, preferably when you make your reservations. Work far enough in advance to receive a faxed or mailed confirmation.

HOW TO GET THE ROOM YOU WANT

MOST HOTELS, INCLUDING DISNEY'S, won't guarantee a specific room when you book, but will post your request on your reservations record and try to accommodate you. Our experience indicates that if you give them your first, second, and third choices, you'll probably get one of the three.

When speaking to the reservationist or your travel agent, it's important to be specific. If you want a room overlooking the pool, say so. Similarly, be sure to clearly state such preferences as a particular floor, a corner room, a room close to restaurants, a room away from elevators and ice machines, a nonsmoking room, a room with a certain type of balcony, or any other preference. If you have a laundry list of preferences, type it up in order of importance, and e-mail, fax, or mail it to the hotel or to your travel agent. Be sure to include your own contact information and, if you've already booked, your reservation confirmation number. If it makes you feel better, call back in a couple of days to make sure your preferences were posted to your reservations record.

About Hotel Renovations

We have inspected almost 100 hotels in the Disneyland Resort area to compile the list of lodging choices presented in this *Unofficial Guide*. Each year we phone each hotel to verify contact information and to inquire about renovations or refurbishments. If a hotel has been renovated or has refurbished its guest rooms, we reinspect that hotel along with any new hotels for the next edition of this book. Hotels that report no improvements are checked out every two years.

Our hotel ratings are provided shortly in the section "Hotels and Motels: Rated and Ranked" (page 43).

TRAVEL PACKAGES

PACKAGE TOURS ARE ROUTINELY AVAILABLE that include lodging, park admission, and other features. Some of these are very good deals if you make use of the features you are paying for.

ONE MORE THING

If your travel plans include a stay in the area of more than two or three days, lodge near Disneyland Resort only just before and on the days you visit the park. The same traffic you avoid by staying close to the park will eat you alive when you begin branching out to other Los Angeles–area attractions. Also, the area immediately around Disneyland is uninspiring, and there is a marked scarcity of decent restaurants.

Finally, a helpful source of regional travel information is:

Anaheim/Orange County Visitor and Convention Bureau
Department C
P.O. Box 4270
Anaheim, CA 92803
☎ 714-765-8888
www.anaheimoc.org

How to Evaluate a Disneyland Travel Package

Hundreds of Disneyland package vacations are offered to the public each year. Some are created by the Walt Disney Travel Sales Center, others by airline touring companies, and some by independent travel agents and wholesalers. Almost all Disneyland packages include lodging at or near Disneyland and theme-park admission. Packages offered by the airlines include air transportation.

Package prices vary seasonally, with mid-June to mid-August and holiday periods being most expensive. Off-season, forget packages; there are plenty of empty rooms and you can negotiate great discounts (at non-Disney properties) yourself. Similarly, airfares and rental cars are cheaper at off-peak times.

Almost all package ads feature a headline stating "Disneyland for Three Days from $298" or some such wording. The key word in the ads is "from." The rock-bottom package price connotes the least desirable hotel accommodations. If you want better or more conveniently located digs, you'll have to pay more, often much more.

At Disneyland, packages offer a wide selection of hotels. Some, like the Disney-owned hotels, are very good. Others, unfortunately, run the quality gamut. Packages with lodging in non-Disney hotels are much less expensive.

Packages should be a win-win proposition for both the buyer and the seller. The buyer only has to make one phone call and deal with a single salesperson to set up the whole vacation: transportation, rental car, admissions, lodging, meals, and even golf and tennis. The seller, likewise, only has to deal with the buyer one time, eliminating the need for separate sales, confirmations, and billing. In addition to streamlining selling, processing, and administration, some packagers also buy airfares in bulk on contract, like a broker playing the commodities market. Buying a large number of airfares in advance allows the packager to buy them at a significant savings from posted fares. The same practice is applied also to hotel rooms. Because selling vacation packages is an efficient way of doing business, and because the packager can often buy individual package components (airfare, lodging, etc.) in bulk at a discount, savings in operating expenses realized by the seller are sometimes passed on to the buyer so that, in addition to convenience, the package is also an exceptional value. In any event, that is the way it is supposed to work.

All too often, in practice, the seller realizes all of the economies and passes on nothing in the way of savings to the buyer. In some instances, packages are loaded with extras that cost the packager next to nothing, but run the retail price of the package sky-high. As you might expect, the savings to be passed along to customers are still somewhere in Fantasyland.

When considering a package, choose one that includes features you are sure to use. Whether you use all the features or not, you will most certainly pay for them. Second, if cost is of greater concern than convenience, make a few phone calls and see what the package would cost if you booked its individual components (airfare, rental car, lodging, etc.) on your own. If the package price is less than the à la carte cost, the package is a good deal. If the costs are about the same, the package is probably worth it for the convenience.

If you buy a package from Disney, do not expect Disney reservationists to offer suggestions or help you sort out your options. As a rule they will not volunteer information, but will only respond to specific questions you pose, adroitly ducking any query that calls for an opinion. A reader from North Riverside, Illinois, wrote to the *Unofficial Guide,* complaining:

> I have received various pieces of literature from [Disney] and it is very confusing to try and figure everything out. My wife made two telephone calls and the [Disney] representatives were very courteous. However, they only answered the questions posed and were not very eager to give advice on what might be most cost-effective. The [Disney] reps would not say if we would be better off doing one thing over the other. I feel a person could spend eight hours on the telephone with [Disney] reps and not have any more input than you get from reading the literature.

If you cannot get the information you need from the Disney people, try a good travel agent. Chances are the agent will be more forthcoming in helping you sort out your options.

Information Needed for Evaluation

For quick reference and to save on phone expenses, write or call Walt Disney Travel Sales Center at ☎ 714-520-7070 and ask that they mail you a current Walt Disney Travel Sales Center California Brochure containing descriptions and room rates for all Disneyland lodging properties. Summarized information sheets on lodging are also available by fax. In addition, ask for a rate sheet listing admission options and prices for the theme parks. With this in hand, you are ready to evaluate any package that appeals to you. Remember that all packages are quoted on a per-person basis, two to a room (double occupancy). Good luck.

HOTELS *and* MOTELS: RATED *and* RANKED

WHAT'S IN A ROOM?

EXCEPT FOR CLEANLINESS, STATE OF REPAIR, AND DECOR, most travelers do not pay much attention to hotel rooms. There is, of course, a discernible standard of quality and luxury that differentiates Motel 6 from Holiday Inn, Holiday Inn from Marriott, and so on. In general, however, hotel guests fail to appreciate that some rooms are better engineered than others.

Contrary to what you might suppose, designing a hotel room is (or should be) a lot more complex than picking a bedspread to match the carpet and drapes. Making the room usable to its occupants is an art, a planning discipline that combines both form and function.

Decor and taste are important, certainly. No one wants to spend several days in a room where the decor is dated, garish, or even ugly.

But beyond the decor, there are variables that determine how "livable" a hotel room is. In Anaheim, for example, we have seen some beautifully appointed rooms that are simply not well designed for human habitation. The next time you stay in a hotel, pay attention to the details and design elements of your room. Even more than decor, these are the things that will make you feel comfortable and at home.

It takes the *Unofficial Guide* researchers up to 40 minutes to inspect a hotel room. Here are a few of the things we check that you may want to start paying attention to, before they bother you:

ROOM SIZE While some smaller rooms are cozy and well designed, a large and uncluttered room is generally preferable, especially for a stay of more than three days.

TEMPERATURE CONTROL, VENTILATION, AND ODOR The guest should be able to control the temperature of the room. The best system, because it's so quiet, is central heating and air-conditioning, controlled by the room's own thermostat. The next best system is a room-module heater and air-conditioner, preferably controlled by an automatic thermostat, but more often by manually operated button controls. The worst system is central heating and air without any sort of room thermostat or guest control.

The vast majority of hotel rooms have windows or balcony doors that have been permanently secured shut. Though there are some legitimate safety and liability issues involved, we prefer windows and balcony doors that can be opened to admit fresh air. Hotel rooms should be odor-free and smoke-free and should not feel stuffy or damp.

ROOM SECURITY Better rooms have locks that require a plastic card instead of the traditional lock and key. Card and slot systems essentially allow the hotel to change the combination or entry code of the lock with each new guest who uses the room. A burglar who has somehow acquired a room key to a conventional lock can afford to wait until the situation is right before using the key to gain access. Not so with a card-and-slot system. Though larger hotels and hotel chains with lock-and-key systems usually rotate their locks once each year, they remain vulnerable to hotel thieves much of the time. Many smaller or independent properties rarely rotate their locks.

unofficial **TIP**
Request a renovated room at your hotel—these can be much nicer than the older rooms.

In addition to the entry-lock system, the door should have a deadbolt, and preferably a chain that can be locked from the inside. A chain by itself is not sufficient. Doors should also have a peephole. Windows and balcony doors, if present, should have secure locks.

SAFETY Every room should have a fire or smoke alarm, clear fire instructions, and preferably a sprinkler system. Bathtubs should have a nonskid surface, and shower stalls should have doors that either open outward or slide side to side. Bathroom electrical outlets should be high on the wall and not too close to the sink. Balconies should have sturdy, high rails.

NOISE Most travelers have been kept awake by the television, partying, amorous activities of people in the next room, or traffic on the street outside. Better hotels are designed with noise control in mind. Wall and ceiling construction are substantial, effectively screening out routine noise. Carpets and drapes, in addition to being decorative, also absorb and muffle sounds. Mattresses mounted on stable platforms or sturdy bed frames do not squeak even when challenged by the most passionate and acrobatic lovers. Televisions enclosed in cabinets, and with volume governors, rarely disturb guests in adjacent rooms.

In better hotels, the air-conditioning and heating system is well maintained and operates without noise or vibration. Likewise, plumbing is quiet and positioned away from the sleeping area. Doors to the hall and to adjoining rooms are thick and well fitted to better keep out noise.

DARKNESS CONTROL Ever been in a hotel room where the curtains would not quite come together in the middle? Thick, lined curtains that close completely in the center and extend beyond the dimensions of the window or door frame are required. In a well-planned room, the curtains, shades, or blinds should almost totally block light at any time of day.

LIGHTING Poor lighting is an extremely common problem in American hotel rooms. The lighting is usually adequate for dressing, relaxing, or watching television, but not for reading or working. Lighting needs to be bright over tables and desks and alongside couches or easy chairs. Because so many people read in bed, there should be a separate light for each person. A room with two queen beds should have individual lights for four people. Better bedside reading lights illuminate a small area, so if you want to sleep and someone else prefers to stay up and read, you will not be bothered by the light. The worst situation by far is a single lamp on a table between beds. In each bed, only the person next to the lamp will have sufficient light to read. This deficiency is often compounded by light bulbs of insufficient wattage.

In addition, closet areas should be well lit, and there should be a switch near the door that turns on lights in the room when you enter. A seldom seen but desirable feature is a bedside console that allows a guest to control all or most lights in the room from bed.

FURNISHINGS At bare minimum, the bed(s) must be firm. Pillows should be made with nonallergenic fillers and, in addition to the sheets and spread, a blanket should be provided. Bedclothes should be laundered with a fabric softener and changed daily. Better hotels usually provide extra blankets and pillows in the room or on request, and sometimes use a second sheet between the blanket and the spread.

There should be a dresser large enough to hold clothes for two people during a five-day stay. A small table with two chairs or a desk with one chair should be provided. The room should be equipped with a luggage rack and a three-quarter- to full-length mirror.

The television should be cable-connected and color; ideally it should have a volume governor and remote control. It should be mounted on a swivel base and preferably enclosed in a cabinet. Local channels should be posted on the set, and a local TV program guide should be supplied.

The telephone should be Touch-Tone and conveniently situated for bedside use. It should have on or near it easily understood dialing instructions and a rate card. Local white and yellow pages should be provided. Better hotels have phones in the bathroom and equip phones with long cords.

Well-designed hotel rooms usually have a plush armchair or a sleeper sofa for lounging and reading. Better headboards are padded for comfortable reading in bed, and there should be a nightstand or table on each side of the bed(s). Nice extras in any hotel room include a small refrigerator, a digital alarm clock, and a coffeemaker.

BATHROOM Two sinks are better than one, and you cannot have too much counter space. A sink outside the bath is a great convenience when one person bathes as another dresses. Sinks should have drains with stoppers.

Better bathrooms have both a tub and shower with nonslip bottoms. Faucet controls should be easy to operate. Adjustable showerheads are preferred. The bath needs to be well lit and should have an exhaust fan and a guest-controlled heater. Bath towels should be large, soft, fluffy, and provided in generous quantities, as should hand towels and washcloths. There should be an electrical outlet per sink, conveniently and safely placed.

Complimentary shampoo, conditioner, soap, and lotion are a plus, as are robes and bathmats. Better hotels supply their bathrooms with tissues and extra toilet paper. Luxurious baths feature a phone, a hair dryer, and sometimes a small television or even a Jacuzzi.

VENDING There should be complimentary ice and a drink machine on each floor. Welcome additions include a snack machine and a sundries (combs, toothpaste) machine. The latter are seldom found in large hotels that have 24-hour restaurants and shops.

ROOM RATINGS

TO SEPARATE PROPERTIES ACCORDING TO the relative quality, tastefulness, state of repair, cleanliness, and size of their standard rooms, we have grouped the hotels and motels into classifications denoted by stars. Star ratings in this guide apply to Anaheim properties only, and do not necessarily correspond to ratings awarded by Mobil, AAA, or other travel critics. Because stars have little relevance when awarded in the absence of commonly recognized standards of comparison, we have tied our ratings to expected levels of quality established by specific American hotel corporations.

Star ratings apply to *room quality only,* and describe the property's standard accommodations. For most hotels and motels a "standard accommodation" is a hotel room with either one king bed or two queen beds. In an all-suite property, the standard accommodation is either a studio or one-bedroom suite. In addition to standard accommodations, many hotels offer luxury rooms and special suites that are not rated in this guide. Star ratings for rooms are assigned without regard to whether a property has a restaurant, recreational facilities, entertainment, or other extras.

In addition to stars (which delineate broad categories), we also employ a numerical rating system. Our rating scale is 0 to 100, with 100 as the best possible rating. Numerical ratings are presented to show the difference we perceive between one property and another. Rooms at the Homewood Suites, Peacock Suites, and Howard Johnson Hotel are all rated as three and one-half stars (★★★½). In the supplemental numerical ratings, the Homewood Suites is rated an 80, the Peacock is rated an 81, and the Howard Johnson a 75. This means that within the three-and-a-half-star category, the Homewood Suites and Peacock Suites are comparable, and both have slightly nicer rooms than the Howard Johnson Hotel.

OVERALL STAR RATINGS		
★★★★★	Superior Rooms	Tasteful and luxurious by any standard
★★★★	Extremely Nice Rooms	What you would expect at a Hyatt Regency or Marriott
★★★	Nice Rooms	Holiday Inn or comparable quality
★★	Adequate Rooms	Clean, comfortable, and functional without frills—like a Motel 6
★	Budget Rooms	Spartan, not aesthetically pleasing

HOW THE HOTELS COMPARE

COST ESTIMATES ARE BASED ON the hotel's published rack rates for standard rooms. Each "$" represents $50. Thus, a cost symbol of "$$$" means a room (or suite) at that hotel will be about $150 a night (it may be less for weekdays or more on weekends).

Following is a hit parade of the nicest rooms in town. We've focused strictly on room quality and have excluded any consideration of location, services, recreation, or amenities. In some instances, a one- or two-room suite can be had for the same price or less than that of a hotel room.

If you used an earlier edition of this guide, you will notice that many of the ratings and rankings have changed. In addition to the inclusion of new properties, these changes are occasioned by such positive developments as guest-room renovation or improved maintenance and housekeeping. A failure to properly maintain guest rooms or a lapse in housekeeping standards can negatively affect the ratings.

Finally, before you begin to shop for a hotel, take a hard look at this letter we received from a couple in Hot Springs, Arkansas:

> We cancelled our room reservations to follow the advice in your book [and reserved a hotel highly ranked by the Unofficial Guide]. We wanted inexpensive, but clean and cheerful. We got inexpensive, but dirty, grim, and depressing. I really felt disappointed in your advice and the room. It was the pits. That was the one real piece of information I needed from your book! The room spoiled the holiday for me aside from our touring.

Needless to say, this letter was as unsettling to us as the bad room was to our reader. Our integrity as travel journalists, after all, is based on the quality of the information we provide to our readers. Even with the best of intentions and the most conscientious research, however, we cannot inspect every room in every hotel. What we do, in statistical terms, is take a sample: we check out several rooms selected at random in each hotel and base our ratings and rankings on those rooms. The inspections are conducted anonymously and without the knowledge of the property's management. Although it would be unusual, it is certainly possible that the rooms we randomly inspect are not representative of the majority of rooms at a particular hotel. Another possibility is that the rooms we inspect in a given hotel are representative but that by bad luck a reader is assigned to an inferior room. When we rechecked the hotel our reader disliked so intensely, we discovered that our rating was correctly representative but that he and his wife had unfortunately been assigned to one of a small number of threadbare rooms scheduled for renovation.

The key to avoiding disappointment is to do some advance snooping around. We recommend that you ask to get a photo of a hotel's standard guest room before you book, or at least a copy of the hotel's promotional brochure. Be forewarned, however, that some hotel chains use the same guest room photo in their promotional literature for all hotels in the chain, and that the guest room in a specific property may not resemble the photo in the brochure. When you or your travel agent call, ask how old the property is and when the guest room you are being assigned was last renovated. If you arrive and are assigned a room inferior to that which you had been led to expect, demand to be moved to another room.

How the Hotels Compare

HOTEL	OVERALL QUALITY RATING	ROOM QUALITY RATING	COST ($=$50)	PHONE
DISNEYLAND AREA				
Disney's Grand Californian Hotel	★★★★	90	$$$$$$$–	☎ 714-635-2300
Disneyland Hotel	★★★★	89	$$$$$+	☎ 714-778-6600
Crowne Plaza Anaheim Resort	★★★★	86	$$+	☎ 714-867-5555
Disney Paradise Pier Hotel	★★★★	86	$$$$$–	☎ 714-999-0990
Hilton Suites Anaheim Orange	★★★★	86	$$$+	☎ 714-938-1111
Ayres Hotel	★★★★	85	$$+	☎ 714-634-2106
Hyatt Regency Orange County	★★★★	85	$$$–	☎ 714-750-1234
Marriott Hotel Main Tower	★★★★	85	$$$+	☎ 714-750-8000
Staybridge Suites Anaheim Resort Area	★★★★	85	$$$–	☎ 714-748-7700
Doubletree Hotel Anaheim	★★★★	84	$$$–	☎ 714-634-4500
The Anabella	★★★★	83	$$	☎ 714-905-1050
Marriott Anaheim Suites	★★★★	83	$$$	☎ 714-750-1000
Sheraton Anaheim Hotel	★★★★	83	$$$	☎ 714-778-1700
Candlewood Suites	★★★½	82	$$$–	☎ 714-808-9000
Marriott Hotel North Tower	★★★½	82	$$$+	☎ 714-750-8000
Portofino Inn & Suites	★★★½	82	$$$–	☎ 714-782-7600
Embassy Suites Anaheim South	★★★½	81	$$$+	☎ 714-539-3300
Hilton Anaheim	★★★½	81	$$$–	☎ 714-750-4321
Peacock Suites Resort	★★★½	81	$$$–	☎ 714-535-8255
Ramada Plaza Hotel Anaheim Resort	★★★½	81	$$$–	☎ 714-991-6868
Holiday Inn Anaheim Resort	★★★½	80	$$$–	☎ 714-748-7777
Homewood Suites by Hilton	★★★½	80	$$$$–	☎ 714-740-1800
Desert Inn & Suites	★★★½	79	$$+	☎ 714-772-5050
Hilton Garden Inn	★★★½	79	$$+	☎ 714-703-9100
Residence Inn Anaheim Resort Area	★★★½	79	$$$$–	☎ 714-591-4000
Residence Inn Anaheim/ Disneyland	★★★½	79	$$$+	☎ 714-533-3555
Anaheim La Quinta Inn & Suites	★★★½	76	$$$–	☎ 714-635-5000
Sheraton Park Hotel	★★★½	76	$$+	☎ 714-750-1811
Howard Johnson Hotel in the Anaheim Resort	★★★½	75	$$$-	☎ 714-776-6120
Candy Cane Inn	★★★	74	$$+	☎ 714-774-5284
Carousel Inn & Suites	★★★	72	$$$–	☎ 714-758-0444

How the Hotels Compare *(continued)*

HOTEL	OVERALL QUALITY RATING	ROOM QUALITY RATING	COST ($=$50)	PHONE
DISNEYLAND AREA (CONTINUED)				
Days Inn & Suites at Anaheim Resort	★★★	72	$$+	☎ 714-971-5000
Jolly Roger Inn	★★★	72	$$+	☎ 714-782-7500
Ramada Suites	★★★	72	$$	☎ 714-971-3553
Katella Palms	★★★	71	$$−	☎ 714-978-8088
Clarion Anaheim Hotel Resort	★★★	70	$$+	☎ 714-750-3131
Holiday Inn Express Anaheim Maingate Hotel	★★★	70	$$+	☎ 714-772-7755
Radisson Maingate	★★★	70	$$+	☎ 714-750-2801
Extended Stay America	★★★	69	$$−	☎ 714-502-9988
Fairfield Inn	★★★	69	$$+	☎ 714-772-6777
Best Western Raffles Inn	★★★	67	$$$−	☎ 714-750-6100
Park Inn & Suites	★★★	67	$$−	☎ 714-635-7275
Ayres Inn	★★★	66	$$	☎ 714-978-9168
Best Western Stovall's Inn	★★★	66	$$	☎ 714-778-1880
Comfort Inn & Suites	★★★	66	$$−	☎ 714-772-8713
Best Western Anaheim Stardust Inn	★★★	65	$$$−	☎ 714-774-7600
Best Western Park Place Inn	★★★	65	$$+	☎ 714-776-4800
Anaheim Vagabond Executive Inn	★★½	64	$$−	☎ 714-971-5556
Best Western Anaheim Sportstown	★★½	64	$$+	☎ 714-634-1920
Comfort Inn Maingate	★★½	64	$$+	☎ 714-703-1220
Holiday Inn Hotel & Suites Anaheim	★★½	64	$$+	☎ 714-535-0300
Anaheim Plaza Hotel and Suites	★★½	63	$$−	☎ 714-772-5900
Best Western Pavillions	★★½	63	$$+	☎ 714-776-0140
Holiday Inn Anaheim at the Park	★★½	63	$$$−	☎ 714-758-0900
Castle Inn & Suites	★★½	62	$$−	☎ 714-774-8111
Anaheim Astoria Inn & Suites	★★½	61	$$−	☎ 714-774-3882
Best Western Anaheim Inn	★★½	61	$$+	☎ 714-774-1050
Days Inn Anaheim	★★½	61	$$$−	☎ 714-520-0101
Desert Palm Inn & Suites	★★½	61	$$$−	☎ 714-535-1133
Ramada Limited	★★½	61	$$−	☎ 714-999-0684
Red Roof Inn Anaheim Maingate	★★½	61	$$−	☎ 714-520-9696
Alpine Inn	★★½	60	$$−	☎ 714-535-2186

How the Hotels Compare (continued)

HOTEL	OVERALL QUALITY RATING	ROOM QUALITY RATING	COST ($=$50)	PHONE
DISNEYLAND AREA (CONTINUED)				
Anaheim Carriage Inn	★★½	60	$	☎ 714-740-1440
Anaheim Del Sol	★★½	60	$$	☎ 714-234-3411
Best Western Courtesy Inn	★★½	60	$$+	☎ 714-772-2470
Quality Inn Parkside	★★½	60	$$−	☎ 714-750-5211
Tropicana Inn & Suites	★★½	58	$$+	☎ 714-635-4082
Anaheim Maingate Rodeway Inn	★★½	57	$$−	☎ 714-533-2500
Econo Lodge Spas & Suites Maingate	★★½	57	$$−	☎ 714-535-7878
Penny Sleeper Inn	★★½	57	$+	☎ 714-991-8100
Anaheim Angel Inn	★★½	56	$+	☎ 714-634-9121
Anaheim Travelodge at the Park	★★½	56	$+	☎ 714-774-7817
Days Inn & Suites	★★½	56	$$−	☎ 714-533-8830
Travelodge International Inn & Suites	★★½	56	$$$+	☎ 714-971-9393
Super 8 Motel Disneyland Drive	★★	55	$$−	☎ 714-778-0350
Anaheim Best Inn	★★	53	$+	☎ 714-533-2570
Alamo Inn	★★	52	$+	☎ 714-635-8070
Super 8 Motel Disneyland	★★	51	$$−	☎ 714-778-6900
Budget Inn	★★	50	$+	☎ 714-535-5524
Hacienda Motel	★½	46	$	☎ 714-750-2101
Fantasy Inn	★½	41	$+	☎ 714-776-2815
Parkside	★	37	$+	☎ 714-971-5511
Econo Lodge at the Park	★	34	$$−	☎ 714-533-4505
UNIVERSAL AREA				
Universal City Hilton & Towers	★★★★	87	$$$$+	☎ 818-506-2500
Sheraton Universal	★★★★	85	$$$$−	☎ 818-980-1212
Chamberlain West Hollywood	★★★½	81	$$$$+	☎ 310-657-7400
Hilton Burbank Airport	★★★½	80	$$$+	☎ 818-843-6000
Holiday Inn Burbank Airport	★★★	68	$$$−	☎ 818-841-4770
Best Western Hollywood Plaza Inn	★★½	62	$$+	☎ 323-851-1800
Colony Inn Hotel	★★½	60	$$	☎ 818-763-2787

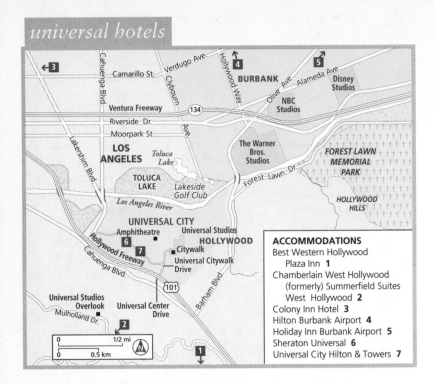

universal hotels

ACCOMMODATIONS

Best Western Hollywood
   Plaza Inn **1**
Chamberlain West Hollywood
   (formerly) Summerfield Suites
   West Hollywood **2**
Colony Inn Hotel **3**
Hilton Burbank Airport **4**
Holiday Inn Burbank Airport **5**
Sheraton Universal **6**
Universal City Hilton & Towers **7**

THE TOP 30 BEST DEALS

HAVING LISTED THE BETTER ROOMS IN TOWN, let's take a look at the best combinations of quality and value in a room. As before, the rankings are made without consideration of location or the availability of restaurants, recreational facilities, entertainment, or amenities.

The Disneyland Hotel, you may notice, is not one of the best deals. This is because you can get more for your money at other properties. The Disneyland and Grand Californian Hotels, however, are two of the most popular hotels in the area, and many guests are willing to pay a higher rate for their convenience, service, and amenities.

We recently had a reader complain to us that he had booked one of our top-ranked rooms for value and had been very disappointed in the room. On checking we noticed that the room the reader occupied had a quality rating of ★★½. We would remind you that the value ratings are intended to give you some sense of value received for your lodging dollar spent. A ★★½ room at $35 may have the same value rating as a ★★★★ room at $85, but that does not mean the rooms will be of comparable quality. Regardless of whether it's a good deal or not, a ★★½ room is still a ★★½ room.

Listed on the facing page are the top 30 room buys for the money,

The Top 30 Best Deals

HOTEL	OVERALL QUALITY RATING	ROOM QUALITY RATING	COST ($=$50)	PHONE (714)
1. The Anabella	★★★★	83	$$	☎ 714-905-1050
2. Crowne Plaza Anaheim Resort	★★★★	86	$$+	☎ 714-867-5555
3. Ayres Hotel	★★★★	85	$$+	☎ 714-634-2106
4. Anaheim Carriage Inn	★★½	60	$	☎ 714-740-1440
5. Hyatt Regency Orange County	★★★★	85	$$$–	☎ 714-750-1234
6. Staybridge Suites Anaheim Resort Area	★★★★	85	$$$–	☎ 714-748-7700
7. Doubletree Hotel Anaheim	★★★★	84	$$$–	☎ 714-634-4500
8. Sheraton Park Hotel	★★★½	76	$$+	☎ 714-750-1811
9. Hilton Garden Inn	★★★½	79	$$+	☎ 714-703-9100
10 Katella Palms	★★★	71	$$–	☎ 714-978-8088
11. Penny Sleeper Inn	★★½	57	$+	☎ 714-991-8100
12. Desert Inn & Suites	★★★½	79	$$+	☎ 714-772-5050
13. Extended Stay America	★★★	69	$$–	☎ 714-502-9988
14. Park Inn & Suites	★★★	67	$$–	☎ 714-635-7275
15. Marriott Anaheim Suites	★★★★	83	$$$	☎ 714-750-1000
16. Sheraton Anaheim Hotel	★★★★	83	$$$	☎ 714-778-1700
17. Peacock Suites Resort	★★★½	81	$$$–	☎ 714-535-8255
18. Hilton Suites Anaheim Orange	★★★★	86	$$$+	☎ 714-938-1111
19. Candlewood Suites	★★★½	82	$$$–	☎ 714-808-9000
20. Comfort Inn & Suites	★★★	66	$$–	☎ 714-772-8713
21. Holiday Inn Anaheim Resort	★★★½	80	$$$–	☎ 714-748-7777
22. Ramada Suites	★★★	72	$$	☎ 714-971-3553
23. Portofino Inn & Suites	★★★½	82	$$$–	☎ 714-782-7600
24. Anaheim La Quinta Inn & Suites	★★★½	76	$$$–	☎ 714-635-5000
25. Hilton Anaheim	★★★½	81	$$$–	☎ 714-750-4321
26. Ramada Plaza Hotel Anaheim Resort	★★★½	81	$$$–	☎ 714-991-6868
27. Red Roof Inn Anaheim Maingate	★★½	61	$$–	☎ 714-520-9696
28. Anaheim Angel Inn	★★½	56	$+	☎ 714-634-9121
29. Marriott Hotel Main Tower	★★★★	85	$$$+	☎ 714-750-8000
30. Anaheim Astoria Inn & Suites	★★½	61	$$–	☎ 714-774-3882

regardless of location or star classification, based on rack rates. Note that sometimes a suite can cost less than a hotel room.

Hotel Information Chart

Alamo Inn ★★
1140 West Katella Avenue
Anaheim, 92802
☎ 714-635-8070
fax 714-778-3307
www.alamoinnandsuites.com

ROOM RATING 52
COST $+

Alpine Inn ★★½
715 West Katella Avenue
Anaheim, 92802
☎ 714-535-2186
fax 714-535-3714
www.alpineinnanaheim.com

ROOM RATING 60
COST $$−

The Anabella ★★★★
1030 West Katella Avenue
Anaheim, 92802
☎ 714-905-1050
fax 714-905-1055
www.anabellahotel.com

ROOM RATING 83
COST $$

Anaheim Carriage Inn ★★½
2125 South Harvor Boulevard
Anaheim, 92802
☎ 714-740-1440
fax 714-971-5330
www.anaheimcarriageinn.com

ROOM RATING 60
COST $

Anaheim Del Sol ★★½
1604 South Harbor Boulevard
Anaheim, 92802
☎ 714-234-3411
fax 714-284-3422
www.delsolinn.com

ROOM RATING 60
COST $$

**Anaheim La Quinta Inn
& Suites** ★★★½
1752 South Clementine Street
Anaheim, 92802
☎ 714-635-5000
fax 714-776-9073
www.laquinta.com

ROOM RATING 76
COST $$$−

**Anaheim Vagabond
Executive Inn** ★★½
2145 South Harbor Boulevard
Anaheim, 92802
☎ 714-971-5556
fax 714-
www.vagabondinn-anaheim-hotel.com

ROOM RATING 64
COST $$−

Ayres Hotel ★★★★
2550 East Katella Avenue
Anaheim, 92806
☎ 714-634-2106
fax 714-634-2108
www.ayreshotels.com

ROOM RATING 85
COST $$+

Ayres Inn ★★★
3737 West Chapman Avenue
Anaheim, 92868
☎ 714-978-9168
fax 714-978-9028
www.ayreshotels.com

ROOM RATING 66
COST $$

**Best Western
Courtesy Inn** ★★½
1070 West Ball Road
Anaheim, 92802
☎ 714-772-2470
fax 714-774-3425
www.bestwestern.com

ROOM RATING 60
COST $$+

**Best Western Hollywood
Plaza Inn** ★★½
2011 North Highland Avenue
Hollywood, 90068
☎ 323-851-1800
fax 323-851-1836
www.bestwestern.com

ROOM RATING 62
COST $$+

**Best Western
Park Place Inn** ★★★
1544 South Harbor Boulevard
Anaheim, 92802
☎ 714-776-4800
fax 714-758-1396
www.bestwestern.com

ROOM RATING 65
COST $$+

Budget Inn ★★
1042 Ball Road
Anaheim, 92802
☎ 714-535-5524
fax 714-999-5900
www.amaheimbudgetinn.com

ROOM RATING 50
COST $+

Candlewood Suites ★★★½
1733 South Anaheim Boulevard
Anaheim, 92805
☎ 714-808-9000
fax 714-808-8989
www.candlewoodssuites.com

ROOM RATING 82
COST $$$−

Candy Cane Inn ★★★
1747 South Harbor Boulevard
Anaheim, 92802
☎ 714-774-5284
fax 714-772-1305
www.candycaneinn.net

ROOM RATING 74
COST $$+

Anaheim Angel Inn ★★½
1800 East Katella Avenue
Anaheim, 92805
☎ 714-634-9121
FAX 714-978-1608

ROOM RATING **56**
COST **$+**

**Anaheim Astoria Inn
& Suites** ★★½
426 West Ball Road
Anaheim, 92805
☎ 714-774-3882
fax 714-234-2164
www.anaheimastoriainn.com

ROOM RATING **61**
COST **$$−**

Anaheim Best Inn ★★
414 West Ball Road
Anaheim, 92805
☎ 714-533-2570
fax 714-635-3322
www.bestinnanaheim.com

ROOM RATING **53**
COST **$+**

**Anaheim Maingate
Rodeway Inn** ★★½
1211 West Place
Anaheim, 92802
☎ 714-533-2500
FAX 714-398-8026

ROOM RATING **57**
COST **$$−**

**Anaheim Plaza Hotel
and Suites** ★★½
1700 South Harbor Boulevard
Anaheim, 92802
☎ 714-772-5900
fax 714-772-8386
www.anaheimplazahotel.com

ROOM RATING **63**
COST **$$−**

**Anaheim Travelodge
at the Park** ★★½
1166 West Katella Avenue
Anaheim, 92802
☎ 714-774-7817
fax 714-
www.anaheimatthepark.com

ROOM RATING **56**
COST **$+**

Best Western Anaheim Inn ★★½
1630 South Harbor Boulevard
Anaheim, 92802
☎ 714-774-1050
fax 714-776-6305
www.bestwestern.com

ROOM RATING **61**
COST **$$+**

**Best Western Anaheim
Sportstown** ★★½
1700 East Katella Avenue
Anaheim, 92805
☎ 714-634-1920
fax 714-634-0366
www.bestwestern.com

ROOM RATING **64**
COST **$$+**

**Best Western Anaheim
Stardust Inn** ★★★
1057 West Ball Road
Anaheim, 92802
☎ 714-774-7600
fax 714-535-6953
www.anaheimstardustinn.com

ROOM RATING **65**
COST **$$$−**

Best Western Pavillions ★★½
1176 West Katella Avenue
Anaheim, 92802
☎ 714-776-0140
fax 714-776-5801
www.bestwestern.com

ROOM RATING **63**
COST **$$+**

Best Western Raffles Inn ★★★
2040 South Harbor Boulevard
Anaheim, 92802
☎ 714-750-6100
fax 714-740-0639
www.bestwestern.com

ROOM RATING **67**
COST **$$$−**

Best Western Stovall's Inn ★★★
1110 West Katella Avenue
Anaheim, 92802
☎ 714-778-1880
fax 714-778-3805
www.bestwestern.com

ROOM RATING **66**
COST **$$**

Carousel Inn & Suites ★★★
1530 South Harbor Boulevard
Anaheim, 92802
☎ 714-758-0444
fax 714-772-9960
www.carouselinnandsuites.com

ROOM RATING **72**
COST **$$$−**

Castle Inn & Suites ★★½
1734 South Harbor Boulevard
Anaheim, 92802
☎ 714-774-8111
fax 714-956-4736
www.castleinn.com

ROOM RATING **62**
COST **$$−**

**Chamberlain
West Hollywood** ★★★½
1000 Westmount Drive
West Hollywood, 90069
☎ 310-657-7400
fax 310-657-1535
www.chamberlainwes
thollywood.com

ROOM RATING **81**
COST **$$$$+**

Hotel Information Chart

Clarion Anaheim Hotel Resort ★★★
616 Convention Way
Anaheim, 92802
☎ 714-750-3131
fax 714-750-9027
www.chidirect.com

ROOM RATING **70**
COST **$$+**

Colony Inn Hotel ★★½
4917 Vineland Avenue
North Hollywood, 91601
☎ 818-763-2787
FAX 818-763-0909

ROOM RATING **60**
COST **$$**

Comfort Inn & Suites ★★★
300 East Katella Way
Anaheim, 92802
☎ 714-772-8713
fax 714-778-1235
www.comfortinnsuites
anaheim.com

ROOM RATING **66**
COST **$$−**

Days Inn & Suites at Anaheim Resort ★★★
2029 South Harbor Boulevard
Anaheim, 92802
☎ 714-971-5000
fax 714-971-5001
www.daysinn.com

ROOM RATING **72**
COST **$$+**

Days Inn Anaheim ★★½
1030 West Ball Road
Anaheim, 92802
☎ 714-520-0101
fax 714-758-9406
www.daysinn.com

ROOM RATING **61**
COST **$$$−**

Desert Inn & Suites ★★★½
1600 South Harbor Boulevard
Anaheim, 92802
☎ 714-772-5050
fax 714-778-2754
www.anaheimdesertinn.com

ROOM RATING **79**
COST **$$+**

Disneyland Hotel ★★★★
1150 West Magic Way
Anaheim, 92802
☎ 714-778-6600
fax 714-520-6079
www.disneyland.com

ROOM RATING **89**
COST **$$$$$+**

Doubletree Hotel Anaheim ★★★★
100 The City Drive
Orange, 92868
☎ 714-634-4500
fax 714-978-2310
www.doubletree,com

ROOM RATING **84**
COST **$$$−**

Econo Lodge at the Park ★
1126 West Katella Avenue
Anaheim, 92802
☎ 714-533-4505
fax 714-533-4545
www.choicehotels.com

ROOM RATING **34**
COST **$$−**

Fairfield Inn ★★★
1460 South Harbor Boulevard
Anaheim, 92802
☎ 714-772-6777
fax 714-999-1727
www.marriott.com

ROOM RATING **69**
COST **$$+**

Fantasy Inn ★½
425 West Katella Avenue
Anaheim, 92802
☎ 714-776-2815
fax 714-533-4037
www.anaheimfantasyinn.com

ROOM RATING **41**
COST **$+**

Hacienda Motel ★½
2176 South Harbor Boulevard
Anaheim, 92802
☎ 714-750-2101
FAX 714-971-1235

ROOM RATING **46**
COST **$**

Hilton Suites Anaheim Orange ★★★★
400 North State College Boulevard
Orange, 92868
☎ 714-938-1111
fax 714-938-0930
www.hilton.com

ROOM RATING **86**
COST **$$$+**

Holiday Inn Anaheim at the Park ★★½
1221 South Harbor Boulevard
Anaheim, 92805
☎ 714-758-0900
fax 714-533-1804
www.holiday-inn.com

ROOM RATING **63**
COST **$$$−**

Holiday Inn Anaheim Resort ★★★½
1915 South Manchester Avenue
Anaheim, 92802
☎ 714-748-7777
fax 714-748-7400
www.holiday-inn.com

ROOM RATING **80**
COST **$$$−**

Comfort Inn Maingate ★★½
2171 South Harbor Boulevard
Anaheim, 92802
☎ 714-703-1220
fax 714-703-1401
www.choicehotels.com

ROOM RATING   64
COST $$+

**Crowne Plaza
Anaheim Resort** ★★★★
12021 Harbor Boulevard
Garden Grove, 92840
☎ 714-867-5555
fax 714-867-5123
www.anaheim.crowneplaza.com

ROOM RATING   86
COST $$+

Days Inn & Suites ★★½
1111 South Harbor Boulevard
Anaheim, 92805
☎ 714-533-8830
fax 714-758-0573
www.daysinn.com

ROOM RATING   56
COST $$−

Desert Palm Inn & Suites ★★½
631 West Katella Avenue
Anaheim, 92802
☎ 714-535-1133
fax 714-491-7409
www.desertpalmshotel.com

ROOM RATING   61
COST $$$−

**Disney Paradise Pier
Hotel** ★★★★
1717 South Disneyland Drive
Anaheim, 92802
☎ 714-999-0990
fax 714-776-5763
www.disneyland.com

ROOM RATING   86
COST $$$$$−

**Disney's Grand Californian
Hotel** ★★★★
1600 South Disneyland Drive
Anaheim, 92802
☎ 714-635-2300
fax 714-300-7300
www.disneyland.com

ROOM RATING   90
COST $$$$$$$−

**Econo Lodge Spas &
Suites Maingate** ★★½
871 South Harbor Boulevard
Anaheim, 92805
☎ 714-535-7878
fax 714-535-8186
www.choicehotels.com

ROOM RATING   57
COST $$−

**Embassy Suites Anaheim
South** ★★★½
11767 Harbor Boulevard
Garden Grove, 92840
☎ 714-539-3300
fax 714-539-4600
www.anaheimsouth.embassy
suites.com

ROOM RATING   81
COST $$$+

Extended Stay America ★★★
1742 South Clementine St.
Anaheim, 92802
☎ 714-502-9988
fax 714-502-9977
www.extendedstayamerica.com

ROOM RATING   69
COST $$−

Hilton Anaheim ★★★½
777 Convention Way
Anaheim, 92802
☎ 714-750-4321
fax 714-740-4460
www.hilton.com

ROOM RATING   81
COST $$$−

Hilton Burbank Airport ★★★½
2500 Hollywood Way
Burbank, 91505
☎ 818-843-6000
fax 818-842-9720
www.hiltonburbank.com

ROOM RATING   80
COST $$$+

Hilton Garden Inn ★★★½
11777 Harbor Boulevard
Garden Grove, 92840
☎ 714-703-9100
fax 714-703-9200
www.hilton.com

ROOM RATING   79
COST $$+

**Holiday Inn Burbank
Airport** ★★★
150 East Angeleno
Burbank, 91502
☎ 818-841-4770
fax 818-566-7886
www.ichotelsgroup.com

ROOM RATING   68
COST $$$−

**Holiday Inn Express Anaheim
Maingate Hotel** ★★★
435 West Katella Avenue
Anaheim, 92802
☎ 714-772-7755
fax 714-772-2727
www.holiday-anaheim.com

ROOM RATING   70
COST $$+

**Holiday Inn Hotel &
Suites Anaheim** ★★½
1240 South Walnut Avenue
Anaheim, 92802
☎ 714-535-0300
fax 714-491-8953
www.holiday-inn.com

ROOM RATING   64
COST $$+

Hotel Information Chart

**Homewood Suites
by Hilton** ★★★½
12005 Harbor Boulevard
Garden Grove, 92840
☎ 714-740-1800
fax 714-740-1867
www.hilton.com

ROOM RATING **80**
COST **$$$$–**

**Howard Johnson Hotel
in the Anaheim Resort** ★★★½
1380 South Harbor Boulevard
Anaheim, 92802
☎ 714-776-6120
fax 714-533-3578
www.hojoanaheim.com

ROOM RATING **75**
COST **$$$–**

**Hyatt Regency
Orange County** ★★★★
11999 Harbor Boulevard
Garden Grove, 92840
☎ 714-750-1234
fax 714-740-0465
www.hyatt.com

ROOM RATING **85**
COST **$$$–**

**Marriott Hotel
Main Tower** ★★★★
700 West Convention Way
Anaheim, 92802
☎ 714-750-8000
fax 714-750-9100
www.marriott.com

ROOM RATING **85**
COST **$$$+**

**Marriott Hotel
North Tower** ★★★½
700 West Convention Way
Anaheim, 92802
☎ 714-750-8000
fax 714-750-9100
www.marriott.com

ROOM RATING **82**
COST **$$$+**

Park Inn & Suites ★★★
1520 South Harbor Boulevard
Anaheim, 92802
☎ 714-635-7275
fax 714-635-7276
www.parkinn-anaheim.com

ROOM RATING **67**
COST **$$–**

Portofino Inn & Suites ★★★½
1831 South Harbor Boulevard
Anaheim, 92802
☎ 714-782-7600
fax 714-782-7619
www.portifinoinnanaheim.com

ROOM RATING **82**
COST **$$$–**

Quality Inn Parkside ★★½
2200 South Harbor Boulevard
Anaheim, 92802
☎ 714-750-5211
fax 208-279-5561

ROOM RATING **60**
COST **$$–**

Radisson Maingate ★★★
1850 South Harbor Boulevard
Anaheim, 92802
☎ 714-750-2801
fax 714-971-4754
www.radisson.com

ROOM RATING **70**
COST **$$+**

**Red Roof Inn Anaheim
Maingate** ★★½
100 Disney Way
Anaheim, 92802
☎ 714-520-9696
fax 714-533-7539
www.redroof.com

ROOM RATING **61**
COST **$$–**

**Residence Inn Anaheim
Resort Area** ★★★½
11931 Harbor Boulevard
Garden Grove, 92840
☎ 714-591-4000
fax 714-591-4048
www.marriott.com

ROOM RATING **79**
COST **$$$$–**

**Residence Inn
Anaheim/Disneyland** ★★★½
1700 South Clementine Street
Anaheim, 92802
☎ 714-533-3555
fax 714-535-7626
www.marriott.com

ROOM RATING **79**
COST **$$$+**

**Staybridge Suites Anaheim
Resort Area** ★★★★
1855 South Manchester Avenue
Anaheim, 92802
☎ 714-748-7700
fax 714-748-4700
www.staybridge.com

ROOM RATING **85**
COST **$$$–**

**Super 8 Motel
Disneyland Drive** ★★
915 South Disneyland Drive
Anaheim, 92802
☎ 714-778-0350
fax 714-778-3878
www.super8motel.net

ROOM RATING **55**
COST **$$–**

**Super 8 Motel
Disneyland** ★★
415 West Katella Avenue
Anaheim, 92802
☎ 714-778-6900
fax 714-535-5659
www.super8.com

ROOM RATING **51**
COST **$$–**

Jolly Roger Inn ★★★
640 West Katella Avenue
Anaheim, 92802
☎ 714-782-7500
fax 714-782-7619
www.jollyrogerhotel.com

ROOM RATING   72
COST $$+

Katella Palms ★★★
1331 East Katella Avenue
Anaheim, 92805
☎ 714-978-8088
FAX 714-937-5622

ROOM RATING   71
COST $$−

Marriott Anaheim Suites ★★★★
12015 Harbor Boulevard
Anaheim, 92802
☎ 714-750-1000
fax 714-750-9000
www.marriott.com

ROOM RATING   83
COST $$$

Parkside ★
1830 South West Street
Anaheim, 92802
☎ 714-971-5511
FAX 714-971-5520

ROOM RATING   37
COST $+

Peacock Suites Resort ★★★½
1745 South Anaheim Boulevard
Anaheim, 92805
☎ 714-535-8255
fax 714-535-8914
www.peacocksuitesresort.com

ROOM RATING   81
COST $$$−

Penny Sleeper Inn ★★½
1441 South Manchester Avenue
Anaheim, 92802
☎ 714-991-8100
fax 714-533-6430
www.anaheimpenny
sleeperinn.com

ROOM RATING   57
COST $+

Ramada Limited ★★½
921 South Harbor Boulevard
Anaheim, 92802
☎ 714-999-0684
fax 714-956-8839
www.ramada.com

ROOM RATING   61
COST $$−

**Ramada Plaza Hotel
Anaheim Resort** ★★★½
515 West Katella Avenue
Anaheim, 92802
☎ 714-991-6868
fax 714-991-6565
www.ramadaplazadisney.com

ROOM RATING   81
COST $$$−

Ramada Suites ★★★
2141 South Harbor Boulevard
Anaheim, 92802
☎ 714-971-3553
fax 714-971-4609
www.ramada.com

ROOM RATING   72
COST $$

Sheraton Anaheim Hotel ★★★★
900 South Disneyland Drive
Anaheim, 92802
☎ 714-778-1700
fax 714-535-3889
www.sheraton.com

ROOM RATING   83
COST $$$

Sheraton Park Hotel ★★★½
1855 South Harbor Boulevard
Anaheim, 92802
☎ 714-750-1811
fax 714-971-1326
www.coasthotels.com

ROOM RATING   76
COST $$+

Sheraton Universal ★★★★
333 Universal Hollywood Drive
Universal City, 91608
☎ 818-980-1212
fax 818-985-4980
www.starwoodhotels.com

ROOM RATING   85
COST $$$$−

**Travelodge International Inn
& Suites** ★★½
2060 South Harbor Boulevard
Anaheim, 92802
☎ 714-971-9393
fax 714-971-2706
www.travelodge.com

ROOM RATING   56
COST $$$+

Tropicana Inn & Suites ★★½
1540 South Harbor Boulevard
Anaheim, 92802
☎ 714-635-4082
fax 714-635-1535
www.tropicanainn-anaheim.com

ROOM RATING   58
COST $$+

**Universal City Hilton &
Towers** ★★★★
555 Universal Hollywood Drive
Universal City, 91608
☎ 818-506-2500
fax 818-509-2058
www.hilton.com

ROOM RATING   87
COST $$$$+

MAKING *the* MOST *of* YOUR TIME

ALLOCATING TIME

THE DISNEY PEOPLE RECOMMEND spending two to four full days at Disneyland Resort. While this may seem a little self-serving, it is not without basis. Disneyland Resort is *huge,* with something to see or do crammed into every conceivable space. In addition, there are now two parks, and touring requires a lot of walking, and often a lot of waiting in line. Moving in and among large crowds all day is exhausting, and often the unrelenting Southern California sun zaps even the most hardy, making tempers short.

During our many visits to Disneyland, we observed, particularly on hot summer days, a dramatic transition from happy, enthusiastic touring on arrival to almost zombie-like plodding along later in the day. Visitors who began their day enjoying the wonders of Disney imagination ultimately lapsed into an exhausted production mentality ("We've got two more rides in Fantasyland, then we can go back to the hotel").

OPTIMUM TOURING SITUATION

WE DON'T BELIEVE THERE IS ONE IDEAL ITINERARY. Tastes, energy levels, and perspectives on what constitutes entertainment and relaxation vary. This understood, here are some considerations for developing your own ideal itinerary.

Optimum touring at Disneyland requires a good game plan, a minimum of three days on-site (excluding travel time), and a fair amount of money. It also requires a fairly prodigious appetite for Disney entertainment. The essence of optimum touring is to see the attractions in a series of shorter, less-exhausting visits during the cooler, less-crowded times of day, with plenty of rest and relaxation between excursions.

Since optimum touring calls for leaving and returning to the theme parks, it makes sense to stay in one of the Disney hotels or in one of the non-Disney hotels within walking distance. If you visit Disneyland during busy times, you need to get up early to beat the crowds. Short lines and stress-free touring are incompatible with sleeping in. If you want to sleep in *and* enjoy your touring, visit Disneyland when attendance is lighter.

THE CARDINAL RULES FOR SUCCESSFUL TOURING

MANY VISITORS DON'T HAVE THREE DAYS to devote to Disneyland Resort. For these visitors, efficient touring is a must. Even the most time-effective plan, however, won't allow you to cover both Disney theme parks in one day. Plan to allocate at least an entire day to each park. If your schedule permits only one day of touring, concentrate on one theme park and save the other for another visit.

One-Day Touring

A comprehensive one-day tour of Disneyland Park or Disney's California Adventure is possible, but requires knowledge of the park, good planning, and plenty of energy and endurance. One-day touring doesn't leave much time for full-service meals, prolonged shopping, or lengthy breaks. One-day touring can be fun and rewarding, but allocating two days per park, especially for Disneyland Park, is always preferable.

Successful touring of Disneyland Park or Disney's California Adventure hinges on three rules:

I. DETERMINE IN ADVANCE WHAT YOU REALLY WANT TO SEE. What rides and attractions most appeal to you? Which additional rides and attractions would you like to experience if you have any time left? What are you willing to forego?

To help you establish your touring priorities, we have described every attraction in detail. In each description, we include the author's critical evaluation of the attraction as well as the opinions of Disneyland Resort guests expressed as star ratings. Five stars is the highest (best) rating possible.

Finally, because Disneyland Resort attractions range in scope from midway-type rides and horse-drawn trolleys to colossal, high-tech extravaganzas spanning the equivalent of whole city blocks, we have developed a hierarchy of categories for attractions to give you some sense of their order of magnitude:

SUPER HEADLINERS The best attractions the theme park has to offer. They are mind-boggling in size, scope, and imagination and represent the cutting edge of modern attraction technology and design.

HEADLINERS Full-blown, multimillion-dollar, full-scale, themed adventure experiences and theater presentations. They are modern in their technology and design and employ a full range of special effects.

MAJOR ATTRACTIONS Themed adventure experiences on a more modest scale, but incorporating state-of-the-art technologies. Or, larger scale attractions of older design.

MINOR ATTRACTIONS Midway-type rides, small-scale "dark rides" (spook house–type rides), minor theater presentations, transportation rides, and elaborate walk-through attractions.

DIVERSIONS Exhibits, both passive and interactive. Also includes playgrounds, video arcades, and street theater.

Though not every attraction fits neatly into the above categories, the categories provide a relative comparison of attraction size and scope. Remember, however, that bigger and more elaborate does not always mean better. Peter Pan's Flight, a minor attraction, continues to be one of the park's most beloved rides. Likewise, for many small children, there is no attraction, regardless of size, that can surpass Dumbo.

2. ARRIVE EARLY! ARRIVE EARLY! ARRIVE EARLY! This is the single most important key to touring efficiently and avoiding long lines. With your admission pass in hand, be at the gate ready to go at least 30 minutes before the theme park's stated opening time. There are no lines and relatively few people first thing in the morning. The same four rides you can experience in one hour in the early morning will take more than three hours to see after 11 a.m. Have breakfast before you arrive so you will not have to waste prime touring time sitting in a restaurant.

3. AVOID BOTTLENECKS. Helping you avoid bottlenecks is what this guide is all about. Bottlenecks occur as a result of crowd concentrations and/or less-than-optimal traffic engineering. Concentrations of hungry people create bottlenecks at restaurants during the lunch and dinner hours; concentrations of people moving toward the exit near closing time create bottlenecks in the gift shops en route to the gate; concentrations of visitors at new and unusually popular rides create bottlenecks and long waiting lines; rides slow to load and unload passengers create bottlenecks and long waiting lines. Avoiding bottlenecks involves being able to predict where, when, and why they occur. To this end, we provide field-tested touring plans to keep you ahead of the crowd or out of its way (see pages 176–192, 218–220, and 238–239). In addition, we provide critical data on all rides and shows that helps you estimate how long you may have to wait in line, compares rides in terms of their capacity to accommodate large crowds, and rates the rides according to our opinions and the opinions of other Disneyland visitors.

TOURING PLANS:
WHAT THEY ARE AND HOW THEY WORK

We followed your plans to the letter—which at times was troublesome to the dad in our party. . . somewhat akin to testing the strength of your marriage by wallpapering together!

—*Unofficial Guide* reader and mother of two
from Milford, Connecticut

WHEN WE INTERVIEWED DISNEYLAND VISITORS who toured the theme park(s) on slow days, they invariably waxed eloquent about the sheer delight of their experience. When we questioned visitors who toured on moderate or busy days, however, they talked at length about the jostling crowds and how much time they stood in line. What a shame, they said, that so much time and energy are spent fighting crowds in a place as special as Disneyland.

Given this complaint, our researchers descended on Disneyland to determine whether a touring plan could be devised that would liberate visitors from the traffic flow and allow them to see any theme park in one day with minimal waiting in line. On some of the busiest days of

the year, our team monitored traffic into and through Disneyland Park, noting how it filled and how patrons were distributed among the attractions. We also observed which rides and attractions were most popular and where bottlenecks were most likely to occur.

After many days of collecting data, we devised preliminary touring plans, which we tested during one of the busiest weeks of the year. Each day, our researchers would tour the park using one of the preliminary plans, noting how long it took to walk from place to place and how long the wait in line was for each attraction. Combining the information gained on trial runs, we devised a master plan that we retested and fine-tuned. This plan, with very little variance from day to day, allowed us to experience all major rides and attractions and most lesser ones in one day, with an average wait in line of less than ten minutes at each.

From this master plan, we developed alternative plans that took into account the varying tastes and personal requirements of different Disneyland patrons. Each plan operated with the same logic as the master plan but addressed the special needs and preferences of its intended users.

Finally, after all of the plans were tested by our staff, we selected (using convenience sampling) Disneyland visitors to test the plans. The only requisite for being chosen to test the plans was that the guests must have been visiting a Disney park for the first time. A second group of patrons was chosen for a "control group." These were first-time visitors who would tour the park according to their own plans but who would make notes about what they did and how much time they spent in lines.

unofficial **TIP**
By using our touring plans you can save as much as 3.5 hours wait in line per day.

When the two groups were compared, the results were amazing. On days when major theme-park attendance exceeded 42,000, visitors touring without our plans *averaged* 2.6 hours more waiting in line per day than the patrons touring with our plans, and they experienced 33% fewer attractions. In 2004, the application of a cutting-edge algorithm to our touring plan software increased the waiting time saved to an average of three-and-a-half hours. We expect additional research to improve the performance of the touring plans again in next year's edition.

General Overview of the Touring Plans

Our touring plans are step-by-step guides for seeing as much as possible with a minimum of standing in line. They're designed to help you avoid crowds and bottlenecks on days of moderate-to-heavy attendance. On days of lighter attendance (see "Selecting the Time of Year for Your Visit," page 21), the plans still save time but aren't as critical to successful touring.

What You Can Realistically Expect from the Touring Plans

Though we present one-day touring plans for both of the theme parks, you should understand that Disneyland Park has more attractions than you can see in one day, even if you never wait in line. If you must cram your visit to Disneyland Park into a single day, the one-day touring plans will allow you to see as much as is humanly possible. Under certain circumstances you may not complete the plan, and you definitely won't be able to see everything. For Disneyland Park, the most comprehensive, efficient, and relaxing touring plans are the two-day plans. Although Disney's California Adventure will undoubtedly grow over the next few years, you should have no problem for the moment seeing everything in one day.

Variables that Will Affect the Success of the Touring Plans

How quickly you move from one ride to another; when and how many refreshment and restroom breaks you take; when, where, and how you eat meals; and your ability (or lack thereof) to find your way around will all have an impact on the success of the plans. Smaller groups almost always move faster than larger groups, and parties of adults generally can cover more ground than families with young children. Switching off (see page 107), among other things, prohibits families with little ones from moving expeditiously among attractions. Plus, some children simply cannot conform to the "early-to-rise" conditions of the touring plans.

A mom from Nutley, New Jersey, writes:

> [Although] the touring plans all advise getting to parks at opening, we just couldn't burn the candle at both ends. Our kids (10, 7, and 4) would not go to sleep early and couldn't be up at dawn and still stay relatively sane. It worked well for us to let them sleep a little

later, go out and bring breakfast back to the room while they slept, and still get a relatively early start by not spending time on eating breakfast out. We managed to avoid long lines with an occasional early morning, and hitting popular attractions during parades, meal-times, and late evenings.

And a family from Centerville, Ohio, says:

The toughest thing about your tour plans was getting the rest of the family to stay with them, at least to some degree. Getting them to pass by attractions in order to hit something across the park was no easy task (sometimes imspossible).

Finally, if you have young children in your party, be prepared for character encounters. The appearance of a Disney character is usually sufficient to stop a touring plan dead in its tracks. What's more, while some characters continue to stroll the parks, it is becoming more the rule to assemble characters in some specific venue (like at Mickey's Toontown) where families must queue up for photos of and auto-graphs from Mickey. Meeting characters, posing for photos, and col-lecting autographs can burn hours of touring time. If your kids are into character-autograph collecting, you will need to anticipate these inter-ruptions to the touring plan and negotiate some understanding with your children about when you will follow the plan and when you will collect autographs. Our advice is to either go with the flow or alterna-tively set aside a certain morning or afternoon for photos and auto-graphs. Be aware, however, that queues for autographs, especially in Mickey's Toontown at Disneyland Park are every bit as long as the queues for major attractions. The only time-efficient way to collect au-tographs is to line up at the character-greeting areas first thing in the morning. Because this is also the best time to experience the more pop-ular attractions, you may have some tough decisions to make.

While we realize that following the touring plans is not always easy, we nevertheless recommend continuous, expeditious touring until around noon. After that hour, breaks and diversions won't affect the plans significantly.

Some variables that can profoundly affect the touring plans are beyond your control. Chief among these is the manner and timing of bringing a particular ride to capacity. For example, Big Thunder Mountain Railroad, a roller coaster in Disneyland Park, has five trains. On a given morning it may begin operation with two of the five, then add the other three if and when they are needed. If the wait-ing line builds rapidly before operators decide to go to full capacity, you could have a long wait, even in early morning.

Another variable relates to the time you arrive for a theater per-formance. Usually, your wait will be the length of time from your arrival to the end of the presentation in progress. Thus, if the *Enchanted Tiki Birds* show is 15 minutes long and you arrive

1 minute after a show has begun, your wait for the next show will be 14 minutes. Conversely, if you arrive as the show is wrapping up, your wait will be only a minute or two.

> **WHAT TO DO IF YOU LOSE THE THREAD**
>
> Anything from a blister to a broken attraction can throw off a touring plan. If unforeseen events interrupt a touring plan, skip one step on the plan for every 20 minutes you're delayed. If you lose your billfold, for example, and spend an hour finding it, skip three steps and pick up from there.

WHAT TO EXPECT WHEN YOU ARRIVE AT THE PARKS

BECAUSE EACH TOURING PLAN IS BASED ON being present when the theme park opens, you need to know a little about opening procedures. Disney transportation to the parks, and the respective theme-park parking lots, open an hour to two hours before official opening time.

Each park has an entrance plaza just outside the turnstiles. Usually you will be held outside the turnstiles until 30 minutes before official opening time. If you are admitted prior to the official opening time, what happens next depends on the season of the year and the anticipated crowds for that day.

1. MOST DAYS You will usually be held at the turnstiles or confined in a small section of the park until the official opening time. At Disneyland Park you might be admitted to Main Street, U.S.A.; at Disney's California Adventure to the Sunshine Plaza. If you proceed farther into a park, you will encounter a rope barrier manned by Disney cast members who will keep you from entering the remainder of the park. You will remain here until the "rope drop," when the rope barrier is removed and the park and all (or most) of its attractions are opened at the official opening time.

2. HIGH SEASON AND HOLIDAYS Sometimes when large crowds are expected, you will be admitted through the turnstiles 30 minutes prior to the official opening time. This time, however, the entire park will be up and running and you will not encounter any rope barriers.

3. VARIATIONS Sometimes, Disney will run a variation of the two opening procedures described above. In this situation, you will be permitted through the turnstiles and will find that one or several specific attractions are open early for your enjoyment.

A Word about the Rope Drop

Until recently, Disney cast members would dive for cover when the rope was dropped as thousands of adrenaline-charged guests stampeded to the most popular attractions. This practice occasioned the legendary Space Mountain Morning Mini-Marathon and the Splash Mountain Rapid Rampage at Disneyland Park.

Well, this scenario no longer exists—at least not in the crazed versions of years past. Recently, Disney has beefed up the number of cast members supervising the rope drop in order to suppress the mayhem. In some cases, the rope is not even "dropped." Instead, it's walked back. In other words, Disney cast members lead you with the rope at a fast walk toward the attraction you're straining to reach, forcing you (and everyone else) to maintain their pace. Not until they come within close proximity of the attraction do the cast members step aside.

So, here's the scoop. If Disney persists in walking the rope back, the only way you can gain an advantage over the rest of the crowd is to arrive early enough to be one of those up front close to the rope. Be alert, though; sometimes the Disney folks will step out of the way after about 50 yards or so. If this happens, you can fire up the afterburners and speed the remaining distance to your destination.

Touring Plan Clip-Out Pocket Outlines

For your convenience, we have prepared outlines of all the touring plans in this guide. These pocket versions present the same itineraries as the detailed plans, but with vastly abbreviated directions. Select the plan appropriate for your party, then familiarize yourself with the detailed version. Once you understand how the plan works, clip the pocket version from the back of this guide and carry it with you as a quick reference at the theme park.

Will the Plans Continue to Work Once the Secret Is Out?

Yes! First, all of the plans require that a patron be there when the theme parks open. Many Disneyland patrons simply refuse to get up early while on vacation. Second, less than one percent of any day's attendance has been exposed to the plans, too little to affect results. Last, most groups tailor the plans, skipping rides or shows according to personal taste.

How Frequently Are the Touring Plans Revised?

Because Disney is always adding new attractions and changing operations, we revise the touring plans every year. Most complaints we receive about them come from readers who are using out-of-date editions of the *Unofficial Guide*. Be prepared, however, for surprises. Opening procedures and show times, for example, may change, and you never know when an attraction might break down.

FASTPASS

IN 1999 DISNEY INITIATED A SYSTEM for moderating the waiting time for popular attractions. Called FASTPASS, it was originally tried at Walt Disney World and then subsequently expanded to cover attractions at all the American Disney parks. Here's how it works.

Your handout park map, as well as signage at respective attractions, will tell you which attractions are included. Attractions operating

FASTPASS will have a regular line and a FASTPASS line. A sign at the entrance will tell you how long the wait is in the regular line. If the wait is acceptable, hop in line. If the wait seems too long, you can insert your park admission pass into a special FASTPASS turnstile and receive an appointment time (for sometime later in the day) to come back and ride. When you return at the appointed time, you will enter the FAST-PASS line and proceed directly to the attraction's preshow or boarding area with no further wait. There is no extra charge to use FASTPASS, but you can get an appointment for only one attraction at a time. Interestingly, this procedure was pioneered by Universal Studios Hollywood many years ago and has been pretty much ignored by major theme parks until recently.

There have been two basic changes made to the original FASTPASS program at the two Disneyland parks. First, instead of having to return during the appointed time window printed on your FASTPASS, you can now return to ride anytime after the beginning of that window. If your return window is 10 to 11 a.m., for example, your FASTPASS is now good from 10 a.m. until the park closes. Thus the window on the FAST-PASS represents only a recommended time to return.

The second change relates to multiday admissions purchased as part of a AAA package that includes lodging at a Disney Resort hotel. These passes allow you to obtain FASTPASSes for as many FASTPASS attractions as you wish and hold them all at the same time. This means you can run around to all the FASTPASS attractions as soon as you enter the park and obtain a FASTPASS for each one. You can only hold one FASTPASS at a time for a particular attraction and the FASTPASSes must be obtained at the individual attraction's FASTPASS kiosk (in other words, you can't obtain a Splash Mountain FASTPASS at the Haunted Mansion kiosk). This multiple FASTPASS privilege was previously available to guests who purchased Disneyland Resort packages from the Walt Disney Travel Sales Center. Interestingly, Disney bequeathed the very powerful perk to AAA, leaving the Walt Disney Travel Sales Center with no purchase incentive that can compete.

FASTPASS works remarkably well, primarily because FASTPASS holders get amazingly preferential treatment.

The effort to accommodate FASTPASS holders makes anyone in the regular line feel like an illegal immigrant. As a telling indication of their status, Disney (borrowing a term from the airlines) refers to those in the regular line as "standby guests." Indeed, we watched guests in the regular line stand by and stand by, shifting despondently from foot to foot while dozens and sometimes hundreds of FAST-PASS holders were ushered into the boarding area ahead of them. Clearly Disney is sending a message here, to wit: FASTPASS is heaven, anything else is limbo at best and probably purgatory. In either event, you'll think you've been in purgatory if you get stuck in the regular line during the hot, crowded part of the day.

FASTPASS, however, doesn't eliminate the need to arrive at the theme park early. Because each park offers at most ten FASTPASS attractions, you still need to get an early start if you want to see as much as possible in a single day. Plus, as we'll discuss later, there's only a limited supply of FASTPASSes available for each attraction on a given day. So, if you don't show up until the middle of the afternoon, you might find that all the FASTPASSes have been distributed to other guests. FASTPASS does, happily, make it possible to see more with less waiting than ever before, and it's a great benefit to those who like to sleep late or who enjoy an afternoon or evening at the theme parks on their arrival day. It also allows you to postpone wet rides like the Grizzly River Run at Disney's California Adventure or Splash Mountain at Disneyland Park until the warmer part of the day.

FASTPASS ATTRACTIONS

DISNEYLAND PARK	DISNEY'S CALIFORNIA ADVENTURE
Autopia	California Screamin'
Big Thunder Mountain	Grizzly River Run
Buzz Lightyear Astro Blasters	Mulholland Madness*
Indiana Jones	Soarin' over California*
Roger Rabbit's CarToon Spin*	*Twilight Zone* Tower of Terror
Space Mountain*	
Splash Mountain*	
Star Tours	

* Denotes rides that routinely issue FASTPASSes for redemption three to seven hours later.

Understanding the FASTPASS System

The basic purpose of the FASTPASS system is to reduce the waiting time for designated attractions by more equally distributing the arrival of guests at those attractions over the course of the day. This is accomplished by providing an incentive, a shorter wait in line, for guests who are willing to postpone experiencing the attraction until sometime later in the day. The system also, in effect, imposes a penalty—that is, being relegated to standby status—to those who opt not to use it (although as we shall see, spreading guest arrivals more equally decreases waiting time for standby guests as well).

When you insert your admission pass into a FASTPASS time clock, the machine spits out a small slip of paper about two-thirds the size of a credit card, small enough to fit in your wallet (but also small enough to lose easily). Printed on the paper will be the name of the attraction and a specific one-hour time window, for example 1:15 to 2:15 p.m. You can return to enjoy the ride anytime from 1:15 until park closing.

Each person in your party must have his/her own FASTPASS.

When you report back to the attraction during your one-hour window, you'll enter a line marked "FASTPASS Return" that will route you more or less directly to the boarding area or preshow area. Each person in your party must have his/her own FASTPASS and be ready to show it to the Disney cast member at the entrance of the FASTPASS return line. Before you enter the boarding area (or theater) another cast member will collect your FASTPASS.

You may show up at any time after the period printed on your FASTPASS begins, and from our observation, no specific time is better or worse. This holds true because cast members are instructed to minimize waits for FASTPASS holders. Thus, if the FASTPASS return line is suddenly inundated (something that occurs more or less by chance), cast members rapidly intervene to reduce the FASTPASS line. This is done by admitting as many as 25 FASTPASS holders for each standby guest until the FASTPASS line is drawn down to an acceptable length. Though FASTPASS will lop off as much as 80% of the wait you'd experience in the regular line, you can still expect a short wait, but usually less than 20 minutes.

You can obtain a FASTPASS anytime after a park opens, though the FASTPASS return lines do not begin operating until about 35 to 50 minutes after opening. Thus, if the attractions at Disneyland Park open at 9 a.m., the FASTPASS time-clock machines will also be available at 9 a.m. and the FASTPASS line will begin operating at about 9:35 a.m.

Whatever time you obtain a FASTPASS, you can be assured of a period of time between when you receive your FASTPASS and the beginning of your return window. The interval can be as short as 30 minutes or as long as seven hours depending on park attendance, the popularity of the attraction, and the attraction's hourly capacity. As a rule of thumb, the earlier in the day you secure a FASTPASS, the shorter the interval between time of issue and the begining of your return window. If on a day that the park opens at 9 a.m., you pick up a FASTPASS for Splash Mountain at say, 9:25 a.m., your recommended window for returning to ride would be something like 10 to 11 a.m., or perhaps 10:10 to 11:10 a.m. The exact time will be determined by how many other guests have obtained FASTPASSes before you.

To more effectively distribute guests over the course of a day, the FASTPASS machines bump the one-hour return period back five minutes for a specific set number of passes issued (usually the number is equal to about 6% of the attraction's hourly capacity). When Splash Mountain opens at 9 a.m., for example, the first 125 people to obtain a FASTPASS will get a 10 to 11 a.m. recommended return window. The next 125 guests are issued FASTPASSes that can be used between 10:05 and 11:05 a.m., with the next 125 assigned a 10:10 to 11:10 a.m. time slot. And so it goes, with the time window dropping back five minutes for every 125 guests. The fewer guests who obtain FASTPASSes for an attraction, the shorter the interval between the receipt of your pass and the return window. Conversely, the more guests issued FASTPASSes, the longer the interval. If an attraction is exceptionally popular, and/or its hourly capacity is relatively small, the return window might be pushed back all the way to park closing time. When this happens the FAST-PASS machines stop pumping out passes. It would not be unusual, for example, for Maliboomer at Disney's California Adventure to distribute an entire day's allocation of FASTPASSes by 2 p.m. When this happens, the machines simply shut down and a sign is posted saying that FASTPASSes are all gone for the day.

Whereas rides routinely exhaust their daily FASTPASS supply, shows almost never do. FASTPASS machines at theaters try to balance attendance at each show so that the audience of any given performance is divided evenly between standby and FASTPASS guests. At shows, consequently, standby guests are not discriminated against to the degree experienced by standby guests at rides. In practice, FASTPASS diminishes the wait for standby guests. Generally, with very few exceptions, using the standby line at theater attractions requires a smaller investment of time than using FASTPASS.

FASTPASS GUIDELINES

- Don't mess with FASTPASS unless it can save you 30 minutes or more.
- If you arrive after a park opens, obtain a FASTPASS for your preferred FASTPASS attraction first thing.
- Do not obtain a FASTPASS for a theater attraction until you have experienced all of the FASTPASS rides on your itinerary (using FAST-PASS at theater attractions usually requires a greater investment of time than using the standby line).
- Always check the FASTPASS return period before obtaining your FASTPASS.
- Obtain FASTPASSes for Space Mountain and Splash Mountain at Disneyland Park, and Soarin' over California and Mulholland Madness at DCA as early in the day as practicable.
- Try to obtain FASTPASSes for rides not mentioned above by 1 p.m.
- Don't depend on FASTPASSes being available for ride attractions after 2 p.m. during busier times of the year.
- Make sure everyone in your party has his or her own FASTPASS.
- Be mindful that you can obtain a second FASTPASS as soon as you enter the return period for your first FASTPASS or after two hours from issuance, whichever comes first.
- Be mindful of your FASTPASS return time and plan intervening activities accordingly.

FASTPASS Rule Changes

Disney stipulates that "you must use your current FASTPASS ticket or wait two hours before getting another FASTPASS ticket for a different attraction." This stipulation represents a change from the program as it was introduced. Previously, you could possess only one FASTPASS at a time and could not obtain another until the first was used. Disney undoubtedly received hundreds of letters similar to one we got from a San Diego reader:

> I got a FASTPASS for Soarin' over California at about two o'clock without paying attention to the return time posted on the sign. When I looked at my FASTPASS ticket, my time to come back and ride was 8:30 that night!

Because situations like this one were legion, Disney amended the rules so that now you can obtain a second FASTPASS two hours from the time your first one was issued, or anytime after the beginning of your return window, whichever is first. Rules aside, the real lesson here is to check out the posted return time before obtaining a FAST-PASS, as a father of two from Cranston, Rhode Island, advises:

> You should always check on the sign above the FASTPASS machines to see the ride time that you will receive. We made the mistake of not looking at the time before we got our FASTPASSes for Space Mountain. The time we received was not for two hours and was at a time when we couldn't ride because of lunch reservations. So we couldn't take advantage of FASTPASS at Space Mountain and couldn't get any other FASTPASSes until after lunch.

Disconnected FASTPASS Attractions

Some attractions' FASTPASS kiosks function independently and are not hooked up to the park-wide FASTPASS distribution system. Because a "disconnected" attraction has no way of knowing if you have a FASTPASS for another attraction, it will issue you a FASTPASS at any time. In Disneyland Park, Roger Rabbit is disconnected. At DCA, Grizzly River Run is disconnected. Disney can connect and disconnect FASTPASS attractions at will so it's possible that the disconnected lineup will vary somewhat during your visit. Finally, the use of disconnected FASTPASS attractions is incorporated in our touring plans.

When to Use FASTPASS

Except as discussed below, there's no reason to use FASTPASS during the first 30 to 40 minutes a park is open. Lines for most attractions are quite manageable during this period. In addition, this is the only time of the day when the FASTPASS attractions exclusively serve those in the regular line. Regardless of time of day, however, if the wait in the regular line at a FASTPASS attraction is 25 to 30 minutes or less, we recommend joining the regular line.

unofficial **TIP**
Use FASTPASS if the wait in the regular line is more than 30 minutes.

Think about it. Using FASTPASS requires two trips to the same attraction: one to obtain the pass and one to use it. This means that you must invest time to secure the pass (by the way, sometimes there are lines at the FASTPASS machines!) and then later interrupt your touring and backtrack in order to use your FASTPASS. The additional time, effort, and touring modification required, therefore, are justified only if you can save more than 30 minutes. And don't forget: even in the FASTPASS line you must endure some waiting.

Tricks of the Trade

Although Disney stipulates that you can hold a FASTPASS to only one attraction at a time, it's possible to acquire a second FASTPASS before using the first. Let's say you obtain a FASTPASS to Buzz Lightyear at Disneyland Park with a return time slot of 10:15 to 11:15 a.m. Any time after your FASTPASS window begins, that is, anytime after 10:15 a.m., you will be able to obtain another FASTPASS, for Splash Mountain, for example. This is possible because the FAST-PASS computer system monitors only the distribution of passes, ignoring whether or when a FASTPASS is used.

When obtaining FASTPASSes, it's faster and more considerate of other guests if one person obtains passes for your entire party. This means entrusting one individual with both your valuable park admission passes and your FASTPASSes, so choose wisely.

Tour Groups from Hell

We have discovered that tour groups of up to 200 people sometimes use our plans. Unless your party is as large as that tour group, this development shouldn't alarm you. Because tour groups are big, they move slowly and have to stop periodically to collect stragglers. The tour guide also has to accommodate the unpredictability of five dozen or so bladders. In short, you should have no problem passing a group after the initial encounter.

"Bouncing Around"

Many readers object to crisscrossing a theme park as our touring plans sometimes require. A lady from Decatur, Georgia, said she "got dizzy from all the bouncing around" and that the "running back and forth reminded [her] of a scavenger hunt." We empathize, but here's the rub, park by park.

In Disneyland Park, the most popular attractions are positioned across the park from one another. This is no accident. It's good planning, a method of more equally distributing guests throughout the park. If you want to experience the most popular attractions in one day without long waits, you can arrive before the park fills and see those attractions first thing (which requires crisscrossing the park), or you can enjoy the main attractions on one side of the park first thing in the morning then use FASTPASS for the popular attractions on the other side. All other approaches will subject you to awesome waits at some attractions if you tour during busy times of year.

The best way to minimize "bouncing around" at Disneyland Park is to use one of our Two-Day Touring Plans, which spread the more popular attractions over two mornings and work beautifully even when the park closes at 8 p.m. or earlier. Using FASTPASS will absolutely decrease your waiting time but will increase bouncing around because you must first go to the attraction to obtain your FASTPASS and then backtrack later to the same attraction to use your pass.

Disney's California Adventure is configured in a way that precludes an orderly approach to touring, or to a clockwise or counterclockwise rotation. Orderly touring is further frustrated by the limited guest capacity of the midway rides in the Paradise Pier district of the park. At DCA, therefore, you're stuck with "bouncing around," whether you use the touring plan or not, if you want to avoid horrendous waits.

We suggest you follow the touring plans religiously, especially in the mornings, if you're visiting Disneyland during busy, more-crowded times. The consequence of touring spontaneity in peak season is hours of otherwise avoidable standing in line. During quieter times of year, there's no need to be compulsive about following the plans.

Touring Plan Rejection

We have discovered you can't implant a touring plan in certain personalities without rapid and often vehement rejection. Some folks just do not respond well to the regimentation. If you bump into this problem with someone in your party, it's best to roll with the punches as did one couple from Maryland:

> The rest of the group was not receptive to the use of the touring plans. They all thought I was being a little too regimented about planning this vacation. Rather than argue, I left the touring plans behind as we ventured off for the parks. You can guess the outcome. We took our camcorder with us and when we returned home, watched the movies. About every five minutes there is a shot of us all gathered around a park map trying to decide what to do next.

Finally, as a Connecticut woman alleges, the touring plans are incompatible with some readers' bladders as well as their personalities:

> I want to know if next year when you write those "day" schedules if you could schedule bathroom breaks in there too. You expect us to be at a certain ride at a certain time and with no stops in between. Like one of the letters in your book a guy writes, "You expect everyone to be theme-park commandos." When I read that I thought, there is a man who really knows what a problem the schedules are if you are a laid-back, slow-moving, careful detail-noticer. What were you thinking when you made these schedules?

A Clamor for Customized Touring Plans

We're inundated by letters urging us to create additional touring plans. These include a plan for ninth- and tenth-graders, a plan for rainy days, a seniors' plan, a plan for folks who sleep late, a plan omitting rides that "bump, jerk, and clonk," a plan for gardening enthusiasts, and a plan for single women.

The touring plans in this book are intended to be flexible. Adapt them to your preferences. If you don't like rides that bump and jerk, skip them when they come up in a touring plan. If you want to sleep in and go to the park at noon, use the afternoon part of a plan. If you're a ninth-grader and want to ride Space Mountain three times in a row, do it. Will it decrease the touring plan's effectiveness? Sure, but the plan was created only to help you have fun. It's your day. Don't let the tail wag the dog.

Saving Time in Line by Understanding the Rides

There are many different types of rides in Disneyland. Some rides, like It's a Small World, are engineered to carry several thousand people every hour. At the other extreme, rides such as Dumbo, the Flying Elephant, can only accommodate around 500 people in an hour. Most rides fall somewhere in between. Lots of factors figure into how long you will have to wait to experience a particular ride: the popularity of the ride, how it loads and unloads, how many people can ride at one time, how many units (cars, rockets, boats, flying elephants, or whatever) of those available are in service at a given time, and how many staff personnel are available to operate the ride. Let's take them one by one:

1. HOW POPULAR IS THE RIDE? Rides like Soarin' over California attract a lot of people, as do longtime favorites such as the Jungle Cruise. If you know a ride is popular, you need to learn a little more about how it operates to determine when might be the best time to ride. But a ride need not be especially popular to form long lines. The lines can be the result of less-than-desirable traffic engineering; that is, it takes so long to load and unload that a line builds up. This is the situation at the Mad Tea Party and Dumbo, the Flying Elephant. Only a small percentage of the visitors to Disneyland Park (mostly children) ride Dumbo, for instance, but because it takes so long to load and unload, this ride can form long waiting lines.

2. HOW DOES THE RIDE LOAD AND UNLOAD? Some rides never stop. They are like a circular conveyor belt that goes around and around. We call these "continuous loaders." The Haunted Mansion is a continuous loader. The more cars or ships or whatever on the conveyor, the more people can be moved through in an hour. The Haunted Mansion has lots of cars on the conveyor belt and consequently can move more than 2,400 people an hour.

Other rides are "interval loaders." This means that cars are unloaded, loaded, and dispatched at certain set intervals (sometimes controlled manually and sometimes by a computer). Matterhorn Bobsleds is an interval loader. It has two separate tracks (in other words, the ride has been duplicated in the same facility). Each track can run up to ten sleds, released at 23-second or greater intervals (the bigger the crowd, the shorter the interval). In another kind of interval loader, like the Jungle Cruise, empty boats return to the starting point, where they line up waiting to be reloaded. In a third type of interval loader, one group of riders enters the vehicle while the last group of riders departs. We call these "in-and-out" interval loaders. Indiana Jones is a good example of an "in-and-out" interval loader. As a troop transport pulls up to the loading station, those who have just completed their ride exit to the left. At almost the same time, those waiting to ride enter the troop transport from the right. The troop transport is released to the dispatch point a few yards down the line where it is launched according to whatever second interval is being used. Interval loaders of both types can be very efficient at moving people if (1) the release (launch) interval is relatively short, and (2) the ride can accommodate a large number of vehicles in the system at one time. Since many boats can be floating through Pirates of the Caribbean at a given time and the release interval is short, almost 2,300 people an hour can see this attraction.

A third group of rides are "cycle rides." Another name for these same rides is "stop-and-go" rides; those waiting to ride exchange places with those who have just ridden. The main difference between "in-and-out" interval rides and cycle rides is that with a cycle ride the whole system shuts down when loading and unloading is in progress. While one boat is loading and unloading in It's a Small World, many other boats are proceeding through the ride. But when Dumbo, the Flying Elephant touches down, the whole ride is at a standstill until the next flight is launched. Likewise, with the Orange Stinger, all riders dismount and the swings stand stationary until the next group is loaded and ready to ride.

In discussing a cycle ride, the amount of time the ride is in motion is called "ride time." The amount of time that the ride is idle while loading and unloading is called "load time." Load time plus ride time equals "cycle time," or the time expended from the start of one run of the ride until the start of the succeeding run. Cycle rides are the least efficient of all the Disneyland rides in terms of traffic engineering. Disneyland Park has eight cycle rides while Disney's California Adventure has six, an astonishing number for a new park.

3. HOW MANY PEOPLE CAN RIDE AT ONE TIME? This figure is defined in terms of "per-ride capacity" or "system capacity." Either way, the figures refer to the number of people who can ride at the same time. Our discussion above illustrates that the greater a ride's carrying capacity (all other things being equal), the more visitors it can accommodate in an hour.

4. HOW MANY "UNITS" ARE IN SERVICE AT A GIVEN TIME? A "unit" is simply a term for the vehicle you sit in during your ride. At the Mad

Cycle Rides

DISNEYLAND PARK

Fantasyland	Mickey's Toontown	Tomorrowland
Casey Jr. Circus Train	**Gadget's Go Coaster**	**Astro Orbiter**
Dumbo, the Flying Elephant	**Goofy's Bounce House**	
King Arthur Carrousel		
Mad Tea Party		

DISNEY'S CALIFORNIA ADVENTURE

A Bug's Land	Paradise Pier
Flick's Flyers	**Golden Zephyr**
Francis Ladybug Boogie	**Jumpin' Jellyfish**
Tuck and Roll's Drive	**Maliboomer**
'Em Buggies	**Orange Stinger**
Sun Wheel	
King Triton's Carousel	

Tea Party the unit is a teacup, and at Alice in Wonderland it's a caterpillar. On some rides (mostly cycle rides), the number of units in operation at a given time is fixed. Thus there are always 16 flying elephant units operating on the Dumbo ride, 72 horses on King Arthur Carrousel, and so on. What this fixed number of units means to you is that there is no way to increase the carrying capacity of the ride by adding more units. On a busy day, therefore, the only way to carry more people each hour on a fixed-unit cycle ride is to shorten the loading time (which, as we will see in number 5 below, is sometimes impossible) or by decreasing the riding time, the actual time the ride is in motion. The bottom line on a busy day for a cycle ride is that you will wait longer and be rewarded for your wait with a shorter ride. This is why we try to steer you clear of the cycle rides unless you are willing to ride them early in the morning or late at night.

Other rides at Disneyland can increase their carrying capacity by adding units to the system as the crowds build. The Big Thunder Mountain Railroad is a good example. If attendance is very light, Big Thunder can start the day by running one of five available mine trains. When lines start to build, more mine trains can be placed into operation. At full capacity, a total of five trains can carry about 2,400 people an hour. Likewise, Pirates of the Caribbean can increase its capacity by adding more boats, and Orange Stinger can do the same by adding more swings. Sometimes a long line will disappear almost instantly when new units are brought on line. When an interval-loading ride places more units into operation, it usually shortens the dispatch interval, so more units are being dispatched more often.

5. HOW MANY CAST MEMBERS ARE AVAILABLE TO OPERATE THE RIDE?
Allocation of additional staff to a given ride can allow extra units to be placed in operation, or additional loading areas or holding areas to be opened. Pirates of the Caribbean and It's a Small World can run two separate waiting lines and loading zones. Haunted Mansion has a short "preshow," which is staged in a "stretch room." On busy days a second stretch room can be activated, thus permitting a more continuous flow of visitors to the actual loading area. Additional staff make a world of difference on some cycle rides. Often, if not usually, one attendant will operate the Golden Zephyr. This single person must clear the visitors from the ride just completed, admit and seat visitors for the upcoming ride, check that all zephyrs are properly secured (which entails an inspection of each zephyr), return to the control panel, issue instructions to the riders, and finally, activate the ride (whew!). A second attendant allows for the division of these responsibilities and has the effect of cutting loading time by 25 to 50%.

SAVING TIME IN LINE BY UNDERSTANDING THE SHOWS

MANY OF THE FEATURED ATTRACTIONS at Disneyland are theater presentations. While not as complex from a traffic-engineering viewpoint as rides, a little enlightenment concerning their operation may save some touring time.

Most of Disneyland theater attractions operate in three distinct phases:

1. First, there are the visitors who are in the theater viewing the presentation.
2. Next, there are the visitors who have passed through the turnstile into a holding area or waiting lobby. These people will be admitted to the theater as soon as the current presentation is concluded. Several attractions offer a preshow in their waiting lobby to entertain the crowd until they are admitted to the main show.
3. Finally, there is the outside line. Visitors waiting here will enter the waiting lobby when there is room and then move into the theater when the audience turns over (is exchanged) between shows.

The theater capacity and popularity of the presentation, along with the level of attendance in the park, determine how long the lines will be at a given theater attraction. Except for holidays and other days of especially heavy attendance, the longest wait for a show usually does not exceed the length of one complete performance.

Since almost all Disneyland theater attractions run continuously, only stopping long enough for the previous audience to leave and the waiting audience to enter, a performance will be in progress when you arrive. If the *Enchanted Tiki Birds* show lasts 15 minutes, the wait under normal circumstances should be 15 minutes if you were to arrive just after the show began.

All Disneyland theaters (except the Main Street Cinema and some amphitheater productions) are very strict when it comes to controlling access. Unlike a regular movie theater, you cannot just walk in during the middle of a performance; you will always have at least a short wait.

HOW TO DEAL WITH OBNOXIOUS PEOPLE

AT EVERY THEATER PRESENTATION AT DISNEYLAND, visitors in the preshow area elbow, nudge, and crowd one another in order to make sure they are admitted to the performance. Not necessary—if you are admitted through the turnstile into the preshow area, a seat has automatically been allocated for you in the theater. When it is time to proceed into the theater don't rush; just relax and let other people jam the doorways. When the congestion has been relieved, simply stroll in and take a seat.

Attendants at many theaters will instruct you to enter a row of seats and move completely to the far side, filling every seat so that each row can be completely filled. And invariably, some inconsiderate, pea-brained dunderhead will plop down right in the middle of the row, stopping traffic or forcing other visitors to climb over him. Take our word for it—there is no such thing as a bad seat. All of the Disney theaters have been designed to provide a nearly perfect view from every seat in the house. Our recommendation is to follow instructions and move to the far end of the row.

The Disney people also ask that visitors not use flash photography in the theaters (the theaters are too dark for the pictures to turn out, plus the flash is disruptive to other viewers). Needless to say, this admonition is routinely ignored. Flashers are more difficult to deal with than row-blockers. You can threaten to turn the offenders over to Disney Security, or better yet, simply hold your hand over the lens (you have to be quick) when they raise their cameras.

GUIDED TOURS AT DISNEYLAND PARK AND DCA

THREE GUIDED TOURS ARE OFFERED. All require a valid park admission in addition to the price of the tour. All three tours can be booked up to 30 days in advance by calling ☎ 714-781-4400.

DISCOVER THE MAGIC A sort of treasure hunt, kids interact with Disney characters to find clues to the treasure and avoid villainous characters. Designed for ages 5 to 9 years, the frenetic, fast-paced family program lasts approximately three hours and includes lunch. Prices are $49 for the first two tickets, $39 for the third and subsequent tickets.

WELCOME TO DISNEYLAND TOUR This two-and-a-half-hour tour provides a warp-speed look at pretty much the entire Disneyland Resort. Guides provide background and history of the parks, attractions, and sights as you tour both theme parks, Downtown Disney, and the Disney-owned hotels. Suffice it to say you'll do a lot of walking. The tour includes special reserved seats for a performance at a stage show or parade (selected locations), two FASTPASSes per person for use after the tour, priority seating at a dining location (selected locations), and a pin lanyard with two trading pins for each ticketed guest. The tour is reasonably priced at $25.

A WALK IN WALT'S FOOTSTEPS This tour offers an historic perspective on both Disneyland Park and the man who created it. A lengthy tour at three and one-half hours, A Walk In Walt's Footsteps provides much more detail as it covers Disney's vision and challenges bringing the groundbreaking theme park to life. The tour includes a private lunch on the patio of the Disney Gallery. Highlights of the tour are an inside look at the Disneyland Railroad, a visit to the park's first animatronic attraction, and a glimpse of the lobby of Club 33 where Disney entertained his friends and dignitaries. Cost is $49 for all ages. The tour is not considered appropriate for younger children.

PART TWO

BASIC ESSENTIALS

THE BARE NECESSITIES

CREDIT CARDS

AMERICAN EXPRESS, MasterCard, VISA, Discover, Japan Credit Bureau (JCB), and of course the Disneyland credit card are accepted for theme park admission. Disneyland shops, fast-food and counter-service restaurants, sit-down restaurants, and the Disneyland resort hotels also accept all the cards listed above. However, no credit cards are accepted in the theme park at vending carts.

RAIN

IF IT RAINS, go anyway; the bad weather will diminish the crowds. Additionally, most of the rides and attractions at the parks are under cover. Likewise, all but a few of the waiting areas are protected from inclement weather. If you get caught in an unexpected downpour, rain gear of varying sorts can be purchased at a number of shops.

VISITORS WITH SPECIAL NEEDS

DISABLED VISITORS Rental wheelchairs are available if needed. Most rides, shows, attractions, restrooms, and restaurants are engineered to accommodate the disabled. For specific inquiries call ☎ 714-781-7290. If you are in Disneyland Park and need some special assistance, go to City Hall on Main Street. At Disney's California Adventure Park (DCA), go to Guest Relations in the entrance plaza. Close-in parking is available for the disabled; inquire when you pay your parking fee.

VISITORS WITH DIETARY RESTRICTIONS Visitors on special or restricted diets, including those requiring kosher meals, can arrange for assistance at City Hall on Main Street at Disneyland Park or at Guest Relations at DCA. For special service at Disneyland resort restaurants, call the restaurant one day in advance for assistance.

FOREIGN LANGUAGE ASSISTANCE Translation services are available to guests who do not speak English. Inquire by calling ☎ 714-781-7290 or by stopping in at City Hall at Disneyland Park or at Guest Relations at DCA.

LOST ADULTS Arrange a plan for regrouping with those in your party should you become separated. Failing this, you can leave a message at City Hall or Guest Relations for your missing person. For information concerning lost children, see page 113.

MESSAGES Messages for your fellow group members can be left at City Hall in Disneyland Park or at DCA Guest Relations.

CAR TROUBLE If you elected to decrease the chance of losing your keys by locking them in your car, or decided that your car might be easier to find if you left your lights on, you may have a little problem to deal with when you return to the parking lot. Fortunately, the security patrols that continually cruise the parking lots are equipped to handle these types of situations and can quickly put you back in business.

LOST AND FOUND If you lose (or find) something at Disneyland Park, the lost and found office is located in the same place where lockers are available (walk down Main Street toward the castle and go to the end of the first cul-de-sac street on the right). At DCA, inquire at Guest Relations. If you do not discover your loss until you have left the parks, call ☎ 714-781-4765.

EXCUSE ME, BUT WHERE CAN I FIND...

SOMEPLACE TO PUT ALL THESE PACKAGES? Lockers are available at both parks. A more convenient solution, if you plan to spend a minimum of two or more hours in the park, is to have the salesperson forward your purchases to Package Pick-Up. When you leave the park, they will be there waiting for you. If you are staying at a Disneyland resort hotel, you can have your purchases delivered directly to your room.

A MIXED DRINK OR BEER? If you are in Disneyland Park, you are out of luck. You will have to exit the park and try one of the hotels. At DCA, alcoholic beverages are readily available.

SOME RAIN GEAR? At Disneyland, rain gear is available at most shops but is not always displayed. As the Disney people say, it is sold "under the counter." In other words, you have to ask for it. If you are caught without protection on a rainy day, don't slog around dripping. Rain gear is one of the few shopping bargains at Disneyland. Ponchos are $6.50 for adults and $5 for kids, and umbrellas are $10 and up.

A CURE FOR THIS HEADACHE? Aspirin and various other sundries can be purchased on Main Street at the Emporium in Disneyland Park and at Greetings from California at the DCA entrance plaza (they keep them behind the counter, so you have to ask).

A PRESCRIPTION FILLED? Unfortunately, there is no place in Disneyland Resort to have a prescription filled.

SUNTAN LOTION? Suntan lotion and various other sundries can be purchased in Disneyland Park on Main Street at the Emporium and at Greetings from California at the DCA entrance plaza (they keep them behind the counter, so you have to ask).

A SMOKE? You won't find cigarettes for sale at Disneyland parks, and you'll have a hard time finding a place to smoke any you bring with you. Smoking is strongly discouraged throughout the parks and resorts, though there are a few designated smoking areas.

FEMININE HYGIENE PRODUCTS? Feminine hygiene products are available in most of the women's restrooms at Disneyland Resort.

CASH? In Disneyland Park, the Bank of Main Street offers the following services:

- Personal checks cashed for $100 or less if drawn on U.S. banks; presentation of a valid driver's license and a major credit card is required
- Cash for traveler's checks
- Exchange of foreign currency for dollars

In addition, cash advances on MasterCard and VISA credit cards are available for a fee at Starcade in Tomorrowland. If the cashier is closed, there are Automatic Teller Machines (ATMs) at these locations:

AT DISNEYLAND PARK

- Outside the main entrance
- On Main Street, next to The Walt Disney Story at the Town Square end
- At the entrance to Frontierland on the left
- Near the Fantasyland Theatre
- In Tommorowland, near Starcade

AT DOWNTOWN DISNEY

- Next to Häagen–Dazs

AT DISNEY'S CALIFORNIA ADVENTURE

- Outside the main entrance
- At the phone and locker complex just inside the main entrance and to the right
- Near the restrooms to the left of the Redwood Creek Challenge Trail
- Near the restrooms at Hollywood Pictures Backlot
- Near the restrooms on Pacific Wharf
- To the left of Mulholland Madness at Paradise Pier
- Near the Sun Wheel at Paradise Pier

A PLACE TO LEAVE MY PET? Cooping up an animal in a hot car while you tour can lead to disastrous results. Additionally, pets are not allowed in the parks (except for seeing-eye dogs). Kennels and holding facilities are provided for the temporary care of your pets and are located at the parking garage. If you are adamant, the folks at the kennels will accept custody of just about any type of animal. Owners of pets, exotic or otherwise, must themselves place their charge in the assigned cage. Small pets (mice, hamsters, birds, snakes, turtles, alligators, etc.) must arrive in their own escape-proof quarters. Kennels cost $10 a day.

In addition to the above, there are several other details you may need to know:

- Advance reservations for animals are not accepted.
- No horses, llamas, or cattle are accepted.
- Kennels' hours are the same as theme-park operating hours.
- Pets may not be boarded overnight.
- Guests leaving exotic pets should supply food for their pet.
- On busy days, there is a one- to two-hour bottleneck at the kennel, beginning half an hour before the park opens. If you need to use the kennels on such a day, arrive at least an hour before the park's stated opening time.
- Pets are fed on request only (yours, not your pet's), and there is no additional charge for food.

CAMERAS AND FILM? If you do not have a camera, you can buy a disposable one, with or without a flash, in both parks. You can buy film throughout the parks. Finally, photo tips, including recommendations for settings and exposures, are provided in the Disneyland Park and DCA maps, both available for free when you enter.

PART THREE

DISNEYLAND *with* KIDS

THE AGONY *and the* ECSTASY

THE NATIONAL MEDIA and advertising presence of Disney is so overwhelming that any child who watches TV or shops with Mom is likely to get all revved up about going to Disneyland Resort. Parents, if anything, are even more susceptible. Almost every parent has brightened with anticipation at the prospect of guiding their children through the wonders of this special place: "Imagine little Tami's expression when she first sees Mickey Mouse. Think of her excitement and awe as she crosses the moat to Sleeping Beauty's Castle, or her small arms around me when Dumbo takes off." Are these not the treasured moments we long to share with our children?

While dreams of visiting the Disney parks are tantamount to nirvana for a three-year-old and dear enough to melt the heart of any parent, the reality of actually taking that three-year-old (particularly during the summer) is usually a lot closer to the "agony" than the "ecstasy."

A mother from Dayton, Ohio, describes taking her five-year-old to the Magic Kingdom in Walt Disney World, but it could just as easily be Disneyland Park:

> I felt so happy and excited before we went. I guess it was all worth it, but when I look back I think I should have had my head examined. The first day we went to Disney World [the Magic Kingdom] and it was packed. By 11 in the morning we had walked so far and stood in so many lines that we were all exhausted. Kristy cried about going on anything that looked or even sounded scary, and was frightened by all of the Disney characters (they are so big!) except Minnie and Snow White.
>
> We got hungry about the same time as everyone else but the lines for food were too long and my husband said we would have to wait. By one in the afternoon we were just plugging along, not seeing anything we were really interested in, but picking rides

because the lines were short, or because whatever it was was air-conditioned. We rode Small World three times in a row and I'll never get that song out of my head (Ha!). At around 2:30 we finally got something to eat, but by then we were so hot and tired that it felt like we had worked in the yard all day. Kristy insisted on being carried and we had 50 fights about not going on rides where the lines were too long. At the end, we were so P.O.'d and uncomfortable that we weren't having any fun. Mostly by this time, we were just trying to get our money's worth.

Before you stiffen in denial, let us assure you that the Ohio family's experience is fairly typical. Most small children are as picky about the rides as they are about what they eat, and more than 50% of preschoolers are intimidated by the friendly Disney characters. Few humans (of any age), moreover, are mentally or physically equipped to march all day in a throng of 40,000 people under the California sun. Finally, would you be surprised to learn that almost 52% of preschoolers said the thing they liked best about their Disneyland vacation was the hotel swimming pool?

REALITY TESTING: WHOSE DREAM IS IT?

REMEMBER WHEN YOU WERE LITTLE and you got that nifty electric train for Christmas, the one your dad wouldn't let you play with? Did you ever wonder who that train was really for? Ask yourself the same question about your vacation to Disneyland. Whose dream are you trying to make come true, yours or your child's?

unofficial **TIP**
When considering a trip to Walt Disney World, think about whether your kids are old enough to enjoy what can be a very fun, but taxing, trip.

Small children are very adept at reading their parents' emotions. When you ask, "Honey, how would you like to go to Disneyland?" your child will be responding more to your smile and excitement, and the idea of doing something with Mom and Dad, than to any notion of what Disneyland is all about. The younger the child in question, the more this is true. For many preschoolers, you could elicit the same enthusiastic response by asking, "Honey, how would you like to go to Cambodia on a dogsled?"

So, is your warm, fuzzy fantasy of introducing your child to the magic of Disney a pipe dream? Not necessarily, but you will have to be practical and open to a little reality testing. For instance, would you increase the probability of a happy, successful visit by holding off a couple of years? Is your child spunky and adventuresome enough to willingly sample the variety of the Disney parks? Will your child have sufficient endurance and patience to cope with long lines and large crowds?

RECOMMENDATIONS FOR MAKING THE DREAM COME TRUE

WHEN CONTEMPLATING a Disneyland Resort vacation with small children, anticipation is the name of the game. Here are some of the things you need to consider:

AGE Although the color and festivity of the Disney theme parks excite children of all ages, and while there are specific attractions that delight toddlers and preschoolers, the Disney entertainment mix is generally oriented to older kids and adults. We believe that children need to be a fairly mature seven years old to *appreciate* the Disney parks.

Not unexpectedly, our readers engage in a lively and ongoing debate over how old a child should be, or what the ideal age is, to go to Disneyland Resort.

A Waldwick, New Jersey, mother reports that:

My kids, not in the least shy or clingy, were very frightened of many attractions. I thought my six-year-old was the "perfect age," but quickly realized this was not the case. Disney makes even the most simple, child-friendly story into a major theatrical production, to the point where my kids couldn't associate their beloved movies with the attraction in front of them.

And a mother of two from Cleveland, Ohio, offers this:

The best advice for parents with young kids is to remember who you are there for and, if possible, accommodate the kids' need to do things again and again. I think you underestimate Disney's appeal to young children.

Finally, a north Alabama woman encourages parents to be more open-minded about taking toddlers:

Parents of toddlers, don't be afraid to bring your little ones! Ours absolutely loved it and we have priceless photos and videos of our little ones and their grandparents together with Mickey and the gang. For all those people in your book who complained about our little sweethearts crying, sorry, but we all found your character-hogging, cursing, ill-mannered, cutting-in-line, screaming-in-our-ears-on-the-roller-coasters teens and preteens much more obnoxious. Guess it's just what you're used to.

Hmmm. . . don't you hate it when people won't tell what they really think?

TIME OF YEAR TO VISIT If there is any way you can swing it, avoid the hot, crowded summer months. Try to go in October, November (except Thanksgiving), early December, March, and April (except Easter and spring break). If your kids are preschoolers, don't even think about going during the summer. If you have children of varying ages and your school-age kids are good students, take the older ones out of school so you can visit during the cooler, less congested off-season. Arrange special study assignments relating to the many educational aspects of the Disney parks. If your school-age children cannot afford to miss any school, take your vacation as soon as the school year ends in late May or early June. Nothing, repeat, nothing will enhance your Disneyland Resort vacation as much as avoiding summer months and holiday periods.

unofficial **TIP**
Coupled with a sense of humor and a little pre-paredness on your part, our touring plans and tips for families ensure a super experience at any time of year.

BUILDING NAPS AND REST INTO YOUR ITINERARY Disneyland Resort is huge. If your schedule allows, try to spread your visit over at least two days. Tour in the early morning and return to your hotel around 11:30 a.m. for lunch, a swim, and a nice nap. Even during the off-season, when the crowds are smaller and the temperature more pleasant, the sheer size of the parks will exhaust most children under age 8 by lunchtime. Go back to the parks in the late afternoon or early evening and continue your touring.

WHERE TO STAY The time and hassle involved in commuting to and from the Disney parks will be somewhat reduced if you can afford to stay at a Disney hotel or at another hotel within easy striking range. But even if, for financial or other reasons, you lodge relatively far away, it remains imperative that you get small children out of the parks each day for a few hours to rest and recuperate. Neglecting to relax and unwind is the best way we know to get the whole family in a snit and ruin the day (or the entire vacation).

unofficial **TIP**
If it takes renting a car to make returning to your hotel practicable, rent the car.

Relief from the frenetic pace of the theme parks, even during the off-season, is indispensable. While it's true that you can gain some measure of peace by retreating to Downtown Disney for lunch or by finding a quiet spot or restaurant in the theme parks, there is really no substitute for returning to the familiarity and security of your own hotel. Regardless of what you may have heard or read, children too large to sleep in a stroller will not relax and revive unless you get them back to your hotel.

Thousands of rooms are available near Disneyland Resort, many of them very affordable. With sufficient lead time you should have no difficulty finding accommodations that fulfill your requirements.

BE IN TOUCH WITH YOUR FEELINGS While we acknowledge that a Disneyland Resort vacation seems like a major capital investment, remember that having fun is not necessarily the same as seeing everything. When you or your children start getting tired and irritable, call a time-out and regroup. Trust your instincts. What would really feel best right now? Another ride, a rest break with some ice cream, going back to the room for a nap? *The way to protect your investment is to stay happy and have a good time, whatever that takes.* You do not have to meet a quota for experiencing a certain number of attractions or watching parades or anything else. It's your vacation; you can do what you want.

LEAST COMMON DENOMINATORS Remember the old saying that a chain is only as strong as its weakest link? The same logic applies to a family touring Disneyland Park or Disney's California Adventure Park (DCA). Somebody is going to run out of steam first, and when they do the whole family will be affected. Sometimes a cold soda and a rest break will get the flagging member back into gear. Sometimes, however, as Marshal Dillon would say, "You just need to get out of Dodge." Pushing the tired or discontented beyond their capacity is like driving on a flat tire: It may get you a few more miles down the road, but you will further damage your car in the process. Accept that energy levels vary among individuals, and be prepared to respond to small children or other members of your group who poop out. *Hint:* "After we've driven 600 miles to take you to Disneyland, you're going to ruin everything!" is not an appropriate response.

unofficial **TIP**
The way to protect your considerable investment in your Disney vacation is to stay happy and have a good time. You don't have to meet a quota for experiencing attractions. Do what you want.

SETTING LIMITS AND MAKING PLANS The best way to avoid arguments and disappointment is to develop a game plan before you go. Establish some general guidelines for the day, and get everybody committed in advance. Be sure to include:

1. Wake-up time and breakfast plans.
2. What time you need to depart for the parks.

3. What you need to take with you.

4. A policy for splitting up the group or for staying together.

5. A plan for what to do if the group gets separated or someone is lost.

6. How long you intend to tour in the morning and what you want to see, including fallback plans in the event an attraction is closed or too crowded.

7. A policy on what you can afford for snacks and refreshments.

8. A target time for returning to the hotel to rest.

9. What time you'll return to the parks, and how late you'll stay.

10. Plans for dinner.

11. Advance agreement concerning bedtimes.

12. A policy for shopping and buying souvenirs, including who pays: mom and dad, or the kids.

BE FLEXIBLE Having a game plan does not mean giving up spontaneity or sticking rigidly to an itinerary. Once again, listen to your intuition. Alter the plan if the situation warrants. Any day at the Disney parks includes some surprises, so be prepared to roll with the punches.

ABOUT THE *UNOFFICIAL GUIDE* TOURING PLANS Parents who embark on one of our touring plans are often frustrated by the various interruptions and delays occasioned by their small children. In case you haven't given the subject much thought, here is what to expect:

1. Many small children will stop dead in their tracks whenever they see a Disney character. Our advice: Live with it. An attempt to haul your children away before they have satisfied their curiosity is likely to precipitate anything from whining to a full-scale revolt.

2. The touring plans call for visiting attractions in a specified sequence, often skipping certain attractions along the way. Children do not like skipping *anything!* If they see something that attracts them they want to experience it *now.* Some children can be persuaded to skip attractions if parents explain things in advance. Other kids severely flip out at the threat of skipping something, particularly something in Fantasyland. A mom from Charleston, South Carolina, had this to say:

Following the Touring Plans turned out to be a train wreck. The main problem with the plan is that it starts in Fantasyland. When we were on Dumbo, my five-year-old saw eight dozen other things in Fantasyland she wanted to see. The long and the short is that after Dumbo, there was no getting her out of there.

3. Children seem to have a genetic instinct when it comes to finding restrooms. We have seen perfectly functional adults equipped with all manner of maps search interminably for a restroom. Small children, on the other hand, including those who cannot read, will head for the nearest restroom with the certainty of a homing pigeon. While you may skip certain attractions, you can be sure that your children will ferret out (and want to use) every restroom in the theme park.

OVERHEATING, SUNBURN, AND DEHYDRATION The most common problems for smaller children at the parks are overheating, sunburn, and dehydration. A small bottle of sunscreen carried in a pocket or fanny pack will help you take precautions against overexposure to the sun. Be sure to put some on children in strollers, even if the stroller has a canopy. Some of the worst cases of sunburn we have seen were on the exposed foreheads and feet of toddlers and infants in strollers. To avoid overheating, rest at regular intervals in the shade or in an air-conditioned restaurant or show.

unofficial **TIP**
Keep little ones well covered in sunscreen and hydrated with fluids. Don't count on hydrating young children with soft drinks and stops at water fountains. Carry plastic bottles of water. Remember: excited children may not tell you when they're thirsty or hot.

Do not count on keeping small children properly hydrated with soft drinks and water fountain stops. Long lines often make buying refreshments problematic, and water fountains are not always handy. What's more, excited children may not realize or inform you that they're thirsty or overheated. We recommend renting a stroller for children age 6 years old and under and carrying plastic water bottles with you. If you forget to bring your own water containers, plastic squeeze bottles with caps are sold at the Emporium on Main Street in Disneyland and at Greetings from California at DCA for about $8.

BLISTERS Sore feet and blisters are common for visitors of all ages, so wear comfortable, well broken-in shoes and a pair of socks that wick moisture away from your feet; Smart Wool socks are one of several brands that will do the trick. If you or your children are unusually susceptible to blisters, carry some precut Moleskin bandages; they offer the best possible protection, stick great, and won't sweat off. When you feel a hot spot, stop, air out your foot, and place a Moleskin over the affected area before a blister forms. Moleskin is available at all drugstores. Sometimes small children won't tell their parents about a developing blister until it's too late. We recommend inspecting the feet of preschoolers two or more times a day.

FIRST AID Registered nurses are on duty at all times in the First Aid Centers of both parks. If you or your children have a medical problem, do not hesitate to use the First Aid Center. It's warmer and friendlier than most doctors' offices, and it's accustomed to treating everything from paper cuts to allergic reactions.

CHILDREN ON MEDICATION For various reasons, some parents of children on medication for hyperactivity elect to discontinue or decrease the child's normal dosage at the close of the school year. Be forewarned that the Disney parks might stimulate such a child to the point of system overload. Consult your physician before altering your child's medication regimen.

SUNGLASSES If you want your smaller children to wear sunglasses, it's a good idea to affix a strap or string to the frames so the glasses will stay on during rides and can hang from the child's neck while indoors.

THINGS YOU FORGOT OR THINGS YOU RAN OUT OF Rain gear, diapers, diaper pins, formula, film, aspirin, topical sunburn treatments, and other sundries are available for sale at the parks. For some reason, rain gear is a bargain, but most other items are pretty expensive. Ask for goods you do not see displayed; some are stored behind the counter.

STROLLER RENTAL Strollers are available for about $8 at Disneyland and DCA. The rental covers the entire day and is good at both parks. If you rent a stroller and later decide to go back to your hotel for lunch, a swim, or a nap, turn in your stroller but hang on to your rental receipt. When you return to either park later in the day, present your receipt. You will be issued another stroller without an additional charge. The rental procedure is fast and efficient. Likewise, returning the stroller is a breeze. Even in the evening, when several hundred strollers are turned in following the laser and fireworks show, there is no wait or hassle.

unofficial **TIP**
Strollers are also great for somewhat older children who run out of steam.

The strollers come with sun canopies and small cargo compartments under the seat. For infants and toddlers, strollers are a must, and we recommend taking a small pillow or blanket with you to help make them more comfortable for your child during what may be long periods in the seat. We have also observed many sharp parents renting strollers for somewhat older children. Strollers prevent parents from having to carry children when they run out of steam and provide an easy, convenient way to carry water, snacks, diaper bags, etc.

When you enter a show or board a ride, you will have to park your stroller, usually in an open, unprotected area. If it rains before you return, you will need a cloth, towel, or spare diaper to dry off the stroller.

STROLLER WARS Sometimes strollers disappear while you are enjoying a ride or a show. Do not be alarmed. You won't have to buy the missing stroller, and you will be issued a new stroller for your continued use. At Disneyland Park, a replacement center is located at the Star Trader in Tomorrowland. At DCA, stroller replacement centers are located across from Soarin' Over California and to the left of the Corn Dog Castle at Paradise Pier. Lost strollers can also be replaced at the main rental facility near the respective park entrances.

unofficial **TIP**
Beware of stroller stealers. With so many identical strollers, it's easy to grab the wrong one. Mark yours with a bandana or some other easily identifiable flag.

While replacing a ripped-off stroller is no big deal, it is an inconvenience. One family complained that their stroller had been taken six times in one day. Even with free replacements,

larceny on this scale represents a lot of wasted time. Through our own experiments, and suggestions from readers, we have developed several techniques for hanging on to your rented stroller:

1. Write your name in Magic Marker on a 6-by-9-inch card, put the card in a transparent freezer bag, and secure the bag to the handle of the stroller with masking or duct tape.

2. Affix something personal (but expendable) to the handle of the stroller. Evidently most strollers are pirated by mistake (since they all look the same) or because it's easier to swipe someone else's stroller (when yours disappears) than to troop off to the replacement center. Since most stroller theft is a function of confusion, laziness, or revenge, the average pram-pincher will balk at hauling off a stroller bearing another person's property. After trying several items, we concluded that a bright, inexpensive scarf or bandanna tied to the handle works well, and a sock partially stuffed with rags or paper works even better (the weirder and more personal the object, the greater the deterrent). Best of all is a dead mackerel dangling from the handle, though in truth, the kids who ride in the stroller prefer the other methods.

Bound and determined not to have her stroller ripped off, an Ann Arbor, Michigan, mother describes her stroller security plan as follows:

> We used a variation on your stroller identification theme. We tied a clear plastic bag with a diaper in it on the stroller. Jon even poured a little root beer on the diaper for effect. Needless to say, no one took our stroller and it was easy to identify.

We receive quite a few letters from readers debating the pros and cons of bringing your own stroller versus renting one of Disney's. A mother from Falls Church, Virginia, with two small children opted for her own pram, commenting:

> I was glad I took my own stroller, because the rented strollers aren't appropriate for infants (we had a five-year-old and a five-month-old in tow). No one said anything about me using a bike lock to secure our brand-new Aprica stroller. However, an attendant came over and told us not to lock it anywhere, because it's a fire hazard! (Outside?) When I politely asked the attendant if she wanted to be responsible for my $300 stroller, she told me to go ahead and lock it but not tell anyone! I observed the attendants constantly moving the strollers. This seems very confusing—no wonder people think their strollers are getting ripped off!

As the reader mentioned, Disney cast members often rearrange strollers parked outside an attraction. Sometimes this is done simply to "tidy up." At other times the strollers are moved to make additional room along a walkway. In any event, do not assume that your stroller is stolen because it is missing from the exact place you left it. Check around. Chances are it will be "neatly arranged" just a few feet away.

BABYSITTING Childcare services are unavailable in the Disney parks and at the resort hotels. An independent organization called the Fullerton Childcare Agency, however, provides in-room sitting for infants and children. If you pay the tab, Fullerton Childcare sitters will even take your kids to Disneyland.

All sitters are experienced and licensed to drive, and the Fullerton Childcare Agency is fully insured. The basic rate for in-room sitting for one or two children is $32 for the first four hours, with a four-hour minimum, and $6.50 each hour thereafter. The charge for each additional child varies with the sitter. Combined families are charged $2 per hour for each additional child from the nonbooking family. There is no transportation fee, but the client is expected to pay for parking when applicable. All fees and charges must be paid in cash at the end of the assignment. To reserve a sitter, one or two days' advance notice is requested. You can reach the Fullerton Childcare Agency by calling ☎ 714-528-1640.

CARING FOR INFANTS AND TODDLERS Both parks have special centralized facilities for the care of infants and toddlers. Everything necessary for changing diapers, preparing formulas, warming bottles and food, etc. is available in ample quantity. A broad selection of baby supplies is for sale, and there are even rockers and special chairs for nursing mothers. Dads in charge of little ones are welcome at the Baby Centers and can avail themselves of most services offered. In addition, babies can be changed without inconvenience in most of the larger restrooms.

DISNEY, KIDS, AND SCARY STUFF

DISNEYLAND PARK and Disney's California Adventure are family theme parks. Yet some of the Disney adventure rides can be intimidating to small children. On certain rides, such as Splash Mountain and the roller coaster rides (California Screamin', Space Mountain, Matterhorn Bobsleds, and Big Thunder Mountain Railroad), the ride itself may be frightening. On other rides, such as the Haunted Mansion and Snow White's Scary Adventures, it is the special effects. We recommend a little parent-child dialogue coupled with a "testing-the-water" approach. A child who is frightened by Pinocchio's Daring Journey should not have to sit through the Haunted Mansion. Likewise, if Big Thunder Mountain Railroad is too much, don't try Space Mountain or California Screamin'.

Disney rides and shows are adventures. They focus on the substance and themes of all adventure, and indeed of life itself: good and evil, beauty and the grotesque, fellowship and enmity, quest, and death. As you sample the variety of attractions at the Disney parks, you transcend the mundane spinning and bouncing of midway rides to a more thought-provoking and emotionally powerful entertainment experience. Though the endings are all happy, the impact of the adventures, with Disney's gift for special effects, is often intimidating and occasionally frightening to small children.

There are rides with menacing witches, rides with burning towns, and rides with ghouls popping out of their graves, all done tongue-in-cheek and with a sense of humor, provided you are old enough to understand the joke. And there are bones, lots of bones—human bones, cattle bones, dinosaur bones, and whole skeletons are everywhere you look. There have to be more bones at Disneyland Park than at the Smithsonian and the UCLA Medical School combined. There is a stack of skulls at the headhunter's camp on the Jungle Cruise; a veritable platoon of skeletons sailing ghost ships in Pirates of the Caribbean; a macabre assemblage of skulls and skeletons in the Haunted Mansion; and more skulls, skeletons, and bones punctuating Snow White's Scary Adventures, Peter Pan's Flight, and Big Thunder Mountain Railroad, to name a few.

One reader wrote us after taking his preschool children on Star Tours:

We took a four-year-old and a five-year-old and they had the *#%^! scared out of them at Star Tours. We did this first thing in the morn-

ing and it took hours of Tom Sawyer Island and It's a Small World to get back to normal.

Our kids were the youngest by far in Star Tours. I assume that either other adults had more sense or were not such avid readers of your book. Preschoolers should start with Dumbo and work up to the Jungle Cruise in the late morning, after being revved up and before getting hungry, thirsty, or tired. Pirates of the Caribbean is out for preschoolers. You get the idea.

The reaction of young children to the inevitable system overload of Disney parks should be anticipated. Be sensitive, alert, and prepared for almost anything, even behavior that is out of character for your child at home. Most small children take Disney's variety of macabre trappings in stride, and others are quickly comforted by an arm around the shoulder or a little squeeze of the hand. For parents who have observed a tendency in their kids to become upset, we recommend taking it slowly and easily by sampling more benign adventures like the Jungle Cruise, gauging reactions, and discussing with children how they felt about the things they saw.

Sometimes, small children will rise above their anxiety in an effort to please their parents or siblings. This behavior, however, does not necessarily indicate a mastery of fear, much less enjoyment. If children come off a ride in ostensibly good shape, we recommend asking if they would like to go on the ride again (not necessarily right now, but sometime). The response to this question will usually give you a clue as to how much they actually enjoyed the experience. There is a lot of difference between having a good time and mustering the courage to get through something.

Evaluating a child's capacity to handle the visual and tactile effects of the Disney parks requires patience, understanding, and experimentation. Each of us, after all, has our own demons. If a child balks at or

Small-Child Fright-Potential Chart

As a quick reference, we provide this Small-Child Fright-Potential Chart to warn you which attractions to be wary of and why. Remember that the chart represents a generalization and that all kids are different. The chart relates specifically to kids 3 to 7 years of age. On average, as you would expect, children at the younger end of the age range are more likely to be frightened than children in their sixth or seventh year.

Disneyland Park

MAIN STREET, U.S.A.

Disneyland Railroad Tunnel with dinosaur display frightens some small children.

Disneyland: The First 50 Years Not frightening in any respect.

Main Street Cinema Not frightening in any respect.

Main Street Vehicles Not frightening in any respect.

ADVENTURELAND

Tarzan's Treehouse Not frightening in any respect.

Jungle Cruise Moderately intense, with some macabre sights; a good test attraction for little ones.

Enchanted Tiki Birds A small thunderstorm momentarily surprises very young children.

Indiana Jones Adventure Visually intimidating, with intense effects and a jerky ride. Switching-off option provided (see page 107).

NEW ORLEANS SQUARE

Pirates of the Caribbean Slightly intimidating queuing area; an intense boat ride with gruesome (though humorously presented) sights and two short, unexpected slides down flumes.

Haunted Mansion Name of attraction raises anxiety, as do sights and sounds of waiting area. An intense attraction with humorously presented macabre sights. The ride itself is gentle.

CRITTER COUNTRY

Splash Mountain Visually intimidating from the outside. Moderately intense visual effects. The ride itself is somewhat hair-raising for all ages, culminating in a 52-foot plunge down a steep chute. Switching-off option provided (see page 107).

Davy Crockett's Explorer Canoes Not frightening in any respect.

The Many Adventures of Winnie the Pooh Not frightening in any respect.

FRONTIERLAND

Big Thunder Mountain Railroad Visually intimidating from the outside with moderately intense visual effects. The roller coaster is wild enough to frighten many adults, particularly seniors. Switching-off option provided (see page 107).

Small-Child Fright-Potential Chart (continued)

Tom Sawyer Island Some very small children are intimidated by dark, walk-through tunnels that can be easily avoided.

Frontierland Shootin' Exposition Not frightening in any respect.

Golden Horseshoe Stage Not frightening in any respect.

Mark Twain **Riverboat** Not frightening in any respect.

Sailing Ship *Columbia* Not frightening in any respect.

FANTASYLAND

Mad Tea Party Midway-type ride can induce motion sickness in all ages.

Mr. Toad's Wild Ride Name of ride intimidates some. Moderately intense spook-house genre attraction with jerky ride. Only frightens a small percentage of preschoolers.

Snow White's Scary Adventures Moderately intense spook-house genre attraction with some grim characters. Absolutely terrifying to many preschoolers.

Dumbo, the Flying Elephant A tame midway ride; a great favorite of most small children.

King Arthur Carousel Not frightening in any respect.

It's a Small World Not frightening in any respect.

Peter Pan's Flight Not frightening in any respect.

Alice in Wonderland Pretty benign, but frightens a small percentage of preschoolers.

Pinocchio's Daring Journey Less frightening than Alice in Wonderland, but scares a few very young preschoolers.

Matterhorn Bobsleds The ride itself is wilder than Big Thunder Mountain Railroad, but not as wild as Space Mountain. Switching off is an option (see page 107).

Casey Jr. Circus Train Not frightening in any respect.

Storybook Land Canal Boats Not frightening in any respect.

MICKEY'S TOONTOWN

Mickey's House Not frightening in any respect.

Minnie's House Not frightening in any respect.

Roger Rabbit's Car Toon Spin Intense special effects, coupled with a dark environment and wild ride; frightens many preschoolers.

Gadget's Go Coaster Tame as far as roller coasters go, frightens some small children.

Chip 'n' Dale Treehouse Not frightening in any respect.

Miss Daisy, **Donald Duck's Boat** Not frightening in any respect.

Goofy's Bounce House Not frightening in any respect.

TOMORROWLAND

Star Tours Extremely intense visually for all ages; the ride itself is one of the wildest in Disney's repertoire. Switching-off option provided (see page 107).

Small-Child Fright-Potential Chart

Disneyland Park (continued)

TOMORROWLAND (CONTINUED)

Honey, I Shrunk the Audience Extremely intense visual effects and the loud volume scare many preschoolers.

Space Mountain Very intense roller coaster in the dark; Disneyland's wildest ride and a scary roller coaster by anyone's standards. Switching-off option provided (see page 107).

Astro Orbiter Waiting area is visually intimidating to preschoolers. The ride is a lot higher, but just a bit wilder, than Dumbo.

Tomorrowland Autopia The noise in the waiting area slightly intimidates preschoolers; otherwise, not frightening.

Disneyland Monorail Not frightening in any respect.

Buzz Lightyear Astro Blasters Intense special effects plus a dark environment frighten some preschoolers.

Disney's California Adventure Park

A BUG'S LAND

Bountiful Valley Farm Not frightening in any respect.

Flik's Fun Fair Rides and Playground Not frightening in any respect.

It's Tough to Be a Bug! Loud and extremely intense with special effects that will terrify children under eight years or anyone with a fear of insects.

Ugly Bug Ball Not frightening in any respect.

GOLDEN STATE

Boudin Bakery Not frightening in any respect.

Golden Dreams Not frightening in any respect.

Golden Vine Winery Not frightening in any respect.

Mission Tortilla Factory Not frightening in any respect.

Redwood Creek Challenge Trail featuring *The Magic of Brother Bear* show. A bit overwhelming to preschoolers but not frightening.

Soarin' over California Frightens some children seven years and under. Really a very sweet ride.

HOLLYWOOD PICTURES BACKLOT

Disney Animation Not frightening in any respect.

Hollywood Backlot Stage Not frightening in any respect.

Hyperion Theater Some productions are both very intense and loud.

MuppetVision 3-D Intense and loud with a lot of special effects. Frightens some preschoolers.

Playhouse Disney—Live on Stage Not frightening in any respect.

Twilight Zone Tower of Terror Frightening to guests of all ages.

Monsters, Inc.: Mike and Sulley to the Rescue Not open at press time.

PARADISE PIER

California Screamin' Frightening to guests of all ages.

Golden Zephyr Frightening to a small percentage of preschoolers.

Small-Child Fright-Potential Chart (continued)

Jumpin' Jellyfish The ride's appearance frightens some younger children. The ride itself is exceedingly tame.

King Triton's Carousel Not frightening in any respect.

Maliboomer Frightening to guests of all ages.

Mulholland Madness Frightening to the under-eight crowd.

Orange Stinger Height requirement keeps preschoolers from riding. Moderately intimidating to younger grade-schoolers.

S.S. Rustworthy Not frightening in any respect.

Sun Wheel The ride's appearance frightens some younger children. The ride itself is exceedingly tame.

is frightened by a ride, respond constructively. Let your children know that lots of people, adults as well as children, are scared by what they see and feel. Help them understand that it is okay if they get frightened and that their fear does not lessen your love or respect. Take pains not to compound the discomfort by making a child feel inadequate; try not to undermine self-esteem, impugn courage, or subject a child to ridicule. Most of all, do not induce guilt, as if your child's trepidation is ruining the family's fun. When older siblings are present, it is sometimes necessary to restrain their taunting and teasing.

A visit to a Disney park is more than an outing or an adventure for a small child. It is a testing experience, a sort of controlled rite of passage. If you help your little one work through the challenges, the time can be immeasurably rewarding and a bonding experience for both of you.

The Fright Factor

While each youngster is different, there are essentially six attraction elements that alone or combined can push a child's buttons:

1. THE NAME OF THE ATTRACTION Small children will naturally be apprehensive about something called the "Haunted Mansion" or "Snow White's Scary Adventures" or "Orange Stinger."

2. THE VISUAL IMPACT OF THE ATTRACTION FROM OUTSIDE Splash Mountain, Maliboomer, the *Twilight Zone* Tower of Terror, and Big Thunder Mountain Railroad look scary enough to give even adults second thoughts. To many small children, these rides are visually terrifying.

3. THE VISUAL IMPACT OF THE INDOOR QUEUING AREA Pirates of the Caribbean, with its dark bayou scene, and the Haunted Mansion, with its "stretch rooms," are capable of frightening small children before they even board the ride.

4. THE INTENSITY OF THE ATTRACTION Some attractions are so intense as to be overwhelming; they inundate the senses with sights, sounds, movement, and even smell. *Honey, I Shrunk the Audience, Muppet Vision 3-D,* and *It's Tough to Be a Bug!,* for instance, combine loud music, laser effects, lights, and 3-D cinematography to create a total sensory experience. For some preschoolers, this is two or three senses too many.

5. THE VISUAL IMPACT OF THE ATTRACTION ITSELF As previously discussed, the sights in various attractions range from falling boulders to lurking buzzards, from grazing dinosaurs to attacking hippos. What one child calmly absorbs may scare the owl poop out of another child the same age.

6. DARK Many Disneyland attractions are "dark" rides—that is, they operate indoors in a dark environment. For some children, this fact alone is sufficient to trigger significant apprehension. A child who is frightened on one dark ride, for example Snow White's Scary Adventures, may be unwilling to try other indoor rides.

7. THE RIDE ITSELF; THE TACTILE EXPERIENCE Some Disney rides are downright wild—wild enough to induce motion sickness, wrench backs, and generally discombobulate patrons of any age.

A Bit of Preparation

We receive many tips from parents relating how they prepared their small children for their Disneyland experience. A common strategy is to acquaint children with the characters and the stories behind the attractions by reading Disney books and watching Disney videos at home. A more direct approach is to rent Disneyland travel videos that actually show the various attractions. Concerning the latter, a father from Arlington, Virginia, reported:

> My kids both loved the Haunted Mansion, with appropriate preparation. We rented a tape before going so they could see it, and then I told them it was all "Mickey Mouse Magic" and that Mickey was just "joking you," to put it in their terms, and that there weren't any real ghosts, and that Mickey wouldn't let anyone actually get hurt.

A mother from Gloucester, Massachusetts, handled her son's preparation a bit more extemporaneously:

> The three-and-a-half-year-old liked It's a Small World, [but] was afraid of the Haunted Mansion. We just pulled his hat over his face and quietly talked to him while we enjoyed [the ride].

A Word about Height Requirements

A number of attractions require children to meet minimum height and age requirements, usually 40 inches tall to ride with an adult, or 40 inches and 7 years of age to ride alone. If you have children too short or too young to ride, you have several options, including switching off (described later in this chapter). Although the alternatives may resolve some practical and logistical issues, be forewarned that your smaller children might nonetheless be resentful of their older (or taller) siblings who qualify to ride. A mom from Virginia bumped into just such a situation, writing:

> *You mention height requirements for rides but not the intense sibling jealousy this can generate. Frontierland was a real problem in that respect. Our very petite five-year-old, to her outrage, was stuck hanging around while our eight-year-old went on Splash Mountain and [Big] Thunder Mountain with Grandma and Grandad, and the nearby alternatives weren't helpful [too long a line for rafts to Tom Sawyer Island, etc.]. If we had thought ahead, we would have left the younger kid back in Mickey's Toontown with one of the grown-ups for another roller coaster ride or two and then met up later at a designated point. The best areas had a playground or other quick attractions for short people near the rides with height requirements.*

The reader makes a valid point, though splitting the group and then meeting later can be more complicated in practical terms than she might imagine. If you choose to split up, ask the Disney greeter at the entrance to the height-restricted attraction(s) how long the wait is. If you tack five minutes for riding onto the anticipated wait, and then add five or so minutes to exit and reach the meeting point, you'll have an approximate sense of how long the younger kids (and their supervising adult) will have to do other stuff. Our guess is that even with a long line for the rafts, the reader would have had more than sufficient time to take her daughter to Tom Sawyer Island while the sibs rode Splash Mountain and Big Thunder Mountain with the grandparents. For sure she had time to tour Tarzan's Treehouse in adjacent Adventureland.

Attractions that Eat Adults

You may spend so much energy worrying about Junior's welfare that you forget to take care of yourself. If the ride component of the attraction (that is, the actual motion and movement of the conveyance itself) is potentially disturbing, persons of any age may be adversely affected. Below are several attractions likely to cause motion sickness or other problems for older children and adults. Fast, jerky rides are also noted with icons in the attraction profiles.

ATTRACTIONS THAT EAT ADULTS	
DISNEYLAND PARK	
Adventureland	Indiana Jones Adventure
Critter Country	Splash Mountain
Fantasyland	Mad Tea Party
	Matterhorn Bobsleds
Frontierland	Big Thunder Mountain Railroad
Tomorrowland	Space Mountain
	Star Tours

MORE ATTRACTIONS THAT EAT ADULTS	
DISNEY'S CALIFORNIA ADVENTURE PARK	
Golden State	**Grizzly River Run**
Paradise Pier	**California Screamin'**
	Maliboomer
	Mulholland Madness
Hollywood Pictures Backlot	*Monsters, Inc.:* **Mike and Sulley to the Rescue**
	Twilight Zone **Tower of Terror**

WAITING-LINE STRATEGIES *for* ADULTS *with* SMALL CHILDREN

CHILDREN HOLD UP BETTER through the day if you minimize the time they have to spend in lines. Arriving early and using the touring plans in this guide will reduce waiting time immensely. There are, however, additional measures you can employ to reduce stress on little ones.

1. LINE GAMES It is a smart parent who anticipates how restless children get waiting in line and how a little structured activity can relieve the stress and boredom. In the morning, kids handle the inactivity of waiting in line by discussing what they want to see and do during the course of the day. Later, however, as events wear on, they need a little help. Watching for, and counting, Disney characters is a good diversion. Simple guessing games like "20 Questions" also work well. Lines for rides move so continuously that games requiring pen and paper are cumbersome and impractical. Waiting in the holding area of a theater attraction, however, is a different story. Here, tic-tac-toe, hangman, drawing, and coloring can really make the time go by.

2. LAST-MINUTE ENTRY If a ride or show can accommodate an unusually large number of people at one time, it is often unnecessary to stand in line. The *Mark Twain* Riverboat in Frontierland is a good example. The boat holds about 450 people, usually more than are waiting in line to ride. Instead of standing uncomfortably in a crowd with dozens of other guests, grab a snack and sit in the shade until the boat arrives and loading is well under way. After the line has all but disappeared, go ahead and board.

In large-capacity theaters, like the one showing *Honey, I Shrunk the Audience* in Tomorrowland, ask the entrance greeter how long it will be until guests are admitted to the theater for the next show. If the answer is 15 minutes or more, use the time for a restroom break or to get a snack; you can return to the attraction just a few minutes before the show starts. You will not be permitted to carry any food or drink into the attraction, so make sure you have time to finish your snack before entering.

To help you determine which attractions to target for last-minute entry, we provide the following chart.

ATTRACTIONS YOU CAN USUALLY ENTER AT THE LAST MINUTE	
Disneyland Park	
Critter Country	Country Bear Playhouse
Frontierland	*Mark Twain* Riverboat
	Sailing Ship *Columbia*
Main Street, U.S.A.	*Disneyland: The First 50 Years*
Tomorrowland	*Honey, I Shrunk the Audience*
Disney's California Adventure	
Golden State	Golden Dreams

3. THE HAIL-MARY PASS Certain waiting lines are configured in such a way that you and your smaller children can pass under the rail to join your partner just before boarding or entry. This technique allows the kids and one adult to rest, snack, cool off, or tinkle, while another adult or older sibling does the waiting. Other guests are understanding when it comes to using this strategy to keep small children content. You are likely to meet hostile opposition, however, if you try to pass older children or more than one adult under the rail. Attractions where it is usually possible to complete a Hail-Mary Pass are listed on the chart below.

ATTRACTIONS WHERE YOU CAN USUALLY COMPLETE A HAIL-MARY PASS	
Disneyland Park	
Adventureland	Jungle Cruise
	Tarzan's Treehouse
Fantasyland	Casey Jr. Circus Train
	Dumbo, the Flying Elephant
	King Arthur Carousel
	Mad Tea Party
	Mr. Toad's Wild Ride
	Peter Pan's Flight
	Snow White's Scary Adventures
	Storybook Land Canal Boats
Tomorrowland	Tomorrowland Autopia
Disney's California Adventure Park	
Paradise Pier	Golden Zephyr
	Jumpin' Jellyfish
	King Triton's Carousel

4. SWITCHING OFF (ALSO KNOWN AS THE BABY SWAP) Several attractions have minimum height and/or age requirements, usually 40

inches tall to ride with an adult, or 7 years of age *and* 40 inches tall to ride alone. Some couples with children too small or too young forego these attractions, while others split up and takes turns riding separately. Missing out on some of Disney's best rides is an unnecessary sacrifice, and waiting in line twice for the same ride is a tremendous waste of time.

A better way to approach the problem is to take advantage of an option known as "switching off" or "The Baby Swap." Switching off requires at least two adults. Everybody waits in line together, both adults and children. When you reach a Disney attendant (known as a "greeter"), say you want to switch off. The greeter will allow everyone, including the small children, to enter the attraction. When you reach the loading area, one adult will ride while the other stays with the kids. The riding adult then disembarks and takes responsibility for the children while the other adult rides. A third adult in the party can ride twice, once with each of the switching-off adults, so they do not have to experience the attraction alone. The 13 attractions where switching off is routinely practiced are listed on the following chart.

An Ada, Michigan, mother who discovered that the procedure for switching off varies from attraction to attraction offered this suggestion:

> *Parents need to tell the very first attendant they come to that they would like to switch off. Each attraction has a different procedure for this. Tell every other attendant too, because they forget quickly.*

ATTRACTIONS WHERE SWITCHING OFF IS COMMON	
Disneyland Park	
Adventureland	**Indiana Jones Adventure**
Critter Country	**Splash Mountain**
Fantasyland	**Matterhorn Bobsleds**
Frontierland	**Big Thunder Mountain Railroad**
Tomorrowland	**Star Tours**
	Space Mountain
Disney's California Adventure Park	
Golden State	**Grizzly River Run**
	Soarin' over California
Paradise Pier	**California Screamin'**
	Maliboomer
	Mulholland Madness
	Orange Stinger
Hollywood Pictures Backlot	***Twilight Zone* Tower of Terror**

5. HOW TO RIDE TWICE IN A ROW WITHOUT WAITING Many small children like to ride a favorite attraction two or more times in succession. Riding the second time often gives the child a feeling of mastery and accomplishment. Unfortunately, repeat rides can be time-consuming, even in the early morning. If you ride Dumbo as soon as Disneyland Park opens, for instance, you will only have a one- or two-minute wait for your first ride. When you come back for your second ride, your wait will be about 12 minutes. If you want to ride a third time, count on a 20-minute or longer wait.

The best way for getting your child on the ride twice (or more) without blowing your whole morning is by using the "Chuck-Bubba Relay" (named in honor of a reader from Kentucky):

1. Mom and little Bubba enter the waiting line.
2. Dad lets a certain number of people go in front of him (32 in the case of Dumbo) and then gets in line.
3. As soon as the ride stops, Mom exits with little Bubba and passes him to Dad to ride the second time.
4. If everybody is really getting into this, Mom can hop in line again, no less than 32 people behind Dad.

The Chuck Bubba Relay will not work on every ride because of differences in the way the waiting areas are configured (i.e., it is impossible in some cases to exit the ride and make the pass). The rides where the Chuck Bubba Relay does work appear on the chart below along with the number of people to count off.

ATTRACTIONS WHERE THE CHUCK-BUBBA RELAY USUALLY WORKS	
Disneyland Park	**Number of people between adults**
Alice in Wonderland **(tough, but possible)**	38 people
Casey Jr. Circus Train	34 people, if 2 trains are operating
Davy Crockett's Explorer Canoes	94 people, if 6 canoes are operating
Dumbo, the Flying Elephant	32 people
King Arthur Carousel	70 people
Mad Tea Party	53 people
Mr. Toad's Wild Ride	32 people
Peter Pan's Flight	25 people
Snow White's Scary Adventures	30 people
Disney's California Adventure Park	
Golden Zephyr	64 people
Jumpin' Jellyfish	16 people
King Triton's Carousel	64 people

When practicing the Chuck-Bubba Relay, if you are the second adult in line, you will reach a point in the waiting area that is obviously the easiest place to make the hand-off. Sometimes this point is where those exiting the ride pass closest to those waiting to board. In any event, you will know it when you see it. Once there, if the first parent has not arrived with little Bubba, just let those behind you slip past until Bubba shows up.

6. LAST-MINUTE COLD FEET If your small child gets cold feet at the last minute after waiting for a ride (where there is no age or height requirement), you can usually arrange with the loading attendant for a switchoff. This situation arises frequently at Pirates of the Caribbean—small children lose their courage en route to the loading area.

There is no law that says you have to ride. If you get to the boarding area and someone is unhappy, just tell a Disney attendant you have changed your mind, and one will show you the way out.

7. ELEVATOR SHOES FOR THE SHORT AND BRAVE If you have a child who is crazy to go on the rides with height requirements, but who is just a little too short, slip heel lifts into his Nikes before he gets to the measuring point. Be sure to leave the heel lifts in because he may get measured again at the boarding area.

A Huntsville, Alabama, mom has the heel-lift problem under control:

Knowing my wild three-year-old child as I do, I was interested in your comment regarding shoe lifts. I don't know about other places, but in the big city of Huntspatch where we live, one has to have a prescription for lifts. Normal shoe repair places don't make them. I couldn't think of a material with which to fashion a homemade lift that would be comfortable enough to stand on while waiting in line. I ended up purchasing some of those painfully ugly, two-inch, chunky-heeled sandals at my local mart where they carried these hideous shoes in unbelievably tiny sizes ($12). Since they didn't look too comfortable, we popped them on her right before we entered the ride lines. None of the height checkers ever asked her to remove them and she clip-clopped onto Splash Mountain, Big Thunder Railroad (Dat BIG Choo-Choo), Star Wars, and The Tower of Terror—twice! ... For adventuresome boys, I would suggest purchasing some of those equally hideous giant-heeled cowboy boots.

A Long Pond, Pennsylvania, mom has this to offer:

Tower of Terror and Star Tours have 40" [height] requirements. Being persistent with a 39" child, we tried these several times. She got on Tower of Terror two of three times, Body Wars one of one time, and Star Tours one of two tries. She wore elevator shoes and a bun hairstyle to increase height.

We should point out that boosting your child's height by a couple inches with a heel lift or the like will not compromise his safety on the ride.

8. THROW YOURSELF ON THE GRENADE, MILDRED! For by-the-book, do-the-right-thing parents determined to sacrifice themselves on behalf of their children, we provide a One-Day Touring Plan for Disneyland Park called the "Dumbo-or-Die-in-a-Day Touring Plan, for Parents with Small Children." This touring plan, detailed on pages 182–185, will ensure that you run yourself ragged. Designed to help you forfeit everything of personal interest for the sake of your children's pleasure, the plan is guaranteed to send you home battered and exhausted with extraordinary stories of devotion and heroic perseverance. By the way, the plan really works. Anyone under eight years old will love it.

9. DISNEY'S CALIFORNIA ADVENTURE This is not a great park for little ones. With the exception of Flik's Fun Fair, three play areas, and a carousel, most preschoolers will find the remaining attractions either boring or too frightening. Elementary school-age children will fare better, but will probably be captivated by the low-capacity/long-line rides at the Paradise Pier district of the park. Although designed to be appealing to the eye, these attractions are simply gussied-up versions of midway rides your kids can enjoy less expensively and with a fraction of the wait at a local amusement park or state fair.

10. CATCH-22 AT THE TOMORROWLAND AUTOPIA Though the Autopia at Disneyland Park is a great treat for small children, they are required to be 52 inches tall in order to drive unassisted. Since very few children age 6 and under top this height, the ride is essentially withheld from the very age group that would most enjoy it. To resolve this catch-22, go on the ride with your small child. The attendants will assume that you will drive. After getting into the car, however, shift your child over behind the steering wheel. From your position you will still be able to control the foot pedals. To your child, it will feel like driving. Because the car travels on a self-guiding track, there is no way your child can make a mistake while steering.

LOST CHILDREN

LOST CHILDREN NORMALLY do not present much of a problem at Disneyland Resort. All Disney employees are schooled in handling such situations should they arise. If you lose a child while touring, report the situation to a Disney employee; then check in at City Hall (Disneyland Park) or Guest Relations (DCA) where lost children "logs" are maintained. In an emergency, an "alert" can be issued throughout the park through internal communications. If a Disney cast member (employee) encounters a lost child, the cast member will escort the child immediately to the Lost Children Office located by First Aid at the central hub end of Main Street in Disneyland Park and at the entrance plaza in DCA.

unofficial **TIP**
We suggest that children younger than eight years be color-coded by dressing them in purple T-shirts or equally distinctive clothes.

It is amazingly easy to lose a child (or two) at a Disney park. It is a good idea to sew a label into each child's shirt that states his or her name, your name, and the name of your hotel. The same thing can be accomplished less elegantly by writing the information on a strip of masking tape; hotel security professionals suggest that the information be printed in small letters, and that the tape be affixed to the outside of the child's shirt five inches or so below the armpit.

HOW KIDS GET LOST

CHILDREN GET SEPARATED from their parents every day at the Disney parks under circumstances that are remarkably similar (and predictable).

1. PREOCCUPIED SOLO PARENT In this scenario the only adult in the party is preoccupied with something like buying refreshments, loading the camera, or using the restroom. Junior is there one second and gone the next.

2. THE HIDDEN EXIT Sometimes parents wait on the sidelines while allowing two or more young children to experience a ride together. As it usually happens, the parents expect the kids to exit the attraction in one place, and, lo and behold, the young ones pop out somewhere else. The exits of some Disney attractions are considerably distant from the entrances. Make sure you know exactly where your children will emerge before letting them ride by themselves.

3. AFTER THE SHOW At the completion of many shows and rides, a Disney staffer will announce, "Check for personal belongings and take small children by the hand." When dozens, if not hundreds, of people leave an attraction at the same time, it is easy for parents to temporarily lose contact with their children unless they have them directly in tow.

4. RESTROOM PROBLEMS Mom tells six-year-old Tommy, "I'll be sitting on this bench when you come out of the restroom." Three situations: One, Tommy exits through a different door and becomes disoriented (Mom may not know there is another door). Two, Mom decides belatedly that she will also use the restroom, and Tommy emerges to find her absent. Three, Mom pokes around in a shop while keeping an eye on the bench, but misses Tommy when he comes out.

If you can't be with your child in the restroom, make sure there is only one exit. Designate a meeting spot more distinctive than a bench, and be specific in your instructions: "I'll meet you by this flagpole. If you get out first, stay right here." Have your child repeat the directions back to you.

5. PARADES There are many special parades and shows at the theme park during which the audience stands. Children, because they are small, tend to jockey around for a better view. By moving a little this way and a little that way, it is amazing how much distance kids can put between themselves and you before anyone notices.

6. MASS MOVEMENTS Another situation to guard against is when huge crowds disperse after shows, fireworks, parades, or at park closing. With between 5,000 and 12,000 people suddenly moving at once, it is very easy to get separated from a small child or others in your party. Extra caution is recommended following the evening parades, fireworks, and *Fantasmic!* Families should develop specific plans for what to do and where to meet in the event they are separated.

7. CHARACTER GREETINGS A fair amount of activity and confusion is commonplace when the Disney characters are on the scene. See the next section on meeting the Disney characters.

THE DISNEY CHARACTERS

FOR YEARS THE COSTUMED, walking versions of Mickey, Minnie, Donald, Goofy, and others have been a colorful supporting cast at Disneyland and Walt Disney World. Known unpretentiously as the "Disney characters," these large and friendly figures help provide a link between Disney animated films and the Disney theme parks.

Audiences, it has been observed, cry during the sad parts of Disney animated films and cheer when the villain is vanquished. To the emotionally invested, the characters in these features are as real as next-door neighbors; never mind that they are simply drawings on plastic. In recent years, the theme-park personifications of Disney characters have likewise become real to us. For thousands of visitors, it is not just some person in a mouse costume they see, it is really Mickey. Similarly, running into Goofy or Snow White in Fantasyland is a memory to be treasured, an encounter with a real celebrity.

About 250 of the Disney animated film characters have been brought to life in costume. Of these, a relatively small number (about 50) are "greeters" (the Disney term for characters who mix with the patrons). The remaining characters are relegated exclusively to performing in shows or participating in parades. Some only appear once or twice a year, usually in Christmas parades or Disney anniversary celebrations.

CHARACTER ENCOUNTERS

CHARACTER-WATCHING has developed into a pastime. Where families were once content to stumble across a character occasionally, they now relentlessly pursue them armed with autograph books and cameras. For those who pay attention, some characters are much more frequently encountered than others. Mickey, Minnie, and Goofy, for example, are seemingly everywhere, while Thumper comes out only on rare occasions. Other characters can be seen regularly, but limit themselves to a specific location.

The fact that some characters are seldom seen has turned character-watching into character-collecting. Mickey Mouse may be the best known and most loved character, but from a collector's perspective he is also the most common. To get an autograph from Mickey is no big deal, but Daisy Duck's signature is a real coup. Commercially tapping into the character-collecting movement, Disney sells autograph books throughout the parks.

PREPARING YOUR CHILDREN TO MEET THE CHARACTERS Since most small children are not expecting Minnie Mouse to be the size of a forklift, it's best to discuss the characters with your kids before you go. Almost all of the characters are quite large, and several, like Brer Bear, are huge! All of them can be extremely intimidating to a preschooler.

unofficial **TIP**
Don't underestimate your child's excitement at meeting the Disney characters—but also be aware that very small children may find the large, costumed characters a little frightening.

On first encounter, it is important not to thrust your child upon the character. Allow the little one to come to terms with this big thing from whatever distance the child feels safe. If two adults are present, one should stay close to the youngster while the other approaches the character and demonstrates that the character is safe and friendly. Some kids warm to the characters immediately, while some never do. Most take a little time, and often require several different encounters.

There are two kinds of characters: those whose costume includes a face-covering headpiece (animal characters plus some human characters like Captain Hook), and "face characters," who are actors who resemble the cartoon characters to such an extent that no mask or headpiece is necessary. Face characters include Mary Poppins, Ariel, Jasmine, Aladdin, Cinderella, Mulan, Tarzan, Jane, Belle, Snow White, and Prince Charming, to name a few.

Only the face characters are allowed to speak. Headpiece characters do not talk or make noises of any kind. Because the cast members could not possibly imitate the distinctive cinema voice of the character, the Disney folks have determined it is more effective to keep them silent. Lack of speech notwithstanding, the headpiece characters are extremely warm and responsive and communicate very effectively with gestures. As with the characters' size, children need to be forewarned that the characters do not talk.

unofficial **TIP**
Explain to your children that the headpiece characters do not talk. Keep in mind too that the characters are clumsy and have limited field of vision.

Parents need to understand that some of the character costumes are very cumbersome and that cast members often suffer from very poor visibility. You have to look closely, but the eye holes are frequently in the mouth of the costume or even down on the neck. What this means in practical terms is that the characters are sort of clumsy and have a limited field of

vision. Children who approach the character from the back or the side may not be noticed, even if the child is touching the character. It is perfectly possible in this situation for the character to accidentally step on the child or knock him or her down. The best way for a child to approach a character is from the front, and occasionally not even this works. For example, the various duck characters (Donald, Daisy, Uncle Scrooge, etc.), have to peer around their bills. If it appears that the character is ignoring your child, pick your child up and hold her in front of the character until the character responds.

It is okay to touch, pat, or hug the character if your child is so inclined. Understanding the unpredictability of children, the characters will keep their feet very still, particularly refraining from moving backwards or to the side. Most of the characters will sign autographs or pose for pictures. Once again, be sure to approach from the front so that the character will understand your intentions. If your child collects autographs, it is a good idea to carry a big, fat pen about the size of a Magic Marker. The costumes make it exceedingly difficult for the characters to wield a smaller pen, so the bigger the better.

THE BIG HURT Many children expect to bump into Mickey the minute they enter a park and are disappointed when he is not around. If your children are unable to settle down and enjoy things until they see Mickey, simply ask a Disney cast member where to find him. If the cast member does not know Mickey's whereabouts, he or she can find out for you in short order.

"THEN SOME CONFUSION HAPPENED" Be forewarned that character encounters give rise to a situation during which small children sometimes get lost. There is usually a lot of activity around a character, with both adults and children touching the character or posing for pictures. In the most common scenario, the parents stay in the crowd while their child marches up to get acquainted. With the excitement of the encounter, all the milling people, and the character moving around, a child may get turned around and head off in the wrong direction. In the words of a Salt Lake City mom: "Milo was shaking hands with Dopey one minute, then some confusion happened and he [Milo] was gone." Families with several small children, and parents who are busy fooling around with cameras, can lose track of a youngster in a heartbeat. Our recommendation for parents of preschoolers is to stay with the kids when they meet the characters, stepping back only long enough to take a picture, if necessary.

MEETING CHARACTERS You can *see* the Disney characters in live shows and in parades. For times, consult your *Times Guide*. If you have the time and money, you can share a meal with the characters (more about this later). But if you want to *meet* the characters, get autographs, and take photos, it's helpful to know where the characters hang out.

Responding to guest requests, Disneyland Resort has added a lot of new information about characters on its handout park maps and *Times Guide*. A listing specifies where and when certain characters will be available and also provides information on character dining. On the maps of the parks themselves, yellow stars are used to denote locations where characters can be found.

At Disney's California Adventure Park, look for characters in Hollywood near the Animation Building, in parades, and in shows at the Hyperion Theater. Elsewhere around the park, characters will be less in evidence than at Disneyland Park, but they will make periodic appearances at Flik's Fun Fair and Sunshine Plaza (the central hub).

The last few years have seen a number of Disney initiatives aimed at satisfying guests' inexhaustible desire to meet the characters. At Disneyland Park, Disney relegated four (Mickey, Minnie, Pluto, and Donald) of the "fab five" to all-day tours of duty in Mickey's Toontown. The fifth "fab," Goofy, works a similar schedule most days in Frontierland. Likewise, Pooh and Tigger can usually be found in Critter Country, Beauty and the Beast in Fantasyland, and Aladdin and Jasmine in Adventureland. Characters less in demand roam the "lands" consistent with their image (Brer Bear and Brer Fox in Critter Country, for example).

While making the characters routinely available has taken the guesswork out of finding them, it has likewise robbed character encounters of much of their surprise and spontaneity. Instead of chancing on a character as you turn a corner, it is much more common now to wait in a queue in order to meet the character. Speaking of which, be aware that lines for face characters move m-u-c-h more slowly than do lines for nonspeaking characters, as you might surmise. Because face characters are allowed to talk, they do, often engaging children in lengthy conversations, much to the consternation of the families stuck in the queue.

If you believe there are already quite enough lines in Disneyland Park, and furthermore, if you prefer to bump into your characters on the run, here's where the bears and chipmunks roam. There will almost always be a character in Town Square on Main Street and often at the central hub. Characters make appearances in all the "lands," but are particularly thick in Fantasyland and Mickey's Toontown. Snow White, Cinderella, and Princess Aurora hang out in the courtyard of the castle; the aforementioned Brers cruise Critter Country; and Pocahontas meets and greets in Frontierland. Characters not specifically mentioned continue to turn up randomly throughout the park.

unofficial **TIP**
Characters make appearances in all the "lands," but are particularly thick in Fantasyland and Mickey's Toontown.

Characters are also featured in the afternoon and evening parades, Frontierland waterfront shows, *Fantasmic!*, and shows on the Fantasyland Theatre stage. Characters also play a major role in shows at the Tomorrowland Terrace stage. Performance times for all of the shows and parades are listed in the Disneyland Park daily entertainment schedule. After the shows, characters will sometimes stick around to greet the audience.

Mickey Mouse is available to meet guests and pose for photos all day long in his dressing room at Mickey's Movie Barn in Mickey's Toontown. To reach the Movie Barn, proceed through the front door of Mickey's House and follow the crowd. If the line extends back to the entrance of Mickey's House, it will take you about 25 to 30 minutes to actually reach Mickey. When you finally get to his dressing room, one or two families at a time are admitted for a short, personal audience with Mickey.

Many children are so excited about meeting Mickey that they cannot relax to enjoy the other attractions. If Mickey looms large in your child's day, board the Disneyland Railroad at the Main Street Station as soon as you arrive at the park, and proceed directly to Mickey's Toontown (half a circuit). If you visit Mickey before 10 a.m., your wait will be short.

Minnie receives guests at her house most of the day as well, and Donald and Pluto are frequently available for photos and autographs in the gazebo situated in front of the Toontown Town Hall. There is, of course, a separate line for each character. Also, be aware that the characters bug out for parades and certain other special performances. Check the daily entertainment schedule on the handout park map for performance times and plan your Toontown visit accordingly.

Character Dining

Fraternizing with Disney characters has become so popular that Disney offers character breakfasts, brunches, and dinners where families can dine in the presence of Mickey, Minnie, Goofy, and other costumed versions of animated celebrities. Besides grabbing customers from Denny's and McDonalds, character meals provide a familiar, controlled setting in which young children can warm gradually to the characters. All meals are attended by several characters. Adult prices apply to persons age 12 or older, children's prices to ages 3 to 11. Little ones under age 3 eat free.

unofficial **TIP**
Arrange priority seating as far in advance as possible. Your wait for a table will usually be less than 15 minutes.

Because character dining is very popular, we recommend that you arrange priority seating as far in advance as possible. A priority seating is Disney's version of a reservation. You arrive at an appointed time and the restaurant will be expecting you, but no specific table will be set aside. Instead, you will be seated at the first available table. The "priority" part simply means that you will be seated ahead of walk-ins. In practice the system works reasonably well, and your wait for a table will usually be less than 15 minutes.

CHARACTER DINING: WHAT TO EXPECT Character meals are bustling affairs, held in hotels' or theme parks' largest table-service or buffeteria restaurants. Character breakfasts (there are five) offer a fixed menu served family style or as a buffet. The typical family-style breakfast includes scrambled eggs; bacon, sausage, and ham; hash browns; waffles, pancakes, or French toast; biscuits, rolls, or pastries; and fruit. The meal is served in large skillets or platters at your table. If you run out of something, you can order seconds (or thirds) at no additional charge. Buffets offer much the same fare, but you have to fetch it yourself. The only character dinner at Disneyland Resort is a buffet serving standard American fare.

Whatever the meal, characters circulate around the room while you eat. During your meal, each of the three to five characters present will visit your table, arriving one at a time to cuddle the kids (and sometimes the adults), pose for photos, and sign autographs. Keep autograph books (with pens) and loaded cameras handy. For the best photos, adults should sit across the table from their children. Always seat the children where characters can reach them most easily. If a table is against a wall, for example, adults should sit with their backs to the wall and children should sit nearest the aisle.

"Casting!" This is George at the character breakfast. There's been a mistake. We were supposed to get the Assorted Character Packages with one Mickey, one Goofy, one Donald, one Pluto . . . "

You will not be rushed to leave after you've eaten. Feel free to ask for seconds on coffee or juice, and stay as long as you wish. Remember, however, that there might be lots of eager children and adults waiting not so patiently to be admitted.

You can dine with Disney characters at the Plaza Inn in Disneyland Park, at Goofy's Kitchen at the Disneyland Hotel, at Ariel's Grotto at DCA, at the Storytellers Cafe at the Grand Californian Hotel, and at the PCH Grill at the Paradise Pier Hotel. For information about character meals and to make priority seatings, call ☎ 714-781-DINE (3463).

PLAZA INN Located at the end of Main Street and to the right, the Plaza Inn character buffet is usually packed because it hosts character breakfasts that are included in vacation packages sold by the Walt Disney Travel Sales Center. Served from opening until 11 a.m., the buffet costs $20 for adults and $11 for children. Characters present usually include Mickey, Minnie, Goofy, Pluto, and Chip and Dale. Priority seating is recommended.

ARIEL'S GROTTO Overlooking Paradise Bay, Avalon Cove restaurant hosts a dinner buffet with Ariel and friends on Friday, Saturday, and Sunday from 5 p.m. until one hour before park closing, as well as a lunch buffet daily. The admission costs are $20 for adults and $13 for children for dinner; $15 for adults and $11 for children for lunch. Priority seating is recommended.

GOOFY'S KITCHEN Located at the Disneyland Hotel, Goofy's Kitchen serves a character brunch buffet from 7 a.m. until 12 p.m. (2 p.m. weekends) and a character dinner buffet 5 to 9 p.m. Brunch is $22 for adults and $12 for kids. Dinners run $29 (!) and $12, respectively. Goofy, of course, is the head character, but he's usually joined by Minnie, Pluto, and others. Priority seating is recommended.

STORYTELLERS CAFE Storytellers Cafe, located at the Grand Californian Hotel, is the most attractive of the character-meal venues. A breakfast buffet is served from 6:30 until 11 a.m. Cost is $20 for adults and $11 for children. Chip and Dale, the featured characters, are usually assisted by Pluto. Priority seating is recommended.

PCH GRILL PCH Grill at the Paradise Pier Hotel serves a breakfast buffet from 6:30 until 11 a.m. that features traditional Japanese breakfast items in addition to the usual American fare. Prices are $20 for adults and $11 for kids. Minnie is the hostess, with Max (Goofy's son) and Daisy Duck also present. Priority seating is recommended.

PART FOUR

DISNEYLAND PARK

ARRIVING *and* GETTING ORIENTED

IF YOU DRIVE, you will probably be directed to the parking garage on West Street near Ball Road. Parking costs $10 for cars, $12 for RVs, and $17 for buses. Be sure to make a note of your section, row, and space. A tram will transport you to a loading/unloading area connected to the entrance by a pedestrian corridor. Because security screening is conducted just before passing through the turnstiles, the lines to enter the park are often quite lengthy. Two entrance gates, 14 and 19, are blocked by trees situated in the entrance plaza about ten feet from the security checkpoint. The trees inhibit the formation of a line in front of both of the obstructed gates. These gates (14 and 19) are staffed nonetheless and draw guests from adjacent lines 13 and 20. This significantly speeds up the entry process for guests waiting in lines 13 and 20. Our advice on arriving, therefore, is to join line 13 or 20. Of the two, 13 is usually shorter than 20. On entering Disneyland Park, stroller and wheelchair rentals are to the right just beyond the turnstile. As you enter Main Street, City Hall is to your left, serving as the center for general information, lost and found, and entertainment information.

If you haven't been given a freebie Disneyland Park map by now, City Hall is the place to pick one up. Also pick up a *Times Guide*. The *Times Guide* contains the daily entertainment schedule for live shows, parades, fireworks, and other events, and tells you where you can find the characters. If a *Times Guide* is not available for the day you visit (a very rare occurrence), the daily entertainment schedule will be included in the park map. The park map lists all the attractions, shops, and eateries and provides helpful information about first aid, baby care, assistance for the disabled, and more.

disneyland park

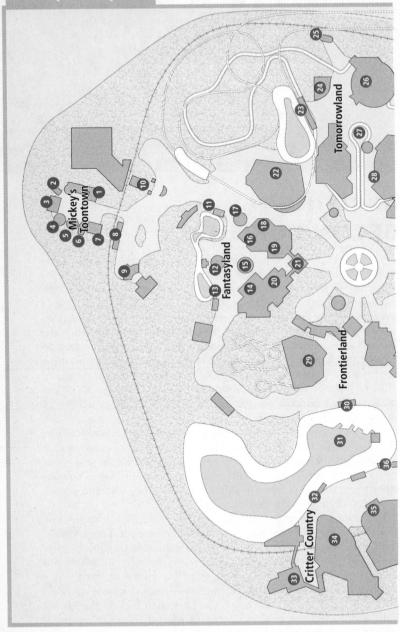

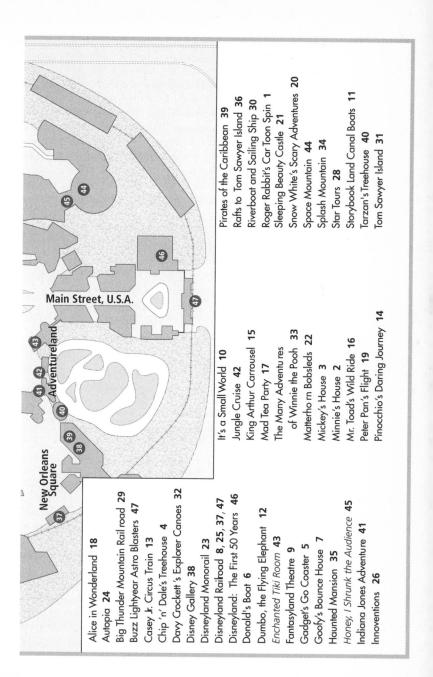

New Orleans
Square

Main Street, U.S.A.

Adventureland

Alice in Wonderland **18**
Autopia **24**
Big Thunder Mountain Rail road **29**
Buzz Lightyear Astro Blasters **47**
Casey Jr. Circus Train **13**
Chip 'n' Dale's Treehouse **4**
Davy Crockett's Explorer Canoes **32**
Disney Gallery **38**
Disneyland Monorail **23**
Disneyland Railroad **8, 25, 37, 47**
Disneyland: The First 50 Years **46**
Donald's Boat **6**
Dumbo, the Flying Elephant **12**
Enchanted Tiki Room **43**
Fantasyland Theatre **9**
Gadget's Go Coaster **5**
Goofy's Bounce House **7**
Haunted Mansion **35**
Honey, I Shrunk the Audience **45**
Indiana Jones Adventure **41**
Innoventions **26**

It's a Small World **10**
Jungle Cruise **42**
King Arthur Carrousel **15**
Mad Tea Party **17**
The Many Adventures
  of Winnie the Pooh **33**
Matterhorn Bobsleds **22**
Mickey's House **3**
Minnie's House **2**
Mr. Toad's Wild Ride **16**
Peter Pan's Flight **19**
Pinocchio's Daring Journey **14**

Pirates of the Caribbean **39**
Rafts to Tom Sawyer Island **36**
Riverboat and Sailing Ship **30**
Roger Rabbit's Car Toon Spin **1**
Sleeping Beauty Castle **21**
Snow White's Scary Adventures **20**
Space Mountain **44**
Splash Mountain **34**
Star Tours **28**
Storybook Land Canal Boats **11**
Tarzan's Treehouse **40**
Tom Sawyer Island **31**

Notice on your map that Main Street ends at a central hub from which branch the entrances to four other sections of Disneyland: Adventureland, Frontierland, Fantasyland, and Tomorrowland. Two other "lands," New Orleans Square and Critter Country, can be reached through Adventureland and Frontierland. Mickey's Toontown is located on the far side of the railroad tracks from It's a Small World in Fantasyland. Sleeping Beauty Castle serves as the entrance to Fantasyland and is a focal landmark and the visual center of the park. The castle is a great place to meet if your group decides to split up for any reason during the day, and it can serve as an emergency meeting place if you are accidentally separated. Keep in mind, however, that the castle covers a lot of territory, so be specific about *where* to meet at the castle. Also be forewarned that parades and live shows sometimes make it difficult to access the entrance of the castle fronting the central hub.

Not to Be Missed at Disneyland Park

Adventureland	Indiana Jones Adventure
Critter Country	Splash Mountain
Frontierland	Big Thunder Mountain Railroad
New Orleans Square	Haunted Mansion
	Pirates of the Caribbean
Tomorrowland	*Honey, I Shrunk the Audience*
	Space Mountain
	Star Tours
Live Entertainment	*Fantasmic!*
	Parade of Dreams

STARTING THE TOUR

EVERYONE WILL SOON FIND his or her own favorite and not-so-favorite attractions in Disneyland Park. Be open-minded and adventuresome. Don't dismiss a particular ride or show as not being for you until *after* you have tried it. Our personal experience as well as our research indicates that each visitor is different in terms of which Disney offerings he or she most enjoys. So don't miss seeing an attraction because a friend from home didn't like it; that attraction may turn out to be your favorite.

We do recommend that you take advantage of what Disney does best—the fantasy adventures like the Indiana Jones Adventure and the Haunted Mansion, and the audio-animatronic (talking robots, that is) attractions such as the Pirates of the Caribbean. Unless you have almost unlimited time, don't burn a lot of daylight browsing through the shops. Except for some special Disney souvenirs, you can find much of the same merchandise elsewhere. Try to minimize the time you spend on midway-type rides, as you've probably got an amusement park, carnival, or state fair close to your hometown. Don't, however, mistake rides like Splash Mountain and the Big Thunder Mountain Railroad for amusement park rides. They may be of the flume-ride or the roller-coaster genre, but they represent pure Disney genius. Similarly, do not devote a lot of time to waiting in lines for meals. Eat a good early breakfast before you come, snack on vendor-sold foods during the touring day, or follow the suggestions for meals incorporated into the various touring plans presented.

ORGANIZATION OF PROFILES

WE HAVE GROUPED ATTRACTIONS into "lands," which are listed geographically—roughly clockwise from the entrance. The attraction profiles are listed alphabetically under their respective "lands" and are followed by comments on eateries and shops.

MAIN STREET, U.S.A.

THIS SECTION OF DISNEYLAND PARK is where you'll begin and end your visit. We have already mentioned that assistance and information are available at City Hall. The Disneyland Railroad stops at the Main Street Station, and you can board here for a grand circle tour of the park, or you can get off the train in New Orleans Square, Mickey's Toontown/Fantasyland, or Tomorrowland.

Main Street is an idealized version of a turn-of-the-century American small-town street. Many visitors are surprised to discover that all the buildings are real, not elaborate props. Attention to detail here is exceptional—interiors, furnishings, and fixtures conform to the period. As with any real Main Street, the Disney version is essentially a collection of shops and eating places, with a city hall, a fire station, and an old-time cinema. A mixed-media attraction combines static exhibits recalling the life of Walt Disney with a patriotic remembrance of Abraham Lincoln. A new exhibit and film chronicling Disneyland's first 50 years has replaced Mr. Lincoln during the 18-month anniversary celebration that commenced on May 5, 2005. Horse-drawn trolleys, fire engines, and horseless carriages give rides along Main Street and transport visitors to the central hub (properly known as the Central Plaza).

Disneyland Railroad

APPEAL BY AGE	PRESCHOOL ★★★★	GRADE SCHOOL ★★★	TEENS ★★
YOUNG ADULTS ★★★½	OVER 30 ★★★½		SENIORS ★★★½

Type of attraction Scenic railroad ride around the park's perimeter; also transportation to New Orleans Square, Mickey's Toontown, Fantasyland, and

Main Street Services

Most of the park's service facilities are centered in the Main Street section, including the following:

Wheelchair and Stroller Rental To the right of the main entrance before you pass under the Railroad Station

Banking Services/Currency Exchange At City Hall at the Railroad Station end of Main Street

Storage Lockers Down Main Street one block (as you walk toward the castle) and to the right

Lost and Found Lost and Found for the entire resort is located east of the entrance of Disney's California Adventures

Live Entertainment and Parade Information City Hall Building at the Railroad Station end of Main Street

Lost Adults and Messages City Hall Building

Lost Children At the central hub end of Main Street near the First Aid Center

Disneyland and Local Attraction Information City Hall Building

First Aid First Aid Center two doors from Plaza Inn at the central hub end of Main Street

Baby Center/Baby Care Needs At the central hub end of Main Street

Tomorrowland. **Scope and scale** Major attraction. **When to go** After 11 a.m. or when you need transportation. **Special comments** The Main Street and Mickey's Toontown/Fantasyland Stations are usually the least-congested boarding points. **Author's rating ★★★. Duration of ride** About 20 minutes for a complete circuit. **Average wait in line per 100 people ahead of you** 8 minutes. **Assumes** 3 trains operating. **Loading speed** Fast.

DESCRIPTION AND COMMENTS A transportation ride that blends an eclectic variety of sights and experiences with an energy-saving way of getting around the park. In addition to providing a glimpse of all the lands except Adventureland, the train passes through the Grand Canyon Diorama (between Tomorrowland and Main Street), a three-dimensional replication of the canyon, complete with wildlife, as it appears from the southern rim. Another sight on the train circuit is Primeval World, a depiction of a prehistoric peat bog and rain forest populated by audio-animatronic (robotic) dinosaurs. Opened in 1966, Primeval World was a precursor to a similar presentation in the Universe of Energy pavilion at Epcot.

TOURING TIPS Save the train ride until after you have seen the featured attractions, or use it when you need transportation. If you have small children who are hell bent to see Mickey first thing in the morning, you might consider taking the train to Mickey's Toontown (a half-circuit) and visiting Mickey in his dressing room as soon as you enter the park. Many families find that this tactic puts the kids in a more receptive frame of mind for the other attractions. On busy days, lines form at the

New Orleans Square and Tomorrowland stations, but rarely at the Main Street or Mickey's Toontown/Fantasyland stations.

Disneyland: The First 50 Years

APPEAL BY AGE	PRESCHOOL ★		GRADE SCHOOL ★★½		TEENS ★★½
YOUNG	ADULTS ★★★	OVER	30 ★★★½	SENIORS	★★★½

Type of attraction Exhibits and film detailing the history of Disneyland. **Scope and scale** Minor attraction. **When to go** Whenever you want. **Author's rating** ★★★½. **Duration of film** 12 minutes.

DESCRIPTION AND COMMENTS This attraction occupies the Main Street Opera House replacing *The Walt Disney Story,* featuring "Great Moments with Mr. Lincoln." Part of the Disneyland 50th Anniversary observance, *Disneyland: The First 50 Years* features Walt Disney and Disneyland memorabilia, early design renderings of the park and of the attractions, and a specially made, nostalgic film about how Disneyland came to be. Following the film, guests view another exhibit showcasing "the Disneyland that never was," highlighting attractions and shows planned but never brought to fruition. The exhibit also offers a glimpse of Disneyland's future.

TOURING TIPS A lovely remembrance. Visit anytime.

Main Street Cinema

APPEAL BY AGE	PRESCHOOL ★★½		GRADE SCHOOL ★★½		TEENS ★★½
YOUNG	ADULTS ★★★½	OVER 30 ★★★½		SENIORS	★★★½

Type of attraction Vintage Disney cartoons. **Scope and scale** Diversion. **When to go** Whenever you want. **Author's rating** Wonderful selection of old-time flicks; ★★. **Duration of presentation** Runs continuously. **Preshow entertainment** None. **Probable waiting time** No waiting.

DESCRIPTION AND COMMENTS Excellent old-time movies including some vintage Disney cartoons. Since the movies are silent, six can be shown simultaneously. No seats; viewers stand.

TOURING TIPS Good place to get out of the sun or rain or to kill time while others in your group shop on Main Street. Fun, but not something you can't afford to miss.

The Walt Disney Story, featuring "Great Moments with Mr. Lincoln" (reopens 2007)

Type of attraction Nostalgic exhibits documenting the Disney success story followed by an audio-animatronic patriotic presentation. **Scope and scale** Minor attraction. **When to go** During the hot, crowded period of the day. **Special comments** *Disneyland: The First 50 Years* replaces *The Walt Disney Story* and Mr. Lincoln during the 18-month Disneyland anniversary celebration that began May 5, 2005. **Author's rating** More emphasis on Lincoln than Disney; ★★★½. **Duration of presentation** 15 minutes including preshow. **Preshow entertainment** Disney exhibits. **Probable waiting time** Usually no wait.

DESCRIPTION AND COMMENTS A warm, well-presented remembrance of the man who started it all. Well worth seeing; especially touching for those old enough to remember Walt Disney himself. The attraction consists of a museum of Disney memorabilia, including a re-creation of Walt's office. Especially interesting are displays illustrating the construction and evolution of Disneyland. Beyond the Disney memorabilia, guests are admitted to a large theater where "Great Moments with Mr. Lincoln" is presented. A patriotic performance, "Great Moments" features an extremely lifelike and sophisticated audio-animatronic Lincoln delivering the Gettysburg Address.

The Walt Disney Story and Mr. Lincoln were pulled out of the lineup for half of 2001, supposedly for a substantial revision and upgrade. Unfortunately, Walt and Abe were caught in a corporate Disney budget cut and some of the more ambitious plans for the attraction were scrapped. There's a lot of new Disney memorabilia in the new rendition and the set surrounding Mr. Lincoln has been improved. In the revised presentation, Civil War photographer Mathew Brady photographs a young Union private before he goes to war. After the shoot, Brady takes the soldier along for an appointment with Lincoln. The presentation is primarily auditory. Wireless earphones make the story unfold three-dimensionally around you. Sounds of scissors, a fly, and Lincoln whispering in your ear are reproduced so realistically that it's almost impossible to differentiate from the real thing. Following the story of Brady, Lincoln, and the private, an audio-animatronic Lincoln delivers the Gettysburg Address.

TOURING TIPS You usually do not have to wait long for this show, so see it during the busy times of day when lines are long elsewhere or as you are leaving the park. The Walt Disney Story and Mr. Lincoln will reopen in 2007.

Transportation Rides

DESCRIPTION AND COMMENTS Trolleys, buses, etc., that add color to Main Street.

TOURING TIPS Will save you a walk to the central hub. Not worth waiting in line for.

MAIN STREET EATERIES AND SHOPS

DESCRIPTION AND COMMENTS Snacks, food, and specialty or souvenir shopping in a nostalgic, happy setting. Incidentally, the **Emporium** on Main Street and the **Star Trader** in Tomorrowland are the two best places for finding Disney trademark souvenirs.

TOURING TIPS The shops are fun but the merchandise can be had elsewhere (except for certain Disney trademark souvenirs). If seeing the park attractions is your objective, save the Main Street eateries and shops until the end of the day. If shopping is your objective, you will find the shops most crowded during the noon hour and near closing time. Remember, Main Street usually opens a half-hour earlier and closes a half-hour to an hour later than the rest of Disneyland Park.

ADVENTURELAND

ADVENTURELAND IS THE FIRST "LAND" to the left of Main Street and embodies a safari–African motif. Since the opening of the Indiana Jones Adventure, the narrow thoroughfares of Adventureland have been mobbed, making pedestrian traffic difficult.

Enchanted Tiki Birds

APPEAL BY AGE	PRESCHOOL ★★½	GRADE SCHOOL ★★★	TEENS ★★
YOUNG ADULTS ★★★	OVER 30 ★★★		SENIORS ★★★

Type of attraction Audio-animatronic Pacific Island musical show. **Scope and scale** Minor attraction. **When to go** Before 11 a.m. and after 6 p.m. **Author's rating** Very, very unusual; ★★★. **Duration of presentation** 14½ minutes. **Preshow entertainment** Talking totem poles. **Probable waiting time** 11 minutes.

DESCRIPTION AND COMMENTS An unusual sit-down theater performance in which more than 200 birds, flowers, and tiki-god statues sing and whistle through a musical program.

TOURING TIPS One of the more bizarre of the Disneyland Park entertainments and sometimes very crowded. We like it in the early evening, when we can especially appreciate sitting for a bit in an air-conditioned theater.

A reader from Cookeville, Tennessee, took exception to the rating for preschoolers and wrote:

I know that visitor reactions vary widely, but the [Enchanted Tiki Birds] was our toddler's favorite attraction. We nearly omitted it because of the rating for preschoolers.

Indiana Jones Adventure (FASTPASS)

Type of ride Motion simulator dark ride. **Scope and scale** Super headliner. **When to go** Before 9:30 a.m. or use FASTPASS. **Special comments** Children must be 46" tall to ride; switching off available (see page 107). **Author's rating** Not to be missed; ★★★★½. **Duration of ride** 3 minutes and 20 seconds. **Average wait in line per 100 people ahead of you** 3 minutes. **Assumes** Full-capacity operation with 18-second dispatch interval. **Loading speed** Fast.

DESCRIPTION AND COMMENTS Indiana Jones Adventure is a combination track ride and motion simulator. Guests ride a military troop transport vehicle. In addition to moving along its path, the vehicle bucks and pitches (the simulator part) in sync with visuals and special effects. Though the plot is complicated and not altogether clear, the bottom line is that if you look into the Forbidden Eye, you're in big trouble. The Forbidden Eye, of course, stands out like Rush Limbaugh in a

Motion Sickness

WARNING!

diaper, and *everybody* stares at it. The rest of the ride consists of a mad race to escape the temple as it collapses around you. In the process, you encounter snakes, spiders, lava pits, rats, swinging bridges, and the house-sized, granite bowling ball that everyone remembers from *Raiders of the Lost Ark.*

The Indiana Jones ride is a Disney masterpiece—nonstop action from beginning to end with brilliant visual effects. Elaborate even by Disney standards, the attraction provides a level of detail and variety of action that makes use of the entire Imagineering arsenal of high-tech gimmickry. Combining a setting as rich as Pirates of the Caribbean with a ride that rivals Star Tours, Indiana Jones is a powerhouse.

Sophisticated in its electronic and computer applications, Indiana Jones purports to offer a different experience on each ride. According to the designers, there are veritable menus of special effects that the computer can mix and match. In practice, however, we could not see much difference from ride to ride. There are, no doubt, subtle variations, but the ride is so wild and frenetic that it's hard to apprehend subtlety. Between explosions and falling rocks your poor, fried brain simply does not register nuance. If you ride twice and your date says, "The rat on the beam winked at me that time," it's probably a good idea to get away from Disneyland for a while.

The adventure begins in the queue, which sometimes extends out the entrance of the attraction and over the bridge leading to Adventureland! When you ultimately work your way into the attraction area, you find yourself at the site of an archaeology expedition with the Temple of Doom entrance beckoning only 50 feet away. After crossing a wooden bridge, you finally step into the temple. The good news is that you are out of the California sun. The bad news is that you have just entered Indiana Jones's indoor queuing area, a system of tunnels and passageways extending to within 50 yards of the Santa Monica pier.

Fortunately, the queuing area is interesting. You wind through caves, down the interior corridors of the temple, and into subterranean rotundas where the archaeologists have been hard at work. Along the way there are various surprises, as well as a succession of homilies etched in an "ancient" language on the temple walls. During our first visit we decoded the messages with feverish intensity, hoping to find one that translated to "restrooms." Trust us on this one: Do *not* chug down Diet Cokes before you get in line for this attraction.

If you are dazed from spending what seems like half of your life in this line and are not up to deciphering the Disney hieroglyphics, not to worry. You will eventually stumble into a chamber where a short movie will explain the plot. From there it's back into the maze and finally on to the loading area. The ride itself is memorable. If you ride with a full bladder, it's absolutely unforgettable.

TOURING TIPS Indiana Jones stays fairly mobbed all day. Try to ride during the first hour the park is open or use FASTPASS. Another alternative, if you don't mind riding alone, is to take advantage of the singles line. Guests from the singles lines are tapped, one at a time, to fill any odd seats remaining in the ride vehicles before they are dispatched. Generally the wait for guests in the singles line is about one-third that of guests in the regular queue. Be forewarned that the singles line at Indiana Jones (the only singles line at Disneyland Park) is a bit of a maze, requiring you to negotiate your way up the exit ramp, up one elevator, across a walkway over the track, then down another elevator to the loading area.

During the first hour or so the park is open, Indiana Jones cast members often employ a line management technique known as "stacking." Simply stated, they allow the line for Indiana Jones to form outside of the attraction, leaving the cavernous inside queuing area virtually empty. Guests, of course, assume that the attraction is packed to the gills and that the outside line is overflow. Naturally, this discourages guests from getting in line. The reality is that the wait is not nearly as bad as it looks, and that it is probably as short as it will be all day. If you arrive in the park early and the Indiana Jones line appears huge, have the rest of your party get in line while you enter Indiana Jones *through the attraction exit* and check out the inside queue. If it is empty or sparsely populated, stacking is being practiced. Join your party in line and enjoy the attraction; your wait will be comparatively short. If the inside queue is bumper to bumper, try Indiana Jones later or use FASTPASS or the singles line. Stacking is also sometimes practiced during the hour just before the park closes.

There is one other thing you should know. Indiana Jones, because it is high-tech, breaks down a lot. The Disney people will announce that the ride is broken but usually will not estimate how long repairs will take. From our experience, most glitches are resolved in approximately 15 to 30 minutes, and probably the best advice is to stick it out.

If you miss Indiana Jones in the early morning and the FASTPASSes are all gone, use the singles line or try again during a parade or *Fantasmic!*, or during the hour before the park closes. Regarding the latter, the Disney folks will usually admit to the attraction anyone in line at closing time. During our last visit to Indiana Jones, Disneyland Park closed at 7 p.m. We hopped in the line for Indiana Jones at 6:45 p.m. and actually got on the ride at 7:30 p.m.

Though the Indiana Jones ride is wild and jerky, it is primarily distinguished by its visual impact and realistic special effects. Thus, we encourage the over-50 crowd to give it a chance: We think you'll like it. As for children, most find the ride extremely intense and action-packed but not particularly frightening. We encountered very few children who met the 46-inch minimum-height requirement who were in any way intimidated.

Jungle Cruise

APPEAL BY AGE	PRESCHOOL ★★★★	GRADE SCHOOL ★★★★	TEENS.★★★
YOUNG ADULTS ★★★		OVER 30 ★★★½	SENIORS ★★★½

Type of ride A Disney outdoor boat-ride adventure. **Scope and scale** Major attraction. **When to go** Before 10 a.m. or after 6 p.m. **Author's rating** A Disney standard; ★★★. **Duration of ride** 7½ minutes. **Average wait in line per 100 people ahead of you** 3½ minutes. **Assumes** 10 boats operating. **Loading speed** Moderate to slow.

The 357th Stroller Squadron: The Mowin' Mamas

DESCRIPTION AND COMMENTS A boat ride through jungle waterways. Passengers encounter elephants, lions, hostile natives, and a menacing hippo. A long-enduring Disney favorite with the boatman's spiel adding measurably to the fun. The ride was shortened by a minute and a half in 1995 when Indiana Jones (next door) commandeered part of the Jungle Cruise's acreage. On the bright side, the Jungle Cruise was spruced up with a nifty new entrance building and queuing area.

As more technologically advanced attractions have been added to the park over the years, the Jungle Cruise has, by comparison, lost some of its luster. Though still a good attraction, it offers few thrills and no surprises for Disneyland Park veterans, many of whom can rattle off the ride's narration right along with the guide. For park first-timers, however, the Jungle Cruise continues to delight.

TOURING TIPS This ride loads slowly and long lines form as the park fills. To compound problems, guests exiting Indiana Jones tend to head for the Jungle Cruise. Go early, or during a parade or a performance of *Fantasmic!*. Be forewarned that the Jungle Cruise has an especially deceptive line: just when you think you are about to board, you are shunted into yet another queuing maze (not visible outside the ride). Regardless how short the line *looks* when you approach the Jungle Cruise, inquire about the length of the wait—at least you will know what you are getting into.

Tarzan's Treehouse

APPEAL BY AGE	PRESCHOOL ★★★★	GRADE SCHOOL ★★★★	TEENS ★★★
YOUNG ADULTS ★★★		OVER 30 ★★★	SENIORS ★★★

Type of attraction Walk-through treehouse exhibit. **Scope and scale** Minor attraction. **When to go** Before 11 a.m. and after 5 p.m. **Special comments**

Requires climbing a lot of stairs. **Author's rating** A very creative exhibit; ★★★. **Duration of tour** 8 to 12 minutes. **Average wait in line per 100 people ahead of you** 7 minutes. **Assumes** Normal staffing. **Loading speed** Does not apply.

DESCRIPTION AND COMMENTS Inspired by Disney's 1999 animated film *Tarzan,* Tarzan's Treehouse replaced the venerable Swiss Family Treehouse that had been an Adventureland icon for 37 years. To enter the new attraction, you climb a rustic staircase and cross a suspension bridge. From there, as they say, it's all downhill. Pages from Jane's sketchbook scattered about tell the Tarzan story and provide insights to the various rooms and levels of the treehouse. At the base of the tree is an interactive play area where characters from Disney's *Tarzan* drop in for photos and autographs.

TOURING TIPS A self-guided, walk-through tour that involves a lot of climbing up and down stairs but with no ropes or ladders or anything fancy. People stopping during the walk-through to look extra long or to rest sometimes create bottlenecks that slow crowd flow. We recommend visiting this attraction in the late afternoon or early evening if you are on a one-day tour schedule.

ADVENTURELAND EATERIES AND SHOPS

DESCRIPTION AND COMMENTS With only one counter-service restaurant (**Bengal Barbeque**), a fruit stand, and a juice bar, pickings are a little slim in Adventureland. Bengal Barbeque offers marinated beef, chicken, bacon, and asparagus, and veggie skewers ranging in price from $4 to $5. Though the skewers are tasty, the portions are small and not a good value for the money. If you find yourself hungry in Adventureland, you will find a much better selection of food in nearby New Orleans Square, Frontierland, or on Main Street.

The shops in Adventureland are set up like an African bazaar and feature safari clothing, tribal crafts, and Disney stuff. If you are on a tight schedule, skip the shops or try them on your second day.

NEW ORLEANS SQUARE

ACCESSIBLE VIA ADVENTURELAND AND FRONTIERLAND, New Orleans Square is one of three lands that do not emanate from the central hub. The architecture and setting are Caribbean colonial, like New Orleans itself, with exceptional attention to detail.

The Disney Gallery

DESCRIPTION AND COMMENTS Located up a set of stairs on the second floor of the building that houses Pirates of the Caribbean, this attraction consists of a collection of paintings, drawings, and models documenting the development and evolution of Disneyland. Included in the collection are design renderings of present and future attractions, as well as sketches for attractions proposed but never constructed. Exhibits showcasing art from Disney animated films and from other Disney theme parks are featured on a temporary basis.

TOURING TIPS Most folks are not aware of the gallery's existence, so it is rarely crowded. See it at your convenience. The gallery has an elevator, so it's wheelchair accessible.

Disneyland Railroad

DESCRIPTION AND COMMENTS The Disneyland Railroad stops in New Orleans Square on its circle tour around the park. See the description of the Disneyland Railroad under Main Street, U.S.A., for additional details regarding the sights en route.

TOURING TIPS A pleasant and feet-saving way to commute to Mickey's Toontown/Fantasyland, Tomorrowland, or Main Street. Be advised, however, that the New Orleans Square station is usually the most congested.

Haunted Mansion

APPEAL BY AGE	PRESCHOOL *varies*	GRADE SCHOOL ★★★★½	TEENS ★★★★
YOUNG ADULTS ★★★★		OVER 30 ★★★★	SENIORS ★★★★

Type of ride Indoor haunted house ride. **Scope and scale** Major attraction. **When to go** Before 11:30 a.m. or after 6:30 p.m. **Special comments** Frightens some very small children. **Author's rating** Some of Disneyland's best special effects; ★★★★. **Duration of ride** 5.5-minute ride plus a 2-minute preshow. **Average wait in line per 100 people ahead of you** 2½ minutes. **Assumes** Both stretch rooms operating. **Loading speed** Fast.

DESCRIPTION AND COMMENTS A fun attraction more than a scary one. An ingenious preshow serves as a vehicle to deliver guests to the ride's boarding area, where they then board "Doom Buggies" for a ride through the mansion's parlor, dining room, library, halls, and attic before descending to an uncommonly active graveyard. Disney employs almost every special effect in its repertoire in the Haunted Mansion, making it one of the most inventive and different of all Disney attractions. Be warned that some youngsters build a lot of anxiety concerning what they think they will see. The actual attraction scares almost nobody.

The Haunted Mansion is one of veteran *Unofficial Guide* writer Eve Zibart's favorite attractions. She warns:

Don't let the childishness of the old-fashioned Haunted Mansion put you off: This is one of the best attractions [in the park]. It's jammed packed with visual puns, special effects, hidden Mickeys, and really lovely Victorian-spooky sets. It's not scary, except in the sweetest of ways, but it will remind you of the days before ghost stories gave way the slasher flicks.

TOURING TIPS This attraction would be more at home in Fantasyland, but no matter, it's Disney at its best; another "not-to-be-missed" feature. Because the Haunted Mansion is in an especially high-traffic corridor (between Pirates of the Caribbean and Splash Mountain), it stays busy all day. Try to see the Haunted Mansion before 11:30 a.m., after 6:30 p.m., or while a parade is in progress. In the evening, crowds for *Fantasmic!* gather in front of the Haunted Mansion, making it very difficult to access.

Pirates of the Caribbean

| APPEAL BY AGE | PRESCHOOL ★★★ | GRADE SCHOOL ★★★★½ | TEENS ★★★★ |
| YOUNG ADULTS ★★★★ | | OVER 30 ★★★★½ | SENIORS ★★★★½ |

Type of ride A Disney indoor adventure boat ride. **Scope and scale** Major attraction. **When to go** Before 11:30 a.m. or after 4:30 p.m. **Special comments** Frightens some small children. **Author's rating** Our pick as one of Disneyland's very best; ★★★★. **Duration of ride** Approximately 14 minutes. **Average wait in line per 100 people ahead of you** 3 minutes. **Assumes** 42 boats operating. **Loading speed** Fast.

DESCRIPTION AND COMMENTS Another boat ride, this time indoors, through a series of sets depicting a pirate raid on an island settlement, from the bombardment of the fortress to the debauchery that follows the victory. Pirates of the Caribbean was the target of a much-publicized political correctness controversy relating to the objectification of women and the "boys will be boys" way in which the pirates' debauchery was depicted. Ultimately, Disney was pressured into revamping the attraction (though not much).

TOURING TIPS Another "not-to-be-missed" attraction. Undoubtedly one of the most elaborate and imaginative attractions in Disneyland Park. Though engineered to move large crowds, this ride sometimes gets overwhelmingly busy in the early and midafternoon. Try to ride before noon or while a parade or *Fantasmic!* is in progress.

NEW ORLEANS SQUARE EATERIES AND SHOPS

DESCRIPTION AND COMMENTS Shops and restaurants in New Orleans Square impart a special realism to the setting. **The Blue Bayou,** the only full-service restaurant in the park, is to the left of the Pirates of the Caribbean exit. With its waterside, bayou-at-dusk setting, the Blue Bayou offers an exotic, romantic atmosphere equaled by few restaurants anywhere. The menu features some Creole and Cajun selections as well as a longtime favorite among visitors, the Monte Cristo sandwich. Priority seatings are generally required and should be made at the door of the restaurant as soon as possible after you enter the park. You can also make priority seatings up to 60 days in advance by calling ☎ 714-781-3463.

Ethnic menu diversification has also improved selections at the **French Market** restaurant. Jambalaya and Cajun chicken breast sandwiches have been added to a lineup that includes angel-hair pasta, fried chicken, and beef stew. Prices run in the $9–$11 range, with children's fried chicken or fettuccine meals available for about $6. More limited fare is available at the **Royal Street Veranda** and at **Café Orleans,** which both serve clam chowder in a bread bowl for $8.

Possibly the most overlooked counter-service restaurant in the park is **La Petite Patisserie.** Consisting of only two modest serving windows mid-block on Royal Street, La Petite Patisserie serves good desserts and coffee to the few guests who stumble upon it.

TOURING TIPS Skip the restaurants and shops if you have only one or two days to visit. If you have some extra time, however, treat yourself to a meal at the Blue Bayou restaurant. The food is a cut above the usual Disney fare and the atmosphere will knock you out.

CRITTER COUNTRY

CRITTER COUNTRY, SITUATED AT THE END of a cul-de-sac and accessible via New Orleans Square, sports a pioneer appearance not unlike that of Frontierland. Critter Country was closed for a major overhaul during much of 2002. Splash Mountain received a face-lift, an improved dock was built for the Davy Crockett canoes, and the Country Bear Playhouse was closed permanently to make way for The Many Adventures of Winnie the Pooh, which opened in 2003.

Davy Crockett's Explorer Canoes

APPEAL BY AGE	PRESCHOOL ★★★★	GRADE SCHOOL ★★★★	TEENS ★★★
YOUNG ADULTS ★★★		OVER 30 ★★★	SENIORS ★★★

Type of ride Scenic canoe ride. **Scope and scale** Minor attraction. **When to go** Before 11 a.m. **Special comments** Skip if the lines are long; closes at dusk. **Author's rating** Most fun way to see Rivers of America; ★★★. **Duration of ride** 8–10 minutes depending on how fast you paddle. **Average wait in line per 100 people ahead of you** 12½ minutes. **Assumes** 6 canoes operating. **Loading speed** Slow.

DESCRIPTION AND COMMENTS Paddle-powered (you paddle) ride around Tom Sawyer Island and Fort Wilderness. Runs the same route with the same sights as the steamboat and the sailing ship. The canoes operate only on busier days and close at dusk. The sights are fun and the ride is a little different in that the patrons paddle the canoe. We think this is the most fun of any of the various river trips. Long lines from about 11 a.m. on reflect the popularity of this attraction.

TOURING TIPS The canoes represent one of four ways to see the same waterways. Since the canoes are slower in loading, we usually opt for the larger steamboat or sailing ship. If you are not up for a boat ride, a different view of the same sights can be had by hoofing around Tom Sawyer Island and Fort Wilderness. Try to ride before 11 a.m. or just before dusk. The canoes operate on selected days and seasonal periods only. If the canoes are a big deal to you, call ahead to make sure they are operating.

Splash Mountain (FASTPASS)

APPEAL BY AGE	PRESCHOOL †	GRADE SCHOOL ★★★★★	TEENS ★★★★★
YOUNG ADULTS ★★★★★		OVER 30 ★★★★½	SENIORS ★★★★½

† Many preschoolers are too short to meet the height requirement, while others are intimidated from watching the ride while standing in line. Of those preschoolers who actually ride, most give the attraction high marks;

WARNING!

For Bouffants, Rug Wearers, and Elvis Impersonators

This Ride Will Muss Your 'Do

Type of ride Water-flume adventure boat ride. **Scope and scale** Headliner. **When to go** Before 9:45 a.m. or use FASTPASS. **Special comments** Children must be 40" tall to ride; those under 7 years of age must ride with an adult; switching off available (see page 107). **Author's rating** A wet winner, not to be missed; ★★★★½. **Duration of ride** About 10 minutes. **Average wait in line per 100 people ahead of you** 3½ minutes. **Assumes** Operation at full capacity. **Loading speed** Moderate.

DESCRIPTION AND COMMENTS Sporting new logs, Splash Mountain is a Disney-style amusement-park flume ride. The ride combines steep chutes with a variety of Disney's best special effects. Covering more than half a mile, the ride splashes through swamps, caves, and back-woods bayous before climaxing in a 52-foot plunge and Brer Rabbit's triumphant return home. The entire ride is populated by more than 100 audio-animatronic characters, including Brer Rabbit, Brer Bear, and Brer Fox, all regaling riders with songs, including "Zip-A-Dee-Doo-Dah."

TOURING TIPS This ride is the most popular ride in Disneyland Park for patrons of all ages—happy, exciting, and adventuresome all at once. Though eclipsed somewhat by the Indiana Jones attraction, crowds nevertheless build quickly during the morning at Splash Mountain, and waits of more than two hours are not uncommon once Disneyland Park fills up on a busy day. To avoid the crowds, arrive at the park before opening time and get in line at Splash Mountain no later than 40 minutes after Disneyland Park opens. Lines persist throughout the day until a few minutes before closing.

There are four ways to experience Splash Mountain without a long wait. The first is to be on hand when the park opens and to sprint over and get in line before anyone else. The second way is to allow the initial mob of Splash cadets to be processed through, and to arrive at Splash Mountain about 20 to 40 minutes after the park opens or after riding Indiana Jones and/or Space Mountain. A third strategy is to get in line for Splash Mountain during a parade and/or a performance of *Fantasmic!* Be advised, however, that huge crowds gathering along the New Orleans Square and Frontierland waterfronts for *Fantasmic!* make getting to Splash Mountain very difficult (if not impossible) just before, during, and just after performances. Fourth, use FASTPASS.

A Suffolk, Virginia mom contends that there are more important considerations than beating crowds:

The only recommendation I do have is to definitely wait to do Splash Mountain at the end of the day. We were seated in the front of the ride and needless to say we were drenched to the bone. If we had ridden the ride [first thing in the morning] according to your plan, I personally would have been miserable for the rest of the day. Parents, beware! It says you will get wet, not drowned.

It is almost a certainty that you will get wet, and possibly drenched, riding Splash Mountain. If you visit on a cool day, you may want to carry a plastic garbage bag. By tearing holes in the bottom and sides, you can fashion a sack dress of sorts to keep you dry. Be sure to tuck the bag under your bottom. By the way, it doesn't matter whether you ride in front or back. You will get wet regardless. If you have a camera, either leave it with a nonriding member of your party or wrap it in a plastic bag.

One final word: This is not just a fancy flume ride; it is a full-blown Disney adventure. The scariest part, by far, is the big drop into the pool (visible from the sidewalk in front of Splash Mountain), and even this plunge looks worse than it really is. Despite reassurances, however, many children wig out after watching it from the sidewalk. A Grand Rapids, Michigan mother recalls her kids rather unique reaction:

We discovered after the fact that our children thought they would go underwater after the five-story drop and tried to hold their breath throughout the ride in preparation. They were really too preoccupied to enjoy the clever Br'er Rabbit story.

Flash Mountain

Type of attraction Water-flume adventure strip show. **Scope and scale** Eye-popper. **When to go** Spring break, weekend nights. **Special comments** A liberating experience. **Author's rating** Author is too near-sighted to rate accurately. **Duration of presentation** About 2 seconds.

DESCRIPTION AND COMMENTS It was reported by the Associated Press that certain female Splash Mountain riders (though we're sure that male riders, not to be outdone, will soon follow their female compatriots in similar fashion) are behaving in a most un-Disneylike manner by "flinging their blouses open" as they plummet down the climactic plunge at the end of the ride. (Fully visible, we might add, to dozens of guests waiting in line in front of the attraction.)

Indeed, automatic cameras shooting souvenir photographs of participants have documented an astounding array of feminine anatomy in free fall. The practice is apparently too spontaneous for Disneyland, which reports that it "has no plans at this time to change the theme of the attraction." Though, ever mindful of guest safety, management has concerns about "undue congestion" in front of the ride and the "possibility of guests catching cold." Disney also initiated what it calls its "Nipple Policy," which decrees that photos of offending guests shall be vaporized immediately. The policy applies to both men and women, so if you want to buy a souvenir pic, keep your shirt on. Cast members, however, some of whom had veritable scrapbooks of the floating strippers, are not unexpectedly irked by the policy.

TOURING TIPS During spring break or weekend nights, spectators should stand on the walkway directly in front of Splash Mountain. Be sure to bring a sign denouncing such unchaste exhibitionist behavior, or, depending on your point of view, a camera with a telescopic lens. If you are a participant, you will have approximately two minutes following the big plunge to get yourself back together before you arrive at the unloading area.

The Many Adventures of Winnie the Pooh

| APPEAL BY AGE | PRESCHOOL ★★★★½ | GRADE SCHOOL ★★★★ | TEENS ★★★ |
| YOUNG   ADULTS   ★★★ | | OVER 30   ★★★ | SENIORS   ★★★ |

Type of ride Indoor track ride. Scope and scale Minor attraction. When to go Before 10 a.m. or in the 2 hours before closing. Author's rating Critter Country's newest attraction; ★★★½. Duration of ride About 3 minutes. Average wait in line per 100 people ahead of you 5 minutes. Loading speed Moderate.

DESCRIPTION AND COMMENTS Opened in the summer of 2003, this addition to Critter Country replaced the alternately praised and maligned Country Bear Playhouse. Pooh is sunny, upbeat, and fun—more in the image of Peter Pan's Flight or Splash Mountain. You ride a "Hunny Pot" through the pages of a huge picture book into the Hundred Acre Wood, where you encounter Pooh, Piglet, Eeyore, Owl, Rabbit, Tigger, Kanga, and Roo as they contend with a blustery day. There's even a dream sequence with Heffalumps and Woozles, a favorite of this 30-something couple from Lexington, Massachusetts, who think Pooh has plenty to offer adults:

The attention to detail and special effects on this ride make it worth seeing even if you don't have children in your party. The Pooh dream sequence was great!

TOURING TIPS You can expect larger-than-average crowds for a while. Try to ride before 10 a.m., during a parade, or in the hours prior to closing. At extremely crowded times of year, Disney has been known to add Pooh to the FASTPASS lineup. Because of the ride's relatively small guest capacity, the daily allocation of FASTPASSes are usually distributed by 1 p.m. or so.

Critter Country Eateries and Shops

DESCRIPTION AND COMMENTS Critter Country restaurants and shops offer the standard array of souvenirs and fast food. The main counter-service venue in Critter Country is the **Hungry Bear Restaurant,** which serves burgers, grilled chicken breasts, fried chicken tenders, and salads. Portions are large. Expect to pay $7 to $8 for a sandwich, fries, and drink. Children's meals featuring chicken tender strips are available for about $5 to $6. In keeping with the park's ongoing evaluation of menus, expect to see some new selections in Critter Country.

TOURING TIPS Even with the tremendous popularity of Splash Mountain, the restaurants in Critter Country remain good bets for avoiding the lunch and dinner rush. The Hungry Bear Restaurant, in addition, offers a spacious open deck with a great view of the New Orleans Square and Frontierland river activity. The **Harbour Galley,** a waterfront dockside eatery near the dock of the *Columbia,* serves McDonald's french fries.

FRONTIERLAND

FRONTIERLAND ADJOINS NEW ORLEANS SQUARE as you move clockwise around the park. The focus here is on the Old West, with log stockades and pioneer trappings. In addition to the attractions listed below there is a small petting farm on the walkway to Fantasyland.

Big Thunder Mountain Railroad (FASTPASS)

APPEAL BY AGE	PRESCHOOL ★★★	GRADE SCHOOL ★★★★	TEENS ★★★★
YOUNG ADULTS ★★★★		OVER 30 ★★★★	SENIORS ★★★

Type of ride Tame roller coaster with exciting special effects. **Scope and scale** Headliner. **When to go** Before 10:30 a.m. and after 6:30 p.m. or use FASTPASS. **Special comments** Children must be 40" tall to ride; those under age 7 must ride with an adult; switching off available (see page 107). **Author's rating** Great effects, though a relatively tame ride; ★★★★. **Duration of ride** 3½ minutes. **Average wait in line per 100 people ahead of you** 3 minutes. **Assumes** 5 trains operating. **Loading speed** Moderate to fast.

DESCRIPTION AND COMMENTS A roller-coaster ride through and around a Disney "mountain." The time is Gold Rush days, and the idea is that you are on a runaway mine train. Along with the usual thrills of a roller-coaster ride (about a five on a "scary scale" of ten), the ride showcases some first-rate examples of Disney creativity: lifelike scenes depicting a mining town, falling rocks, and an earthquake, all humorously animated.

TOURING TIPS A superb Disney experience, but not too wild a roller coaster. The emphasis here is much more on the sights than on the thrill of the ride itself. Regardless, it's a "not-to-be-missed" attraction.

As an example of how differently guests experience Disney attractions, consider this letter we received from a lady in Brookline, Massachusetts:

Being in the senior citizens' category and having limited time, my friend and I confined our activities to those attractions rated as four or five stars for seniors.

Because of your recommendation and because you listed it as "not to be missed," we waited for one hour to board the Big Thunder Mountain Railroad, which you rated a "5" on a scary scale of "10." After living through 3½ minutes of pure terror, I will rate that attraction a "15" on a scary scale of "10." We were so busy holding on and screaming and even praying for our

WARNING!
For Bouffants, Rug Wearers, and Elvis Impersonators
This Ride Will Muss Your 'Do

safety that we did not see any falling rocks, a mining town, or an earthquake. In our opinion the Big Thunder Mountain Railroad should not be recommended for seniors or preschool children.

A woman from New England discovered that there's more to consider about Big Thunder than being scared:

Big Thunder Mountain Railroad was rated "5" on the scary scale. I won't say it warranted a higher scare rating, but it was much higher on the loose-your-lunch meter. One more sharp turn and the kids in front of me would have needed a dip in Splash Mountain!

Frontierland Shootin' Exposition

APPEAL BY AGE	PRESCHOOL ★★★½		GRADE SCHOOL ★★★½		TEENS ★★★½
YOUNG ADULTS ★★★		OVER 30 ★★★		SENIORS ★★★	

Type of attraction Electronic shooting gallery. **Scope and scale** Diversion. **When to go** Whenever convenient. **Special comments** Not included in your admission; costs extra. **Author's rating** A very nifty shooting gallery; ★★.

DESCRIPTION AND COMMENTS A very elaborate shooting gallery that costs 50¢ to play. One of the few attractions in Disneyland Park not included in the admission pass.

TOURING TIPS Good fun for those who like to shoot, but definitely not a place to blow time if you are on a tight schedule. Try it on your second day if time allows.

Golden Horseshoe Stage

APPEAL BY AGE	PRESCHOOL ★★★★		GRADE SCHOOL ★★★★		TEENS ★★★★½
YOUNG ADULTS ★★★★½		OVER 30 ★★★★½		SENIORS ★★★★½	

Type of attraction Western dance-hall stage show. **Scope and scale** Minor attraction. **When to go** Catch a show and lunch at the same time. **Special comments** Food is available. **Author's rating** Delightfully zany show; ★★★★½. **Duration of presentation** 30 minutes.

DESCRIPTION AND COMMENTS The Golden Horseshoe has always offered a decent show, hardy sandwiches, and a nice air-conditioned respite from the sun. In 2004, however, either intentionally or accidentally, Disney signed up an act so good that it turned the humble venue into one of the best attractions in either park. The new talent, unfortunately named Billy Hill and the Hillbillies, consists of a quartet of master bluegrass fiddlers who also happen to be born comics. The show is double-over funny, zany, and totally engaging. And did I mention, the fiddling is phenomenal. At the end of the show I witnessed something I've never seen at any Disney stage production—the audience refused to leave. Instead, they stood clapping and cheering like at a rock concert, trying to bring back the performers for an encore. They stayed at it so long that the fiddlers were forced to return and take a second bow (though they didn't perform another song). Still the audience lingered, departing only reluctantly after many minutes. If Disney has the good sense to hold on to this act, we rate the Golden Horseshoe ★★★★½ and classify it as "not to be missed."

TOURING TIPS The Golden Horseshoe has changed its reservations system to first-come, first-served seating. Performance times are listed in the daily *Times Guide*. We recommend taking in a show and having lunch at the same time. Portions are plenty big enough for kids to split. Be forewarned that guests seated on the first floor are likely to be conscripted into the show.

Mark Twain Riverboat

APPEAL BY AGE	PRESCHOOL ★★★	GRADE SCHOOL ★★★	TEENS ★★½
YOUNG ADULTS ★★★		OVER 30 ★★★	SENIORS ★★★

Type of ride Scenic boat ride. **Scope and scale** Minor attraction. **When to go** Between 11 a.m. and 5 p.m. **Special comments** Suspends operation at dusk. **Author's rating** Provides an excellent vantage point; ★★★. **Duration of ride** About 14 minutes. **Average wait to board** 10 minutes. **Assumes** Normal operations. **Loading method** En masse.

DESCRIPTION AND COMMENTS Large-capacity, paddle-wheel riverboat that navigates the waters around Tom Sawyer Island and Fort Wilderness. A beautiful craft, the riverboat provides a lofty perch from which to see Frontierland and New Orleans Square.

TOURING TIPS One of two regularly operating boat rides that survey the same real estate. Since the Explorer Canoes are slower in loading, we think the riverboat makes more efficient use of touring time. If you are not in the mood for a boat ride, many of the same sights can be seen by hiking around Tom Sawyer Island and Fort Wilderness.

Sailing Ship *Columbia*

APPEAL BY AGE	PRESCHOOL ★★★★	GRADE SCHOOL ★★★½	TEENS ★★★
YOUNG ADULTS ★★★½		OVER 30 ★★★	SENIORS ★★★

Type of ride Scenic boat ride. **Scope and scale** Minor attraction. **When to go** Between 11 a.m. and 5 p.m. **Special comments** Pirates on extremely busy days. **Author's rating** A stunning piece of workmanship; ★★★½. **Duration of ride** About 14 minutes. **Average wait to board** 10 minutes. **Assumes** Normal operations. **Loading method** En masse.

DESCRIPTION AND COMMENTS The *Columbia* is a stunning replica of a three-masted 18th-century merchant ship. Both its above and below decks are open to visitors, with below decks outfitted to depict the life and work environment of the ship's crew in 1787. The *Columbia* operates only on busier days and runs the same route as the canoes, keelboats, and the riverboat. As with the other river craft, the *Columbia* suspends operations at dusk.

An Oregon reader, who liked the *Columbia* but had some problems with its officers, wrote:

It is truly a beautiful ship and would have been a pleasant ride but for the incessant jabbering of the "captain." A little humorous banter is always appreciated, but we were ready to strangle this guy. We went below deck for awhile to get away from him, and would recommend to others to do this, even

with a more restrained captain, as it is a little museum complete with outfit-
ted bunks and other sailing paraphernalia.

TOURING TIPS The *Columbia,* along with the *Mark Twain* Riverboat, provides
a short-wait, high-carrying-capacity alternative for cruising the Rivers
of America. We found the beautifully crafted *Columbia* by far the most
aesthetically pleasing and historically interesting of any of the three
choices of boat rides on the Rivers of America.

If you have time to be choosy, ride aboard the *Columbia.* After boarding, while waiting for the cruise to begin, tour below deck. Once the
ride begins, come topside and stroll the deck, taking in the beauty and
complexity of the rigging.

The *Columbia* does not usually require a long wait, making it a good
bet during the crowded afternoon hours.

Tom Sawyer Island and Fort Wilderness

APPEAL BY AGE	PRESCHOOL ★★★★★	GRADE SCHOOL ★★★★★	TEENS ★★★½
YOUNG ADULTS ★★★		OVER 30 ★★★	SENIORS ★★★

Type of attraction Walk-through exhibit and rustic playground. **Scope and scale**
Minor attraction. **When to go** Midmorning through late afternoon. **Special comments** Closes at dusk; muddy following a hard rain. **Author's rating** The place
for rambunctious kids; ★★★.

DESCRIPTION AND COMMENTS Tom Sawyer Island manages to impart something of a sense of isolation from the rest of the park. It has hills to
climb, a cave and a treehouse to explore, tipsy bridges to cross, and
paths to follow. A new "rock-climbing" play area was added in 2003. It's
a delight for adults but a godsend for children who have been in tow all
day. They love the freedom of the exploration and the excitement of
firing air guns from the walls of Fort Wilderness. Be advised that due to
the scuffling of millions of tiny feet, there is not a blade of grass left
intact on the entire island. Thus, after a good rain, Tom Sawyer Island is
miraculously transformed into Disney's Muddy Wallow. Parents should
feel free within reasonable limits to allow their children to explore
unfettered. In addition to the fact that the island is designed for rowdy
kids, there are a good number of Disney security people (dressed as
cavalry soldiers) to referee the transient cowboys and Indians.

As an aside, a mother of four from Duncan, South Carolina, found
Tom Sawyer Island as much a refuge as an attraction, writing:

I do have one tip for parents. In the afternoon, when the crowds were at their
peak, the weather was hottest, and the kids started lagging behind, our orga-
nization began to suffer. We then retreated over to Tom Sawyer Island, which
proved to be a true haven. My husband and I found a secluded bench and
regrouped.

Meanwhile, the kids were able to run freely in the shade. Afterwards, we
were ready to tackle the park again refreshed and with direction once more.
Admittedly, I got this tip from another guidebook.

TOURING TIPS Tom Sawyer Island is not one of Disneyland Park's more celebrated attractions, but it's certainly one of the most well done. Attention to detail is excellent and kids particularly revel in its adventuresome frontier atmosphere. We think it's a must for families with children ages 5 to 15. If your party has only adults, visit the island on your second day, or stop by on your first day if you have seen the attractions you most wanted to see. We like Tom Sawyer Island from about noon until the island closes at dusk. Access is by raft from Frontierland, and you may have to stand in line to board both coming and going. Two or three rafts operate simultaneously, however, and the round-trip is usually pretty time-efficient. Tom Sawyer Island takes about 35 minutes or so to see, but many children could spend a whole day.

Raft to and from Tom Sawyer Island

Type of ride Transportation ride to Tom Sawyer Island. Scope and scale Minor attraction. Special comments Same information applies to return trip. Duration of ride A little over a minute one way. Average wait in line per 100 people ahead of you 4½ minutes. Assumes 3 rafts operating. Loading speed Moderate.

FRONTIERLAND EATERIES AND SHOPS

DESCRIPTION AND COMMENTS More specialty and souvenir shopping await visitors in Frontierland. One of our favorite restaurants in the park is **Rancho del Zocalo.** Good Mexican fare is available as you would expect, but the Rancho also serves the best barbecue chicken, ribs, and beef in the park. The restaurant is located across from the entrance of Big Thunder Mountain. Prices are in the $9–$15 range.

We also like the **River Belle Terrace** (roast chicken, pasta, salad). With prices ranging from $8 to $12 per person for a meal and a drink, all four Frontierland eateries are somewhat more expensive than Disney's fast-food burgers and hot dogs. Children's meals, running about $6, are available at all four restaurants.

TOURING TIPS Most guests do not know that the Golden Horseshoe serves food until they stop by for a show. This means that the Golden Horseshoe goes virtually unnoticed by the lunch crowd between shows.

FANTASYLAND

TRULY AN ENCHANTING PLACE, spread gracefully like a miniature alpine village beneath the towers of Sleeping Beauty Castle, Fantasyland is the heart of the park.

Alice in Wonderland

APPEAL BY AGE	PRESCHOOL ★★★½	GRADE SCHOOL ★★★½	TEENS ★★★
YOUNG ADULTS ★★★		OVER 30 ★★★	SENIORS ★★★

Type of ride Track ride in the dark. **Scope and scale** Minor attraction. **When to go** Before 11 a.m. or after 5 p.m. **Special comments** Do not confuse with Mad Tea Party ride. **Author's rating** Good characterization and story line; ★★★. **Duration of ride** Almost 4 minutes. **Average wait in line per 100 people ahead of you** 12 minutes. **Assumes** 16 cars operating. **Loading speed** Slow.

DESCRIPTION AND COMMENTS This attraction recalls the story of *Alice in Wonderland* with some nice surprises and colorful effects. Guests ride nifty caterpillar cars in this Disney spook-house adaptation.

TOURING TIPS This is a very well-done ride in the best Disney tradition, with familiar characters, good effects, and a theme you can follow. Unfortunately, it loads very slowly.

Casey Jr. Circus Train

APPEAL BY AGE	PRESCHOOL ★★★★	GRADE SCHOOL ★★★	TEENS ★½
YOUNG ADULTS ★★★	OVER 30 ★★★		SENIORS ★★★

Type of ride Miniature train ride. **Scope and scale** Minor attraction. **When to go** Before 11 a.m. or after 5 p.m. **Author's rating** A quiet, scenic ride; ★★½. **Duration of ride** A little over 3 minutes. **Average wait in line per 100 people ahead of you** 12 minutes. **Assumes** 2 trains operating. **Loading speed** Slow.

DESCRIPTION AND COMMENTS A long-standing attraction and a pet project of Walt Disney, Casey Jr. circulates through a landscape of miniature towns, farms, and lakes. There are some stunning bonsai specimens visible from this ride, as well as some of the most manicured landscaping you are ever likely to see.

TOURING TIPS This ride covers the same sights as the Storybook Land Canal Boats, but does it faster and with less of a wait. Accommodations for adults, however, are less than optimal on this ride, with some passengers having to squeeze into diminutive caged cars (after all, it is a circus train). If you do not have children in your party, you can enjoy the same sights more comfortably by riding the Storybook Land Canal Boats.

Disneyland Railroad

DESCRIPTION AND COMMENTS The Disneyland Railroad stops in Fantasyland/Mickey's Toontown on its circuit around the park. The station is located to the left of It's a Small World, next to the Fantasyland Theatre. From this usually uncrowded boarding point, transportation is available to Tomorrowland, Main Street, and New Orleans Square.

Dumbo, the Flying Elephant

APPEAL BY AGE	PRESCHOOL ★★★★★	GRADE SCHOOL ★★★½	TEENS ★★
YOUNG ADULTS ★½	OVER 30 ★½		SENIORS ★½

Type of ride Disneyfied midway ride. **Scope and scale** Minor attraction. **When to go** Before 10 a.m. or during late evening parades, fireworks, and *Fantasmic!* performances. **Author's rating** An attractive children's ride; ★★★½. **Duration of ride** 1 minute and 40 seconds. **Average wait in line per 100 people ahead of you** 12 minutes. **Assumes** Normal staffing. **Loading speed** Slow.

DESCRIPTION AND COMMENTS A nice, tame, happy children's ride based on the lovable Disney flying elephant. An upgraded rendition of a ride that can be found at state fairs and amusement parks across the country. Shortcomings notwithstanding, Dumbo is the favorite Disneyland Park attraction of most preschoolers. A lot of readers take us to task for lumping Dumbo in with state fair midway rides. These comments from a reader in Armdale, Nova Scotia, are representative:

I think you have acquired a jaded attitude. I know [Dumbo] is not for everybody, but when we took our oldest child (then just four), the sign at the end of the line said there would be a 90-minute wait. He knew and he didn't care, and he and I stood in the hot afternoon sun for 90 blissful minutes waiting for his 90-second flight. Anything that a 4-year-old would wait for that long and that patiently must be pretty special.

TOURING TIPS This is a slow-load ride that we recommend you bypass unless you are on a very relaxed touring schedule. If your kids are excited about Dumbo, try to get them on the ride before 10 a.m., during the parades and *Fantasmic!*, or just before the park closes. Also, consider this advice from an Arlington, Virginia, mom:

Grown-ups beware! Dumbo is really a tight fit with one adult and two kids. My kids threw me out of their Dumbo and I had to sit in a Dumbo all by myself. Pretty embarassing, and my husband got lots of pictures.

It's a Small World

APPEAL BY AGE	PRESCHOOL ★★★★★	GRADE SCHOOL ★★★½	TEENS ★★½
YOUNG ADULTS ★★★	OVER 30 ★★★		SENIORS ★★★½

Type of ride World brotherhood–themed indoor boat ride. **Scope and scale** Major attraction. **When to go** Anytime except after a parade. **Author's rating** A pleasant change of pace; ★★★. **Duration of ride** 11–14 minutes. **Average wait in line per 100 people ahead of you** 2½ minutes. **Assumes** Busy conditions with 56 boats operating. **Loading speed** Fast.

DESCRIPTION AND COMMENTS A happy, upbeat attraction with a world brotherhood theme and a catchy tune that will roll around in your head for weeks. Small boats convey visitors on a tour around the world, with singing and dancing dolls showcasing the dress and culture of each nation. Almost everyone enjoys It's a Small World (well, there are those jaded folks who are put off by the dolls' homogeneous appearance, especially in light of the diversity theme), but it stands, along with the *Enchanted Tiki Birds*, as an attraction that some could take or leave while others consider it one of the real masterpieces of Disneyland Park. In any event, a woman from Holbrook, New York, wrote with this devilish suggestion for improvement:

Small World would be much better if each person got a few softballs on the way in!

A mom from Castleton, Vermont, added this:

It's a Small World at Fantasyland was like a pit stop in the Twilight Zone. They were very slow unloading the boats, and we were stuck in a line of about

six boats waiting to get out while the endless chanting of that song grated on my nerves. I told my husband I was going to swim for it just to escape one more chorus.

TOURING TIPS Though an older Disney attraction, It's a Small World is a fast-loading ride that's usually a good bet during the busier times of the day. The boats are moved along by water pressure, which increases as boats are added. Thus, the more boats in service when you ride (up to a maximum total of 60), the shorter the duration of the ride (and wait).

King Arthur Carousel

APPEAL BY AGE	PRESCHOOL ★★★★	GRADE SCHOOL ★★½	TEENS ★★
YOUNG ADULTS ★★½		OVER 30 ★★★	SENIORS ★★★

Type of ride Merry-go-round. **Scope and scale** Minor attraction. **When to go** Before 11:30 a.m. or after 5 p.m. **Special comments** Adults enjoy the beauty and nostalgia of this ride. **Author's rating** A showpiece carousel; ★★★. **Duration of ride** A little over 2 minutes. **Average wait in line per 100 people ahead of you** 8 minutes. **Assumes** Normal staffing. **Loading speed** Slow.

DESCRIPTION AND COMMENTS A merry-go-round to be sure, but certainly one of the most elaborate and beautiful you will ever see, especially when lit at night.

TOURING TIPS Unless there are small children in your party, we suggest you appreciate this ride from the sidelines. If your children insist on riding, try to get them on before 11:30 a.m. or after 5 p.m. While nice to look at, the carousel loads and unloads very slowly.

Mad Tea Party

APPEAL BY AGE	PRESCHOOL ★★★½	GRADE SCHOOL ★★★★	TEENS ★★★★
YOUNG ADULTS ★★★		OVER 30 ★★	SENIORS ★★

Type of ride Midway-type spinning ride. **Scope and scale** Minor attraction. **When to go** Before 11 a.m. and after 5 p.m. **Special comments** You can make the teacups spin faster by turning the wheel in the center of the cup. **Author's rating** Fun but not worth the wait; ★★. **Duration of ride** 1½ minutes. **Average wait in line per 100 people ahead of you** 8 minutes. **Assumes** Normal staffing. **Loading speed** Slow.

DESCRIPTION AND COMMENTS Well done in the Disney style, but still just an amusement park ride. *Alice in Wonderland's* Mad Hatter provides the theme and patrons whirl around feverishly in big teacups. A rendition of this ride, sans Disney characters, can be found at every local carnival and fair.

TOURING TIPS This ride, aside from not being particularly unique, loads notoriously slow. Skip it on a busy schedule if the kids will let you. Ride in the morning of your second day if your schedule is more relaxed. A warning for parents who have not given this ride much thought: Teenagers like nothing better than to lure an adult onto the teacups and then turn the wheel in the middle (which makes the cup spin faster) until the adults are plastered against the side of the cup and are on the verge of throwing up. Unless your life's ambition is to be the test subject in a human centrifuge, do not even consider getting on this ride with anyone younger than 21 years of age.

Matterhorn Bobsleds

APPEAL BY AGE	PRESCHOOL †	GRADE SCHOOL ★★★★	TEENS ★★★★
YOUNG ADULTS ★★★★		OVER 30 ★★★★	SENIORS ★★★

† Some preschoolers loved Matterhorn Bobsleds; others were frightened.

Type of ride Roller coaster. **Scope and scale** Major attraction. **When to go** During the first 90 minutes the park is open or during the hour before it closes. **Special comments** 35" minimum-height requirement. **Author's rating** Fun ride but not too scary; ★★★. **Duration of ride** 2½ minutes. **Average wait in line per 100 people ahead of you** 13 minutes. **Assumes** Both tracks operating with 10 sleds per track with 23-second dispatch intervals. **Loading speed** Moderate.

DESCRIPTION AND COMMENTS The Matterhorn is the most distinctive landmark on the Disneyland scene, visible from almost anywhere in the
park. Updated and renovated in 1995, the Matterhorn maintains its
popularity and long lines year in and year out. The Matterhorn Bobsleds is a roller-coaster ride with an alpine motif. On the scary scale, the
ride ranks about six on a scale of ten (a little less intimidating than
Space Mountain). The special effects cannot compare to Space Mountain, but they do afford a few surprises.

TOURING TIPS Lines for the Matterhorn form as soon as the gates open and
persist throughout the day. Ride first thing in the morning or just
before the park closes. If you are a roller-coaster person, ride Space
Mountain and then hurry over and hop on the Matterhorn. If roller
coasters are not the end-all for you, we recommend choosing one or
the other of the roller coasters, or saving one for a second day.

One of the things we like about the Matterhorn is that the entire
queuing area is visible. This makes the lines look more oppressive than
they actually are (causing newly arrived guests to bypass the attraction), and also provides an opportunity to closely approximate the time
of your wait. If the line extending toward Tomorrowland reaches a
point across from the Kodak Photo Spot, your wait to ride the Matterhorn Bobsleds will be about 16 minutes.

Mr. Toad's Wild Ride

| APPEAL BY AGE | PRESCHOOL ★★★½ | GRADE SCHOOL ★★★½ | TEENS ★★★½ |
| YOUNG ADULTS ★★★ | | OVER 30 ★★★ | SENIORS ★★★ |

Type of ride Track ride in the dark. **Scope and scale** Minor attraction. **When to go** Before 11 a.m. **Author's rating** Past its prime; ★★½. **Duration of ride** Almost 2 minutes. **Average wait in line per 100 people ahead of you** 9 minutes. **Assumes** 12 cars operating. **Loading speed** Slow.

DESCRIPTION AND COMMENTS Mr. Toad is a twisting, curving ride in the dark
that passes two-dimensional sets and props. There are a couple of
clever effects, but basically it's at the technological basement of the
Disney attraction mix. Its sister attraction at Walt Disney World was
scrapped in 1999.

TOURING TIPS Not a great but certainly a popular attraction. Lines build
early in the day and never let up. Catch Mr. Toad before 11 a.m.

Peter Pan's Flight

| APPEAL BY AGE | PRESCHOOL ★★★★ | GRADE SCHOOL ★★★★ | TEENS ★★★½ |
| YOUNG ADULTS ★★★★ | | OVER 30 ★★★★ | SENIORS ★★★★ |

Type of ride Indoor fantasy adventure ride. **Scope and scale** Minor attraction. **When to go** Before 10 a.m. and after 6 p.m. **Author's rating** Happy and mellow; ★★★★. **Duration of ride** Just over 2 minutes. **Average wait in line per 100 people ahead of you** 11 minutes. **Assumes** 13 ships operating. **Loading speed** Slow.

DESCRIPTION AND COMMENTS Though not considered to be one of the major
attractions, Peter Pan's Flight is superbly designed and absolutely

delightful, with a happy theme, a reunion with some unforgettable Disney characters, beautiful effects, and charming music.

TOURING TIPS Though not a major feature of Disneyland Park, we nevertheless classify it as the best attraction in Fantasyland. Try to ride before 10 a.m. or after 6 p.m., during the afternoon or evening parade(s), or during a performance of *Fantasmic!*. Peter Pan at Walt Disney World is a FASTPASS attraction and should be here as well.

Pinocchio's Daring Journey

| APPEAL BY AGE | PRESCHOOL ★★★ | GRADE SCHOOL ★★★ | TEENS ★★½ |
| YOUNG ADULTS ★★½ | | OVER 30 ★★½ | SENIORS ★★½ |

Type of ride Track ride in the dark. **Scope and scale** Minor attraction. **When to go** Before 11:30 a.m. and after 4:30 p.m. **Author's rating** A big letdown; ★★. **Duration of ride** Almost 3 minutes. **Average wait in line per 100 people ahead of you** 8 minutes. **Assumes** 15 cars operating. **Loading speed** Slow.

DESCRIPTION AND COMMENTS Another twisting, curving track ride in the dark, this time tracing the adventures of Pinocchio as he tries to find his way home. The action is difficult to follow and lacks continuity. Although the sets are three-dimensional and more visually compelling than, say, Mr. Toad, the story line is dull and fails to engage the guest. Definitely the least interesting of the Fantasyland dark rides.

TOURING TIPS The word must be out about Pinocchio, because the lines are seldom very long. Still, you will encounter the longest waits between 11:30 a.m. and 4:30 p.m.

Sleeping Beauty Castle

DESCRIPTION AND COMMENTS Disneyland Park's most famous icon, Sleeping Beauty Castle, is at the heart of Disneyland's 50th anniversary festivities that began on May 5, 2005. Decked with bunting, banners, and flags, and with each of its five turrets adorned by a crown, the castle serves as a stage for any number of shows and special commemorative events. At night, the castle transforms into a tapestry of lights with constantly changing colors and imagery projected on its facade.

Snow White's Scary Adventures

| APPEAL BY AGE | PRESCHOOL ★★★ | GRADE SCHOOL ★★★ | TEENS ★★½ |
| YOUNG ADULTS ★★★ | | OVER 30 ★★★ | SENIORS ★★★ |

Type of ride Track ride in the dark. **Scope and scale** Minor attraction. **When to go** Before 11 a.m. and after 5 p.m. **Special comments** Quite intimidating for preschoolers. **Author's rating** Worth seeing if the wait is not long; ★★★. **Duration of ride** Almost 2 minutes. **Average wait in line per 100 people ahead of you** 9 minutes. **Assumes** 10 cars operating. **Loading speed** Slow.

DESCRIPTION AND COMMENTS Here you ride in a mining car in the dark through a series of sets drawn from *Snow White and the Seven Dwarfs*. The attraction has a *Perils of Pauline* flavor and features Snow White (whom you never see), as she narrowly escapes harm at the hands of the wicked witch. The action and effects are a cut above Mr. Toad's Wild Ride but not as good as Peter Pan's Flight.

TOURING TIPS Enjoyable but not particularly compelling. Experience it if the lines are not too long or on a second-day visit. Ride before 11 a.m. or after 5 p.m. if possible. Also, don't take the "scary" part too seriously. The witch looks mean, but most kids take her in stride. Or maybe not. A mother from Knoxville, Tennessee, commented:

The outside looks cute and fluffy, but inside, the evil witch just keeps coming at you. My five-year-old, who rode Space Mountain three times [and took other scary rides] right in stride, was near panic when our car stopped unexpectedly twice during Snow White. [After Snow White] my six-year-old niece spent a lot of time asking "if a witch will jump out at you" before other rides. So I suggest that you explain a little more what this ride is about. It's tough on preschoolers who are expecting forest animals and dwarfs.

In point of fact, we receive more mail from parents about this ride than about all other Disneyland Park attractions combined. The bottom line is that it really punches the buttons of the six-and-under crowd, when other more traditionally scary rides don't. Many kids, once frightened by Snow White's Scary Adventures, balk at trying any other attractions that go into the dark, regardless how benign.

Storybook Land Canal Boats

APPEAL BY AGE	PRESCHOOL ★★★	GRADE SCHOOL ★★½	TEENS ★★½
YOUNG ADULTS ★★★½	OVER 30 ★★★½		SENIORS ★★★½

Type of ride Scenic boat ride. **Scope and scale** Minor attraction. **When to go** Before 10:30 a.m. and after 5:30 p.m. **Author's rating** Pretty, tranquil, and serene; ★★★. **Duration of ride** 9½ minutes. **Average wait in line per 100 people ahead of you** 16 minutes. **Assumes** 7 boats operating. **Loading speed** Slow.

DESCRIPTION AND COMMENTS Guide-operated boats wind along canals situated beneath the same miniature landscapes visible from the Casey Jr. Circus Train. This ride, offering stellar examples of bonsai cultivation, selective pruning, and miniaturization, is a must for landscape gardening enthusiasts. Updated in 1994, the landscapes now include scenes from more recent Disney features, in addition to those from such classics as *The Wind in the Willows* and *The Three Little Pigs*.

TOURING TIPS The boats are much more comfortable than the train; the view of the miniatures is better; and the pace is more leisurely. On the down side, the lines are long, and if not long, definitely slow-moving. The ride itself also takes a lot of time. Our recommendation is to ride Casey Jr. if you have children or are in a hurry. Take the boat if your party is all adults or your pace is more leisurely. If you ride the canal boats, try to get on before 10:30 a.m.

Fantasyland Theatre

DESCRIPTION AND COMMENTS Originally installed as a teen nightspot called Videopolis, this venue has been converted into a sophisticated amphitheater where concerts and elaborate stage shows are performed according to the daily entertainment schedule. Better productions that have played the Fantasyland Theatre stage include *Beauty and the Beast Live, Snow White,* and *The Spirit of Pocahontas,* all musical stage adaptations of the respective Disney animated features. The year 2005 saw the continuing run of *Snow White–An Enchanting New Musical,* an elaborate adaptation of the Snow White story. The production touches all the bases covered by Disney's animated feature in a nostalgic yet hip sort of way. The musical is scheduled to run through the entire 18-month Disneyland 50th anniversary that began on May 5, 2005. We rate the musical as "not to be missed."

TOURING TIPS　Most of the shows produced here are first-rate and definitely worth your time. On busy days, many guests arrive 45 to 60 minutes in advance to get good seats. Because the shows tend to be less than a half-hour in duration, however, it is no hardship to watch the show standing, and standing room is usually available up to five minutes before show time. In the summer, evening performances are more comfortable.

FANTASYLAND EATERIES AND SHOPS

DESCRIPTION AND COMMENTS　Fantasyland offers the most attractions of any of the "lands" and the fewest places to eat. With the exception of the **Village Haus** counter-service restaurant, most of the food service in Fantasyland is supplied by street vendors. Add the daylong congestion to the scenario and Fantasyland ties with Mickey's Toontown as the best place in the park *not* to eat. If you are hungry, it's much easier to troop over to Frontierland, New Orleans Square, or even back to Main Street than to grab a bite in Fantasyland. Plus, the Village Haus, the only full-scale eatery in Fantasyland, specializes in burgers, pizza, and the like—that is, nothing distinctive, different, or worth the hassle. If you are in the Fantasyland/Toontown area and feeling hungry the smart move is to go for the bratwurst, knockwurst, or cinnamon crisps at the **Enchanted Cottage** counter-service restaurant. The Enchanted Cottage is part of the Fantasyland Theatre complex and is largely overlooked except when guests are gathering prior to a show.

TOURING TIPS　Fast food is anything but in Fantasyland, and shopping is ho-hum. Don't bother with the shops unless you have a relaxed schedule or shopping is a big priority.

MICKEY'S TOONTOWN

MICKEY'S TOONTOWN IS SITUATED across the Disneyland Railroad tracks from Fantasyland. Its entrance is a tunnel that opens into Fantasyland just to the left of It's a Small World. As its name suggests, Toontown is a fanciful representation of the wacky cartoon community where all of the Disney characters live. Mickey's Toontown was inspired by the Disney animated feature *Who Framed Roger Rabbit?,* in which humans were able to enter the world of cartoon characters.

Mickey's Toontown consists of a colorful collection of miniature buildings, all executed in exaggerated cartoon style with rounded edges and brilliant colors. Among the buildings are Mickey's and Minnie's houses, both open to inspection inside and out.

In addition to serving as a place where guests can be certain of finding Disney characters at any time during the day, this newest land also serves as an elaborate interactive playground where it's OK for the kids to run, climb, and let off steam.

Mickey's Toontown is rendered with masterful attention to artistic humor and detail. The colorful buildings each have a story to tell or a gag to visit upon an unsuspecting guest. There is an explosion at the Fireworks Factory every minute or so, always unannounced. Across the street, the sidewalk is littered with crates containing strange contents addressed to exotic destinations. If you pry open the top of one of the crates (easy to do), the crate will emit a noise consistent with its contents. A box of "train parts," for example, broadcasts the sound of a racing locomotive when you lift the top.

Everywhere in Mickey's Toontown are subtleties and absurdities to delight the imagination. Next to Goofy's Bounce House there is an impact crater, shaped like Goofy, marking the spot where he missed his swimming pool while high diving. A sign in front of the local garage declares, "If we can't fix it, we won't."

While adults will enjoy the imaginative charm of Mickey's Toontown, it will quickly become apparent that there is not much for them to do there. Most of the attractions in Mickey's Toontown are for kids, specifically smaller children. Attractions open to adults include a dark ride drawn from *Who Framed Roger Rabbit?* (sort of a high-tech rendition of Mr. Toad's Wild Ride), a diminutive roller coaster, and a trolley that is more decorative than functional. Everything else in Mickey's Toontown is for children.

In many ways, Mickey's Toontown is a designer playground, a fanciful cousin to Tom Sawyer Island in Frontierland. What distinguishes Mickey's Toontown is that the play areas are specially designed for smaller children; it's much cleaner than Tom Sawyer Island (that is, no dirt—though this does not guarantee a dirt-free child upon leaving the area). Finally, in the noblest Disney tradition, you must wait in line for virtually everything.

Also, be forewarned that Mickey's Toontown is not very large, especially in comparison with neighboring Fantasyland. A tolerable crowd in most of the other lands will seem like Times Square on New Year's Eve in Mickey's Toontown. Couple this congestion with the unfortunate fact that none of the attractions in Mickey's Toontown are engineered to handle huge crowds, and you come face-to-face with possibly the most attractive traffic jam the Disney folks have ever created. Our advice is to see Mickey's Toontown earlier in the day, before 11 a.m., or in the evening while the parades and *Fantasmic!* are going on.

Chip 'n' Dale's Treehouse

APPEAL BY AGE	PRESCHOOL ★★★★		GRADE SCHOOL ★★★½		TEENS —
YOUNG ADULTS	—	OVER 30	— °	SENIORS	—

Type of ride Imaginative children's play area. **Scope and scale** Diversion. **When to go** Before 10:30 a.m. and after 5:30 p.m. **Author's rating** Good exercise for the small fry; ★★. **Duration of play** Varies.

DESCRIPTION AND COMMENTS The play area consists of a treehouse with slides.

TOURING TIPS Located in the most remote corner of Mickey's Toontown and obscured by the crowd waiting to ride the roller coaster next door, the Treehouse is frequently overlooked. Of all the attractions in Mickey's Toontown, this is the easiest to get the kids into without much of a wait. Most any child that can fit is allowed to rummage around in the Treehouse.

Disneyland Railroad

DESCRIPTION AND COMMENTS Mickey's Toontown and Fantasyland share a station on the Disneyland Railroad's route around the perimeter of the park. Usually the wait to board is short.

Gadget's Go Coaster

APPEAL BY AGE	PRESCHOOL ★★★★		GRADE SCHOOL ★★★½		TEENS ★★½
YOUNG ADULTS	★★½	OVER 30	★★½	SENIORS	★★

Type of ride Small roller coaster. **Scope and scale** Minor attraction. **When to go** Before 10:30 a.m., during the parades and *Fantasmic!* in the evening, and just before the park closes. **Special comments** Minimum-height requirement of 35". **Author's rating** Great for little ones but not worth the wait for adults; ★★. **Duration of ride** About 50 seconds. **Average wait in line per 100 people ahead of you** 10 minutes. **Assumes** Normal staffing. **Loading speed** Slow.

DESCRIPTION AND COMMENTS Gadget's Go Coaster is a very small roller coaster; the idea is that you are miniaturized and riding around in an acorn shell. The ride itself is pretty zippy, but it is over so quickly you hardly know you've been anywhere. In fact, of the 52 seconds the ride is in motion, 32 seconds are consumed in exiting the loading area, being ratcheted up the first hill, and braking into the off-loading area. The actual time you spend careening around the track is a whopping 20 seconds.

TOURING TIPS Because the cars of this dinky roller coaster are too small for most adults, there is a fair amount of whiplashing for taller people. Add to that the small carrying capacity of the ride (the track is too short for more than one train to operate) and you have a real engineering brain fart. Unfortunately, the ride is visually appealing. All the kids want to ride, subjecting the whole family to incarceration in a line whose movement can only be discerned by time-lapse photography. Our recommendation to parties touring without children: Skip Gadget's Go Coaster. If there are children in your group, you've got a problem.

Goofy's Bounce House

APPEAL BY AGE	PRESCHOOL ★★★★		GRADE SCHOOL ★★★★	TEENS —
YOUNG ADULTS	—	OVER 30 —		SENIORS —

Type of attraction A play area where children jump in an inflated enclosure. **Scope and scale** Diversion. **When to go** Before 10:30 a.m., during the evening parades and *Fantasmic!,* and during the 2 hours before the park closes. **Special comments** Maximum height 52". **Author's rating** A rambunctious child's dream; ★★½. **Bouncing time** 3 minutes. **Average wait in line per 100 people ahead of you** 28 minutes. **Assumes** 2 minutes between jumping sessions. **Loading speed** Slow.

DESCRIPTION AND COMMENTS   Goofy's Bounce House is a house with a totally inflated interior. Up to 15 children are admitted at a time for three minutes of jumping, lunging, tumbling, and careening off the walls, floor, and furniture. A Disney cast member supervises the activity and endeavors to prevent midair collisions.

TOURING TIPS   One of Toontown's most popular attractions, the Bounce House is the exclusive domain of children over three years old and shorter than 52". Children enter the house from the side and remove their shoes. Adults can observe the mayhem from windows at the front of the house. Goofy's Bounce House is another example of an appealing idea executed on a scale too small to handle the attraction's great popularity and demand. On a crowded day, a small child can grow beyond the height limit in the time it takes him to get to the front of the line.

Mickey's House

APPEAL BY AGE	PRESCHOOL ★★★★★	GRADE SCHOOL ★★★★½	TEENS ★★★½
YOUNG ADULTS ★★★½		OVER 30 ★★★½	SENIORS ★★★½

Type of attraction Walk-through tour of Mickey's House and Movie Barn, ending with a personal visit with Mickey. **Scope and scale** Minor attraction and character-greeting opportunity. **When to go** Before 10:30 a.m. and after 5:30 p.m. **Author's rating** Well done; ★★★. Duration of attraction 15–30 minutes (depending on the crowd). **Average wait in line per 100 people ahead of you** 20 minutes. **Assumes** Normal staffing. **Touring speed** Slow.

DESCRIPTION AND COMMENTS   Mickey's House is the starting point of a self-guided tour that winds through the famous mouse's house, into his backyard and past Pluto's doghouse, and then into Mickey's Movie Barn. This last stop hearkens back to the so-called "barn" studio where Walt Disney created a number of the earlier Mickey Mouse cartoons. Once in the Movie Barn, guests watch vintage Disney cartoons while awaiting admittance to Mickey's Dressing Room.

In small groups of one or two families, guests are ultimately conducted into the dressing room where Mickey awaits to pose for photos and sign autographs. The visit is not lengthy (two to four minutes), but there is adequate time for all of the children to hug, poke, and admire the star.

TOURING TIPS The cynical observer will discern immediately that Mickey's House, backyard, Movie Barn, etc., are no more than a cleverly devised queuing area designed to deliver guests to Mickey's Dressing Room for the Mouse Encounter. For those with some vestige of child in their personalities, however, the preamble serves to heighten anticipation while providing the opportunity to get to know the corporate symbol on a more personal level. Mickey's House is well conceived and contains a lot of Disney memorabilia. You will notice that children touch everything as they proceed through the house, hoping to find some artifact that is not welded or riveted into the set (an especially tenacious child during one of our visits was actually able to rip a couple of books from a bookcase).

Meeting Mickey and touring his house is best done during the first two hours the park is open, or alternatively, in the evening during *Fantasmic!* performances. If meeting Mickey is at the top of your child's list, you might consider taking the Disneyland Railroad from Main Street to the Toontown/Fantasyland station as soon as you enter the park. Some children are so obsessed with seeing Mickey that they cannot enjoy anything else until they get Mickey in the rearview mirror.

Minnie's House

APPEAL BY AGE	PRESCHOOL ★★★★	GRADE SCHOOL ★★★½	TEENS ★★½
YOUNG ADULTS ★★½	OVER 30 ★★½		SENIORS ★★½

Type of attraction Walk-through exhibit. **Scope and scale** Minor attraction and character-greeting opportunity. **When to go** Before 11:30 a.m. and after 4:30 p.m. **Author's rating** OK but not great; ★★½. **Duration of tour** About 10 minutes. **Average wait in line per 100 people ahead of you** 12 minutes. **Touring speed** Slow.

DESCRIPTION AND COMMENTS Minnie's House consists of a self-guided tour through the various rooms and backyard of Mickey Mouse's main squeeze. Similar to Mickey's House, only predictably more feminine, Minnie's House likewise showcases some fun Disney memorabilia. Among the highlights of the short tour are the fanciful appliances in Minnie's kitchen. Like Mickey, Minnie is usually present to receive guests.

TOURING TIPS The main difference between Mickey's House and Minnie's House is that Minnie's House cannot accommodate as many guests. See Minnie early and before Mickey to avoid waiting outdoors in a long queue. Be advised that neither Mickey nor Minnie is available during parades.

Miss Daisy, Donald's Boat

APPEAL BY AGE	PRESCHOOL ★★★★	GRADE SCHOOL ★★★½	TEENS —
YOUNG ADULTS —	OVER 30 —		SENIORS —

Type of attraction Creative play area with a boat theme. **Scope and scale** Diversion. **When to go** Before 10:30 a.m. and after 4:30 p.m. **Author's rating** Designer play area; ★★. **Duration of play** Varies. **Average wait in line per 100 people ahead of you** Usually no waiting.

DESCRIPTION AND COMMENTS Another children's play area, this time with a tugboat theme. Children can climb nets, ring bells, survey Toontown from the captain's bridge, and scoot down slides. The idea is that Donald Duck (who, as everyone knows, lives in Duckburg) is visiting Toontown.

TOURING TIPS Kids more or less wander on and off of the *Miss Daisy,* and usually there is not any sort of organized line or queuing area. Enjoy this play area at your leisure and stay as long as you like.

Roger Rabbit's Car Toon Spin (FASTPASS)

APPEAL BY AGE	PRESCHOOL ★★★	GRADE SCHOOL ★★★★	TEENS ★★★½
YOUNG ADULTS ★★★½	OVER 30 ★★★½		SENIORS ★★★½

Type of ride Track ride in the dark. **Scope and scale** Major attraction. **When to go** Before 10:30 a.m. and after 6:30 p.m. **Special comments** Ride with your kids, if you can stomach it. **Author's rating** ★★★. **Duration of ride** A little over 3 minutes. **Average wait in line per 100 people ahead of you** 7 minutes. **Assumes** Full capacity operation. **Loading speed** Moderate.

Motion Sickness

WARNING!

DESCRIPTION AND COMMENTS A so-called dark ride where guests become part of a cartoon plot. The idea is that you are renting a cab for a tour of Toontown. As soon as your cab gets underway, however, weasels throw a slippery glop (known as "dip") on the road, sending the cab into a more or less uncontrollable spin. This spinning continues as the cab passes through a variety of sets populated by cartoon and audio-animatronic characters and punctuated by simulated explosions. As a child of the 1960s put it, "It was like combining Mr. Toad's Wild Ride with the Mad Tea Party while tripping on LSD."

The main problem with the Car Toon Spin is that, because of the spinning, you are often pointed in the wrong direction to appreciate (or even see) many of the better visual effects. Furthermore, the story line is loose. The attraction lacks the continuity and humor of Splash Mountain or the suspense of the Haunted Mansion or Snow White's Scary Adventures.

A reader from Milford, Michigan, echoed our sentiments, lamenting:

The most disappointing ride to me was Roger Rabbit's Car Toon Spin. I stood 45 minutes for a fun-house ride and the wheel was so difficult to operate that I spent most of my time trying to steer the bloody car and missed the point of the ride.

TOURING TIPS The ride is popular for its novelty, and it is one of the few Mickey's Toontown attractions that parents (with strong stomachs) can enjoy with their children. Because the ride stays fairly thronged with people all day long, ride before 10:30 a.m., during parades and *Fantasmic!,* or in the hour before the park closes. Otherwise, use FASTPASS.

The spinning, incidentally, can be controlled by the guests. If you don't want to spin, you don't have to. If you do elect to spin, you still will not be able to approach the eye-popping speed attainable on the teacups at the Mad Tea Party. Sluggish spinning aside, our advice for those who are at all susceptible to motion sickness is not to get near this ride if you are touring with anyone under 21 years of age.

CHARACTER-WATCHING

DESCRIPTION AND COMMENTS If you want to see characters, Mickey's Toontown is the place to go. In addition to Mickey, who receives guests all
day (except during parades) in his dressing room, and Minnie, who
entertains in her house, you are also likely to see Goofy and Pluto in
front of Toontown Hall and bump into such august personages as
Daisy, Roger Rabbit, and a host of others lurking around the streets. It
would be a rare event to visit Toontown without bumping into a few
characters. From time to time, horns sound and whistles blow atop the
Toontown City Hall, followed by a fanfare rendition of the Mickey
Mouse Club theme song. This indicates, as a mom from Texas
explained to us, that "some characters are fixin' to come out." And
there you have it.

TOONTOWN EATERIES AND SHOPS

DESCRIPTION AND COMMENTS Food service in Mickey's Toontown is limited to
drinks, snacks, hot dogs, frozen yogurt, and pizza. The **Gag Factory,**
which sells Disney souvenirs, is one of the park's more entertaining
shopping venues. Even if you do not buy anything, the place is fun to
walk through.

TOMORROWLAND

TOMORROWLAND IS A FUTURISTIC MIX of rides and experiences
that relates to technological development and what life will be like in
the years to come.

An exhaustive renovation of Tomorrowland was begun in 1996 and
completed in 2000. Before the renovation, Tomorrowland's 40-year-old
buildings more resembled 1970s motel architecture than anyone's vision of the future. Tomorrowland's renovated design is more enduring,
reflecting a nostalgic vision of the future as imagined by dreamers and
scientists in the 1920s and 1930s. Frozen in time, Tomorrowland now
conjures up visions of Buck Rogers (who nobody under 50 remembers),
fanciful mechanical rockets, and metallic cities spread beneath towering obelisks. Disney refers to the "new" Tomorrowland as the "Future
That Never Was." *Newsweek* dubs it "retro-future."

In the new Tomorrowland, *Honey, I Shrunk the Audience*
replaced *Captain EO.* The large circular building that once housed
America Sings now contains Innoventions, a collection of hands-on
exhibits featuring cutting-edge consumer products, including virtual
reality games. The Rocket Jets ride, reincarnated as the Astro
Orbiter, sports a campy Jules Verne look, but it still goes around in
circles. Star Tours has been retained, as has the recently updated
Tomorrowland Autopia. Buzz Lightyear Astro Blasters, sort of a
combination dark ride and shooting gallery, opened in 2005, followed
by a completely redesigned Space Mountain.

Astro Orbiter

APPEAL BY AGE	PRESCHOOL ★★★★	GRADE SCHOOL ★★★½	TEENS ★★★
YOUNG ADELTS ★★		OVER 30 ★	SENIORS ★

Type of ride Very mild midway-type thrill ride. **Scope and scale** Minor attraction. **When to go** Before 10 a.m. or during the hour before the park closes. **Author's rating** Not worth the wait; ★. **Duration of ride** 1½ minutes. **Average wait in line per 100 people ahead of you** 13 minutes. **Assumes** Normal staffing. **Loading speed** Slow.

DESCRIPTION AND COMMENTS Though the look is different and the attraction has been relocated at the central-hub entrance to Tomorrowland, the new Astro Orbiter ride is essentially a makeover of the old Rocket Jets—that is, a visually appealing midway-type ride involving small rockets that rotate on arms around a central axis. Be aware that the Astro Orbiter flies higher and faster than Dumbo and that

Motion Sickness

WARNING!

it frightens some small children. The ride also apparently messes with certain adults, as a mother from Israel attests:

I think your assessment of the Rocket Jets [Astro Orbiter] as "very mild" is way off. I was able to sit through all the "Mountains" and the "Tours" . . . without my stomach reacting even a little, but after the Rocket Jets [Astro Orbiter] I thought I would be finished for the rest of the day. Very quickly I realized that my only chance for survival was to pick a point on the toe of my shoe and stare at it (and certainly not lift my eyes out of the "jet") until the ride was over. My four-year-old was my copilot, and she loved the ride (go figure) and she had us up high the whole time. It was a nightmare—people should be forewarned.

TOURING TIPS Astro Orbiter is essentially the same ride as the old Rocket Jets: slow to load and expendable on any schedule. If you take a preschooler on this ride, place your child in the seat first and then sit down yourself.

Buzz Lightyear Astro Blasters (FASTPASS)

APPEAL BY AGE	PRESCHOOL ★★★	GRADE SCHOOL ★★★★½	TEENS ★★★★½
YOUNG ADULTS ★★★★½		OVER 30 ★★★★½	SENIORS ★★★★

Type of ride Space-travel interactive dark ride. **Scope and scale** Major attraction. **When to go** Before 10:30 a.m. or after 6 p.m. **Author's rating** A real winner! ★★★★. **Duration of ride** About 4½ minutes. **Average wait in line per 100 people ahead of you** 3 minutes. **Loading speed** Fast.

DESCRIPTION AND COMMENTS This attraction is based on the space-commando character of Buzz Lightyear from the film *Toy Story*. The marginal story line has you and Buzz Lightyear trying to save the universe from the evil Emperor Zurg. The indoor ride is interactive to the extent that you can spin your car and shoot simulated "laser cannons" at Zurg and his minions.

A similar attraction at the Magic Kingdom at Walt Disney World opened with little fanfare in 1998 but immediately became one of the most popular attractions in the park. The Disneyland version, situated across from Star Tours, is much the same except for one high-tech twist: folks at home can play along with guests on the ride in real time via the Internet. Through Web-cam technology, guests on the attraction are virtually paired up with Internet partners.

Praise for Buzz Lightyear is almost universal. This comment from a Massachusetts couple is typical:

Buzz Lightyear was the surprise hit of our trip! My husband and I enjoyed competing for the best score so much that we went on this ride several times during our stay. Definitely a must, especially when there's no wait.

TOURING TIPS Each car is equipped with two laser cannons and a scorekeeping display. Each scorekeeping display is independent, so you can compete with your riding partner. A joy stick allows you to spin the car to line up the various targets. Each time you pull the trigger you'll release a red laser beam that you can see hitting or missing the target. Most folks' first ride is occupied with learning how to use the equipment (fire off individual shots as opposed to keeping the trigger depressed) and figuring out how the targets work. The next ride (like certain potato chips, one is not enough) you'll surprise yourself by how much better you do. *Unofficial* readers are unanimous in their praise of Buzz Lightyear. Some guests, in fact, spend several hours on the attraction, riding again and again. See Buzz Lightyear after riding Space Mountain first thing in the morning or use FASTPASS.

Disneyland Monorail System

APPEAL BY AGE	PRESCHOOL ★★★	GRADE SCHOOL ★★★	TEENS ★★★
YOUNG ADULTS ★★★		OVER 30 ★★★	SENIORS ★★

Type of ride Scenic transportation. **Scope and scale** Major attraction. **When to go** During the hot, crowded period of the day (11:30 a.m.–5 p.m.). **Special comments** Take the monorail to Downtown Disney for lunch. **Author's rating** Nice relaxing ride with some interesting views of the park; ★★★. **Duration of ride** 12–15 minutes round-trip. **Average wait in line per 100 people ahead of you** 10 minutes. **Assumes** Three monorails operating. **Loading speed** Moderate to fast.

DESCRIPTION AND COMMENTS The monorail is a futuristic transportation ride that affords the only practical opportunity for escaping the park during the crowded lunch period and early afternoon. Boarding at the Tomorrowland monorail station, you can commute to the Disneyland resort hotels and Downtown Disney complex, where it's possible to have a nice lunch without fighting the crowds. For those not interested in lunch, the monorail provides a tranquil trip with a nice view of Downtown Disney, Disney's California Adventure theme park, Fantasyland, and Tomorrowland.

TOURING TIPS We recommend using the monorail to commute to Downtown Disney for a quiet, relaxing lunch away from the crowds and the heat. If you only want to experience the ride, go whenever you wish; the wait to board is usually 15 to 25 minutes except in the 2 hours before closing.

Disneyland Railroad

DESCRIPTION AND COMMENTS The Disneyland Railroad makes a regular stop at the Tomorrowland Railroad Station. For additional details about the railroad see the Disneyland Railroad write-up in the Main Street, U.S.A. section.

TOURING TIPS This station becomes fairly crowded on busy days. If you are interested primarily in getting there, it may be quicker to walk.

Honey, I Shrunk the Audience

APPEAL BY AGE	PRESCHOOL ★★★½	GRADE SCHOOL ★★★★½	TEENS ★★★★½
YOUNG ADULTS ★★★★	OVER 30 ★★★★		SENIORS ★★★★½

Type of attraction 3-D film with special effects. **Scope and scale** Headliner. **When to go** Before 11 a.m. or during the late afternoon and evening. **Special comments** Routinely freaks out kids ages 8 and under. **Author's rating** An absolute hoot! Not to be missed; ★★★★½. **Duration of presentation** Approximately 17 minutes. **Preshow entertainment** 8 minutes. **Probable waiting time** 12 minutes (at suggested times).

DESCRIPTION AND COMMENTS *Honey, I Shrunk the Audience* is a 3-D offshoot of Disney's feature film, *Honey, I Shrunk the Kids. Honey, I Shrunk the Audience* features a stupifying array of special effects, including simulated explosions, smoke, fiber optics, lights, water spray, and even moving seats. Clever, frenetic, and uproarious, we think *Honey, I Shrunk the Audience* is the best theater attraction in the Disney repertoire. We rate it as "not to be missed."

TOURING TIPS The audio level is earsplitting for productions in this theater. Small children are sometimes frightened by the sound volume, and many adults report that the loud soundtrack is distracting and even uncomfortable. While *Honey, I Shrunk the Audience* is a huge hit, it overwhelms children as old as seven or eight. A dad from Lexington, South Carolina, writes:

Honey, I Shrunk the Audience *is too intense for kids. Our four-year-old took off his [3-D] glasses five minutes into the movie. Because of this experience, he would not wear the glasses in the Muppet movie.*

An Arizona mom agrees, offering this report:

Our three- and four-year-olds loved all the rides. They giggled through Thunder Mountain three times, squealed with delight on Splash Mountain, thought Space Mountain was the coolest, and begged to ride Star Tours over and over. They even "fought ghosts" at the Haunted Mansion. But Honey, I Shrunk the Audience *dissolved them into sobbing, shaking terrified preschoolers.*

Honey, I Shrunk the Audience is an exceptionally popular attraction. Try to work the production into your touring schedule before 11 a.m. or in the late afternoon or evening. The theater is large, so don't be intimidated if the line is long. Finally, try to avoid seats in the first several rows. If you are too close to the screen, the 3-D images do not focus properly.

Innoventions

APPEAL BY AGE	PRESCHOOL ★½	GRADE SCHOOL ★★★	TEENS ★★★★
YOUNG ADULTS ★★★★		OVER 30 ★★★	SENIORS ★★★

Type of attraction Multifaceted attraction featuring static and hands-on exhibits relating to products and technologies of the near future. **Scope and scale** Major diversion. **When to go** On your second day or after you have seen all the major attractions. **Special comments** Most exhibits demand time and participation to be rewarding; not much gained here by a quick walk-through. **Author's rating** Very commercial, but well presented; ★★★.

DESCRIPTION AND COMMENTS Innoventions is housed in the large circular building last occupied by the audio-animatronic musical *America Sings*. Modeled after a similar attraction at Epcot in Walt Disney World, Innoventions was part of the 1996–2000 Tomorrowland renovation. The attraction consists of a huge, busy collection of industry-sponsored walk-through, hands-on exhibits. Dynamic, interactive, and forward-looking, Innoventions most closely resembles a high-tech trade show. Featured products provide guests with a preview of consumer and industrial goods of the near future. Electronics, communications, and entertainment technologies, as you would expect, play a prominent role. Exhibits, many of which change each year, demonstrate such products as virtual reality games, high-definition TV, voice-activated appliances, and various CD-ROM applications, among others. There are several major exhibit areas, each sponsored by a different manufacturer or research lab. The emphasis in the respective exhibits is on the effect of the product or technology on daily living. One of the exhibits drawing the most interest is a demonstration by Honda of ASIMO, the world's most advanced humanoid robot. ASIMO has two arms and two hands, allowing him to reach for things, switch lights on and off, and do the hokey pokey (just kidding).

TOURING TIPS Guests display a wide range of reactions to the many Innoventions exhibits. We can only suggest that you form your own opinion. In terms of touring strategy, we recommend you spend time at Innoventions on your second day. If you only have one day, visit sometime during the evening if you have the time and endurance. Be warned, however, that many Innoventions exhibits are technical in nature and may not be compatible with your mood or level of energy toward the end of a long day. Also be advised that you cannot get much of anything out of a quick walk-through of Innoventions; you have to invest a little time to understand what is going on. Finally, and predictably, teens, computer-savvy younger adults, and other electronic game buffs will enjoy Innoventions more than the average guest.

Space Mountain (FASTPASS)

APPEAL BY AGE	PRESCHOOL —*	GRADE SCHOOL ★★★★	TEENS ★★★★½
YOUNG ADULTS ★★★★½		OVER 30 ★★★★	SENIORS —*

* Sample size too small to derive rating

Type of attraction Roller coaster in the dark. **Scope and scale** Super headliner. **When to go** Right aftere the park opens or use FASTPASS. **Author's rating** Much improved ★★★★. **Duration of ride** 2 minutes and 45 seconds. **Average wait in line per 100 people ahead of you** 3 minutes. **Loading speed** Moderate.

DESCRIPTION AND COMMENTS After operating continuously for more than 25 years, Space Mountain was shut down in 2003 for a total rehab including replacement of the track system. Disneyland Park's most popular attraction reopened in July of 2005 with new ride vehicles, a new soundtrack, redesigned queuing and preshow areas, enhanced special effects (especially on launch and reentering the atmosphere), a revised narrative, and a very, very smooth ride. Retained of course is the essential theme of high-speed interstellar travel, or as more simply stated by a Space Mountain fan, "being flung around in the dark."

TOURING TIPS Space Mountain was the park's most popular attraction before it shut down for renovation. Now, answering the pent up demand and high expectations of its many faithful, it will be (if possible) even more popular. Experience it immediately after the park opens or use FASTPASS.

Starcade

DESCRIPTION AND COMMENTS Starcade is nothing more or less than a large electronic games arcade. The pièce de résistance is the SEGA jet combat simulator game—players actually roll upside down in the course of play. Though the game is expensive—$4 for about 2 minutes of play—many teens and young adults regard it as the highlight of their Disneyland day.

TOURING TIPS Enjoy your time in the area with a pocket full of quarters.

Star Tours (FASTPASS)

APPEAL BY AGE	PRESCHOOL ★★★	GRADE SCHOOL ★★★★	TEENS ★★★★
YOUNG ADULTS ★★★★		OVER 30 ★★★★	SENIORS ★★★★

Type of attraction Space-flight simulation ride. **Scope and scale** Major attraction. **When to go** Before 10 a.m. **Special comments** Frightens many small children; expectant mothers are also advised against riding; minimum-height requirement of 40". **Author's rating** A blast; not to be missed; ★★★★. **Duration of ride** Approximately 7 minutes. **Average wait in line per 100 people ahead of you** 6 minutes. **Assumes** 4 simulators operating. **Loading speed** Moderate.

DESCRIPTION AND COMMENTS The attraction consists of a ride in a flight simulator modeled after those used for training pilots and astronauts. Guests, supposedly on a little vacation outing in space, are piloted by a droid (short for android, a.k.a. humanoid, a.k.a. robot) on his first flight with real passengers. Mayhem ensues almost immediately as scenery flashes by at supersonic speed and the simulator bucks and pitches. You could swear you are moving at light speed. After several minutes of this, the droid somehow gets the spacecraft landed and you discover you're grinning from ear to ear.

Motion Sickness

WARNING!

TOURING TIPS After many years this ride still draws large crowds. Either ride in the first hour the park is open or use FASTPASS.

Be aware that the crowds in Tomorrowland are larger on cold or rainy days, when many guests skip Splash Mountain (a water-flume ride in Critter Country). Also, note that children must be at least 35 inches tall and three years of age to ride Star Tours.

Tomorrowland Autopia (FASTPASS)

APPEAL BY AGE	PRESCHOOL ★★★½		GRADE SCHOOL ★★★	TEENS ★
YOUNG ADULTS ½		OVER 30 ½		SENIORS ½

Type of ride Drive-'em-yourself miniature cars. **Scope and scale** Minor attraction. **When to go** Before 10 a.m. and after 5 p.m. or use FASTPASS. **Author's rating** Boring for adults (★); great for preschoolers. **Duration of ride** Approximately 4½ minutes. **Average wait in line per 100 people ahead of you** 6 minutes. **Assumes** 35 cars operating on each track. **Loading speed** Slow.

DESCRIPTION AND COMMENTS An elaborate miniature freeway with gasoline-powered cars that will travel at speeds of up to seven miles an hour. The attraction design, with its sleek cars, auto noises, highway signs, and even an "off-road" section, is quite alluring. In fact, however, the cars poke along on a track that leaves the driver with little to do. Pretty ho-hum for most adults and teenagers. Of those children who would enjoy the ride, many are excluded by the requirement that drivers be 52 inches tall.

TOURING TIPS This ride is appealing to the eye, but definitely expendable on a schedule for adults. Preschoolers, however, love it. If your preschooler is too short to drive, ride along and allow him or her to steer (the car runs on a guide rail) while you work the foot pedal.

A mom from North Billerica, Massachusetts, writes:

I was truly amazed by the number of adults in the line. Please emphasize to your readers that these cars travel on a guided path and are not a whole lot of fun. The only reason I could think of for adults to be in line was an insane desire to go on absolutely every ride. The other feature about the cars is that they tend to pile up at the end, so it takes almost as long to get off as it did to get on. Parents riding with their preschoolers should keep the car going as slow as it can without stalling. This prolongs the preschooler's joy and decreases the time you will have to wait at the end.

TOMORROWLAND EATERIES

DESCRIPTION AND COMMENTS **Redd Rocket's Pizza Port** in the old Mission to Mars building serves pizza, pasta, garlic bread, and salad. The ancient Tomorrowland Terrace is now **Club Buzz,** featuring burgers, salads, chicken nuggets, and a sappy little drama titled, *Calling All Space Scouts. . . A Buzz Lightyear Adventure.* Little ones will enjoy it, but most adults will find it grating, especially as an accompaniment to dining. See the daily entertainment schedule in the park handout map for showtimes.

LIVE ENTERTAINMENT *and* SPECIAL EVENTS

LIVE ENTERTAINMENT IN THE FORM OF BANDS, Disney character appearances, parades, singing and dancing, and ceremonies further enliven and add color to Disneyland Park on a daily basis. For specific information about what's happening on the day you visit, check the daily entertainment schedule in the *Times Guide*. Be forewarned, however, that if you are on a tight schedule, it is impossible to both see the park's featured attractions and take in the numerous and varied live performances offered. In our One-Day Touring Plans (see pages 179–185), we exclude the live performances in favor of seeing as much of the park as time permits. This is a considered tactical decision based on the fact that the parades and *Fantasmic!*, Disneyland Park's river spectacular, siphon crowds away from the more popular rides, thus shortening waiting lines.

The color and pageantry of live events around the park are an integral part of the Disneyland Park entertainment mix and a persuasive argument for second-day touring. Though live entertainment is varied, plentiful, and nearly continuous throughout the day, several productions are preeminent.

Fantasmic!

DESCRIPTION AND COMMENTS   *Fantasmic!* is a mixed-media show presented one or more times each evening the park is open late (10 p.m. or later). Staged at the end of Tom Sawyer Island opposite the Frontierland and New Orleans Square waterfronts, *Fantasmic!* is far and away the most extraordinary and ambitious outdoor spectacle ever attempted in any theme park. Starring Mickey Mouse in his role as the sorcerer's apprentice from *Fantasia*, the production uses lasers, images projected on a shroud of mist, fireworks, lighting effects, and music in combinations so stunning you can scarcely believe what you have seen.

The plot is simple: good versus evil. The story gets lost in all the special effects at times, but no matter—it is the spectacle, not the story line, that is so overpowering. While beautiful, stunning, and powerful are words that immediately come to mind, they fail to convey the uniqueness of this presentation. It could be argued, with some validity, that *Fantasmic!* alone is worth the price of Disneyland Park admission. Needless to say, we rate *Fantasmic!* as "not to be missed."

TOURING TIPS   It is not easy to see *Fantasmic!*. For the first show particularly, guests begin staking out prime viewing spots along the edge of the New Orleans Square and Frontierland waterfronts as much as four hours in advance. Similarly, good vantage points on raised walkways and terraces are also grabbed up early on. A mom from Lummi Island, Washington, dismantled her Disney stroller to make a nest:

We used the snap-off cover on the rental stroller to sit on during Fantasmic!, *since the ground was really cold.*

disneyland parade route

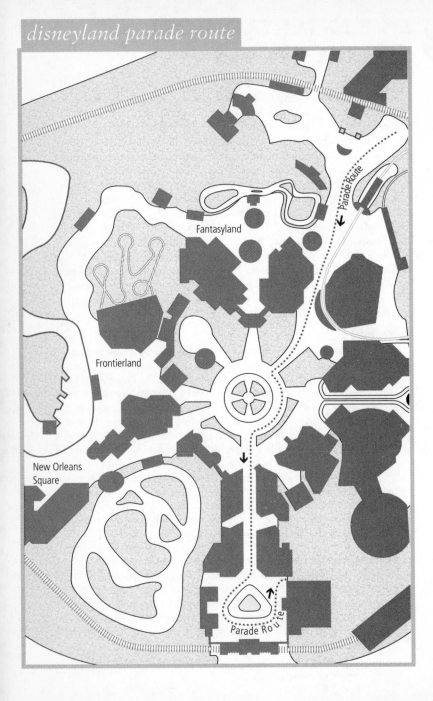

Fantasyland

Frontierland

New Orleans
Square

Parade Route

Parade Route

The Smith family from East Wimple stakes out their viewing spot for Fantasmic!.

Along similar lines, a middle-aged New York man wrote, saying:

Your excellent guidebook also served as a seat cushion while seated on the ground waiting for the show to begin. Make future editions thicker for greater comfort.

The best seats in the house are at the water's edge. For adults, it is really not necessary to have an unobstructed view of the staging area because most of the action is high above the crowd. Children standing in the closely packed crowd, however, are able to catch only bits and pieces of the presentation.

Probably the most painless strategy for seeing *Fantasmic!* is to attend the second show. Usually, the second performance follows the first performance by about an hour and a half. If you let the crowd for the first show clear out and then take up your position, you should be able to find a good vantage point. The evening parade, which winds through Fantasyland and down Main Street, often runs concurrently with *Fantasmic!* for the first and second shows of the evening, essentially splitting the crowd between the two events. At the second *Fantasmic!* and second parade, however, there are fewer people in the park and viewing conditions are less crowded.

Rain and wind conditions sometimes cause *Fantasmic!* to be canceled. Unfortunately, Disney officials usually do not make a final decision about whether to proceed or cancel until just before show time. We have seen guests wrapped in ponchos sit stoically in rain or drizzle for more than an hour with no assurance that their patience and sacrifice would be rewarded. Unless you can find a covered viewing spot, we do not recommend staking out vantage points on rainy or especially windy nights. On nights like these, pursue your own agenda until ten minutes or so before show time, and then head to the waterfront to see what happens.

You can view *Fantasmic!* from the balcony of the Disney Gallery (in New Orleans Square), easily the best vantage point available. Because the balcony can accommodate only 20 guests, each show sells out fast. A second private viewing area is located near the Tom Sawyer's Island Raft Dock. If you want to be one of the elite, call ☎ 714-781-4400 at 8 a.m. exactly 30 days in advance. The price for the balcony is $56 for both adults and children, while the dock viewing area runs $56 for adults and $46 for children 3 to 9 years. A dessert buffet is included at both venues.

Finally, make sure to hang on to children during *Fantasmic!* and to give them explicit instructions for regrouping in the event you are separated. Be especially vigilant when the crowd disperses after the show.

PARADES

DESCRIPTION AND COMMENTS Disney theme parks the world over are famous for their parades. On days when the park closes early there is an afternoon parade. On days when the park closes late (10 p.m. to 1 a.m.), there are always evening parades, and often an afternoon parade as well.

The parades are full-blown Disney productions with some combination of floats, huge inflated balloons of the characters, marching bands, old-time vehicles, dancers, and, of course, literally dozens of costumed Disney characters. Themes for the parades vary from time to time, and special holiday parades are always produced for Christmas and Easter.

Parade of Dreams

For the Disneyland 50th Anniversary Celebration, Disney launched a stunning parade called Parade of Dreams. Consisting of eight floats and just about every Disney character you've ever heard of, it's possibly the most stunning Disney parade ever. Each float has a different dream-related theme such as Dreams of Imagination (Alice in Wonderland float) or Dreams of Adventure (Lion King float). Ringed by dancers, Disney characters, and various performers, the floats are both immense and elaborate. At three locations, Small World Mall, the central hub, and Main Street Town Square, each three-float segment of the parade stops and performs a two-minute show. If you station yourself at one of these viewing areas, you'll see all of the shows. However, if you're positioned elsewhere along the parade route you'll only see the parade in passing. In keeping with the 50th Anniversary, the Parade of Dreams is perhaps the most nostalgic and sentimental Disney parade ever produced. Parents will relive moments from their own childhood as well as from that of their children.

TOURING TIPS Though Parade of Dreams has lights, it is really designed to be a daytime spectacle. Most days it runs at 3 p.m and 7 p.m. with the first parade starting at Small World Mall and ending at Main Street Town Square. The later parade flows in the opposite direction.

Parades always draw thousands of guests from the attraction lines. We recommend, therefore, watching from the departure point. With this strategy you can enjoy the parade, and then while the parade is continuing on its route, take advantage of the diminished lines at the attractions. Watching a parade that begins in Fantasyland from Small World Mall affords the greatest mobility in terms of accessing other areas of the park when the parade has passed.

Main Street is the most crowded area from which to watch a parade when it begins at Town Square. The opposite is true when the parade begins in Fantasyland. The upper platform of the Main Street train station affords the best viewing perspective along the route. The best time to get a position on the platform is when the parade begins in Fantasyland. When this happens, good spots on the platform are available right up to the time the parade begins. When you are at the end of the parade route, you can assume it will take the parade 15 to 18 minutes to get to you.

Keep an eye on your children during parades and give them explicit instructions for regrouping in the event you get separated. Children constantly jockey for better viewing positions. A few wiggles this way and a few wiggles the other, and presto, they are lost in the crowd. Finally, be especially vigilant when the crowd starts dispersing after the parade. Thousands of people suddenly strike out in different directions, creating a perfect situation for losing a child or two.

Live Entertainment Throughout the Park

Parades and *Fantasmic!* make up only a part of the daily live entertainment offerings at Disneyland Park. The following is an incomplete list of other performances and events that are scheduled with some regularity and that require no reservations.

FANTASYLAND THEATRE The park's premier venue for full-fledged musical productions starring the Disney characters. See the *Times Guide* for show times.

GOLDEN HORSESHOE VARIETY SHOW A Western saloon–style show alternates with a "hillbilly" show at the Golden Horseshoe stage in Frontierland. Check the *Times Guide* for show times.

CLUB BUZZ Short dramas based on the Disney/Pixar feature *Toy Story* are performed outdoors in Tomorrowland adjacent to the restaurant of the same name. See the *Times Guide* for show times.

ALADDIN'S OASIS Aladdin and Jasmine act out stories of their adventures with the assistance of guests chosen (drafted) from the audience.

PLAZA GARDENS This tented venue, located just beyond the central hub and to the left of the castle, hosts visiting high school and university bands, as well as swing dance bands.

STREET ENTERTAINMENT Various bands, singers, comics, and strolling musicians entertain in spontaneous (that is, unscheduled) street performances throughout the park. Musical styles include banjo, Dixieland, steel drum, marching, and fife-and-drum.

DISNEY ROCK GROUPS High-energy Disney rock groups perform daily in Tomorrowland according to the *Times Guide*.

RETREAT CEREMONY Daily at around dusk in Town Square a small band and honor guard lower the flag and release a flock of white homing pigeons.

FIREWORKS *REMEMBER . . . DREAMS COME TRUE* Tinker Bell kicks off this sentimental fireworks spectacle with a new, zany flight path that makes you wonder what she's on besides pixie dust. Part of the Disneyland 50th Anniversary celebration, *Remember . . . Dreams Come True* is the most elaborate and ambitious fireworks program in the park's history. Fireworks are seamlessly integrated with the voices of Walt Disney and dozens of Disney characters in the story of how the dream of Disneyland came true. Theme music from each of the park's lands as well as from Disney classic films combine to create a surprisingly moving production.

The show consists of five "acts" as Disney describes them. Julie Andrews' introduction leads to several famous Disney characters sharing their dreams. Then comes Tinker Bell's loopy flight followed by Walt Disney telling the story of his Disneyland dream. Finally Tink reappears for the heart-tugging finale, called "Wishes Everlasting." Each act is naturally accompanied by an Armageddon of fireworks, including some custom patterns created expressly for this production.

TOURING TIPS Without a doubt, the central hub is the best vantage point for watching Remember . . . Dreams Come True. Unfortunately, every guest in the park won't fit in the hub at the same time. Next best positions are any open (that is, not canopied by trees) spots facing Sleeping Beauty Castle, followed by any open spot without something really big, like a Disney mountain, in the way. Concerning the latter, you'll be able to see the fireworks fine but will miss Tinkerbelle.

SWORD IN THE STONE CEREMONY An audience-participation ceremony based on the Disney animated feature of the same name. Merlin the

Magician selects youngsters from the audience to test their courage and strength by removing the sword Excalibur from the stone. Staged each day near King Arthur Carrousel according to the *Times Guide.*

DISNEY CHARACTER APPEARANCES Disney characters appear at random throughout the park but are routinely present in Mickey's Toontown, Fantasyland, and on Main Street. A greeting area featuring Disney princesses is located between the castle and the Plaza Gardens Stage. Princesses also read fairy tales at the **Tinker Bell Toy Shop** located behind the castle and to the left. If you like your princesses wet, you can visit Ariel (the Little Mermaid) at Triton's Garden located off the path connecting the Matterhorn to the central hub.

DISNEY CHARACTER BREAKFASTS AND DINNERS Disney characters join guests for breakfast each morning until 11 a.m. at the **Plaza Inn** on Main Street, **Storyteller's Café** at the Grand Californian Hotel, and **PCH Grill** at Paradise Pier Hotel. Disney characters also join guests for breakfast and dinner at **Goofy's Kitchen** at the Disneyland Hotel, and **Ariel's Grotto** in California Adventure Park serves character meals with Ariel and friends.

TRAFFIC PATTERNS *inside* DISNEYLAND PARK

WHEN WE BEGAN OUR RESEARCH on Disneyland, we were very interested in traffic patterns throughout the park, specifically:

1. WHAT ATTRACTIONS AND WHICH SECTIONS OF THE PARK DO VISITORS HEAD FOR WHEN THEY FIRST ARRIVE? When guests are admitted to the various lands, the flow of people to Tomorrowland (Space Mountain, Buzz Lightyear, and Star Tours) is heaviest. The next most crowded land is Fantasyland, though the crowds are distributed over a large number of attractions. Critter Country is likewise crowded with its small area and only two attractions (Splash Mountain and Pooh). Adventureland, Frontierland, and New Orleans Square fill more slowly, with Mickey's Toontown not really coming alive until later in the morning. In our research we tested the assertion, often heard, that most people turn right into Tomorrowland and tour Disneyland in an orderly, counterclockwise fashion, and we found it without basis. As the park fills, visitors appear to head for specific favored attractions that they wish to ride before the lines get long. This, more than any other factor, determines traffic patterns in the mornings and accounts for the relatively equal distribution of visitors throughout Disneyland.

ATTRACTIONS HEAVILY ATTENDED IN EARLY MORNING	
Adventureland	Indiana Jones
	Jungle Cruise
Critter Country	Splash Mountain
	The Many Adventures of Winnie the Pooh
Fantasyland	Dumbo
	Matterhorn Bobsleds
Mickey's Toontown	Car Toon Spin
Tomorrowland	Space Mountain
	Star Tours
	Buzz Lightyear Astro Blasters (opens 2005)

2. HOW LONG DOES IT TAKE FOR THE PARK TO REACH PEAK CAPACITY FOR A GIVEN DAY? HOW ARE THE VISITORS DISPERSED THROUGHOUT THE PARK? There is a surge of "early birds" who arrive before or around opening time but are quickly dispersed throughout the empty park. After the initial onslaught is absorbed, there is a bit of a lull that lasts until about an hour after opening. Following the lull, the park is inundated with arriving guests for about two hours, peaking between 10 and 11 a.m. Guests continue to arrive in a steady but diminishing stream until around 2 p.m.

Sampled lines reached their longest length between noon and 3 p.m., indicating more arrivals than departures in the early afternoon. For general touring purposes, most attractions develop substantial lines between 9:30 and 11 a.m. In the early morning, Tomorrowland, Critter Country, and Fantasyland fill up first. By late morning and into early afternoon, attendance is fairly equally distributed throughout all of the "lands." Mickey's Toontown, because it is comparatively small, stays mobbed from about 11 a.m. on. By midafternoon, however, we noted a concentration of visitors in Fantasyland, New Orleans Square, and Adventureland, and a slight decrease of visitors in Tomorrowland. This pattern did not occur consistently day to day, but happened often enough for us to suggest Tomorrowland as the best bet for mid-afternoon touring.

In the late afternoon and early evening, attendance is normally more heavily distributed in Tomorrowland, Critter Country, and Fantasyland. Though Space Mountain, Buzz Lightyear, Splash Mountain, and Winnie the Pooh remain inundated throughout the day, most of the other attractions in Tomorrowland and Critter Country have reasonable lines. In New Orleans Square, the Haunted Mansion, the Pirates of the Caribbean, and the multitudes returning from nearby Critter Country keep traffic brisk. Frontierland and Adventureland (except for the Indiana Jones ride) become less congested as the afternoon and evening progress.

3. HOW DO MOST VISITORS GO ABOUT TOURING THE PARK? IS THERE A DIFFERENCE IN THE TOURING BEHAVIOR OF FIRST-TIME VISITORS AND REPEAT VISITORS? Many first-time visitors accompany friends or relatives who are familiar with Disneyland and who guide their tour. These tours sometimes do and sometimes do not proceed in an orderly (clockwise or counterclockwise) touring sequence. First-time visitors without personal touring guidance tend to be more orderly in their touring. Many first-time visitors, however, are drawn to Sleeping Beauty Castle on entering the park and thus commence their rotation from Fantasyland. Repeat visitors usually proceed directly to their favorite attractions or to whatever is new.

4. WHAT EFFECT DO SPECIAL EVENTS, SUCH AS PARADES, FIREWORKS, AND *FANTASMIC!* HAVE ON TRAFFIC PATTERNS? Special events such as parades, fireworks, and *Fantasmic!* pull substantial numbers of visitors from the lines for rides, especially when *Fantasmic!* and a parade are staged at the same time. Unfortunately, however, the left hand taketh what the right hand giveth. A parade and *Fantasmic!* kicking off simultaneously snarls traffic flow throughout Disneyland so much that guests find themselves captive wherever they are. Attraction lines in Tomorrowland, Mickey's Toontown, Adventureland, and Fantasyland (behind the castle) diminish dramatically, making Space Mountain, Buzz Lightyear, Star Tours, the Jungle Cruise, the

Indiana Jones Adventure, Peter Pan's Flight, and Snow White's Scary Adventures particularly good choices during the evening festivities. The remainder of the park (Critter Country, New Orleans Square, Frontierland, Main Street) is so congested with guests viewing the parade and *Fantasmic!* that it is almost impossible to move.

5. WHAT ARE THE TRAFFIC PATTERNS NEAR TO AND AT CLOSING TIME?
On our sample days, which were recorded in and out of season, park departures outnumbered arrivals beginning in midafternoon, with a substantial number of guests leaving after the afternoon parade. Additional numbers of visitors departed during the late afternoon as the dinner hour approached. When the park closed early, there were steady departures during the two hours preceding closing, with a mass exodus of remaining visitors at closing time.

When the park closed late, departures were distributed throughout the evening hours, with waves of departures following the evening parade(s), fireworks, and *Fantasmic!* performances. Though departures increased exponentially as closing time approached, a huge throng was still on hand when the park finally shut down. The balloon effect of this last throng at the end of the day generally overwhelmed the shops on Main Street, the parking lot, trams, and the hotel shuttle, and the exits onto adjoining Anaheim streets. In the hour before closing in the lands other than Main Street, touring conditions were normally uncrowded except at the Indiana Jones attraction in Adventureland and Splash Mountain in Critter Country.

DISNEYLAND PARK TOURING PLANS

THE DISNEYLAND PARK TOURING PLANS are step-by-step plans for seeing as much as possible with a minimum of time wasted standing in line. They are designed to assist you in avoiding crowds and bottlenecks on days of moderate to heavy attendance. On days of lighter attendance (see "Selecting the Time of Year for Your Visit," page 21), the plans will still save you time but will not be as critical to successful touring.

Choosing the Right Touring Plan

Six different touring plans are presented:

- One-Day Touring Plan for Adults
- Author's Select One-Day Touring Plan
- Dumbo-or-Die-in-a-Day Touring Plan for Adults with Small Children
- Two-Day Touring Plan for Adults with Small Children
- Two-Day Touring Plan A for Daytime Touring or for When the Park Closes Early (before 8 p.m.)

- Two-Day Touring Plan B for Morning and Evening Touring or for When the Park Is Open Late (after 8 p.m.)

If you have two days to spend at Disneyland Park, the two-day touring plans are by far the most relaxed and efficient. Two-Day Touring Plan A takes advantage of early morning touring, when lines are short and the park has not yet filled with guests. This plan works well all year and is particularly recommended for days when Disneyland Park closes before 8 p.m. On the other hand, Two-Day Touring Plan B combines the efficiencies of early morning touring on the first day with the splendor of Disneyland Park at night on the second day. This plan is perfect for guests who wish to sample both the attractions and the special magic of Disneyland Park after dark, including *Fantasmic!,* parades, and fireworks. The Two-Day Touring Plan for Adults with Small Children spreads the experience over two more-relaxed days and incorporates more attractions that both children and parents will enjoy.

If you have only one day but wish to see as much as possible, use the One-Day Touring Plan for Adults. This plan will pack as much into a single day as is humanly possible, but it is pretty exhausting. If you prefer a more relaxed visit, try the Author's Select One-Day Touring Plan. This plan features the best Disneyland Park has to offer (in the author's opinion), eliminating some of the less impressive attractions.

If you have small children, you may want to use the Dumbo-or-Die-in-a-Day Touring Plan for Adults with Small Children. This plan includes most of the children's rides in Fantasyland and Mickey's Toontown, and omits roller-coaster rides and other attractions that small children cannot ride (because of Disney's age and height requirements), as well as rides and shows that are frightening for small children. Because this plan calls for adults to sacrifice many of the better Disney attractions, it is not recommended unless you are touring Disneyland Park primarily for the benefit of your children. In essence, you pretty much stand around, sweat, wipe noses, pay for stuff, and watch the children have fun. It's great.

An alternative (to the Dumbo Plan) would be to use the One-Day Touring Plan for Adults, or the Author's Select One-Day Touring Plan, and take advantage of "switching off," a technique whereby children accompany adults to the loading area of rides with age and height requirements, but do not actually ride (see page 107). Switching off allows adults to enjoy the wilder rides while keeping the whole group together.

The Single-Day Touring Conundrum

Touring Disneyland Park in a single day is complicated by the fact that Disneyland's premier attractions, Splash Mountain in Critter Country, Indiana Jones in Adventureland, and Space Mountain and Buzz Lightyear in Tomorrowland are almost at opposite ends of the park, making it virtually impossible to ride all five without encountering a long line at one attraction or another. If you ride Space Mountain right after the park opens, you will ride with little if any wait. By the time you exit Tomorrowland and hustle over to Indiana Jones or Splash Mountain, those lines will have grown to frightening proportions. The same situation prevails if you ride Indiana Jones and Splash Mountain first: Indiana Jones and Splash Mountain—no problem; Space Mountain—big lines. From ten minutes after opening until just before closing, you can expect long waits for these headliner attractions.

The best way to experience all of Disneyland Park's wilder rides in one day, with the least amount of waiting, is to ride in the following sequence:

1. Space Mountain
2. Matterhorn Bobsleds
3. Splash Mountain
4. Big Thunder Mountain

Park Opening Procedures

Your progress and success during your first hour of touring will be affected by the particular opening procedure the Disney people use that day.

A. All guests are held at the turnstiles until the park opens (which may or may not be at the official opening time). On admittance, all "lands" are open. If this is the case on the day you visit, blow right past Main Street and head for the first attraction on whatever touring plan you are following.

B. Guests are admitted to Main Street a half hour to an hour before the remaining "lands" open. Access to the other lands is blocked by a rope barrier at the central hub end of Main Street on these days. On admittance, move to the rope barrier and stake out a position as follows:

(1) If you are going to Indiana Jones or Splash Mountain first, take up a position in front of the Plaza Pavilion restaurant at the central-hub end of Main Street on the left. Wait next to the rope barrier blocking the walkway to Adventureland. When the rest of the park opens (and the rope drops), proceed quickly to Adventureland for Indiana Jones, or Critter Country by way of Adventureland and New Orleans Square for Splash Mountain.

(2) If you are going to Space Mountain first, wait on the right at the central-hub end of Main Street. When the rope drops at opening time, bear right and zip into Tomorrowland.

(3) If you are going to Fantasyland or Frontierland first, proceed to the end of Main Street and line up at the rope right of center.

(4) If you are going to Mickey's Toontown first, ascend to the platform of the Main Street Station of the Disneyland Railroad and board the first train of the day. Ride half a circuit, disembarking at the Fantasyland/Toontown Station. The train pulls out of the Main Street Station at the same time the rope is dropped at the central-hub end of Main Street.

Touring Plan Clip-Out Pocket Outlines

For your convenience, we have prepared outline versions of all the touring plans presented in this guide. These pocket outlines present the same touring itineraries as the detailed touring plans, but with vastly abbreviated directions. First, select the touring plan that is most appropriate for your party, and then familiarize yourself with the detailed version of the plan. Once you understand how the touring plan works, clip out the pocket-outline version of your selected plan from the back of this guide and carry it with you as a quick reference when you visit the theme park.

PRELIMINARY INSTRUCTIONS FOR ALL DISNEYLAND PARK TOURING PLANS

ON DAYS OF MODERATE to heavy attendance, follow the touring plans exactly, deviating only when you do not wish to experience a listed show or ride. For instance, the touring plan may direct you to go next to Big Thunder Mountain, a roller-coaster ride. If you do not like roller coasters, simply skip that step and proceed to the next.

1. Buy your admission in advance (see "Admission Options" on page 17).
2. Call ☎ 714-781-7290 the day before you go for the official opening time.
3. Become familiar with the park-opening procedures (described on page 178), and read over the touring plan of your choice so that you will have a basic understanding of what you are likely to encounter as you enter the park.

DISNEYLAND PARK ONE-DAY TOURING PLAN FOR ADULTS

FOR Adults without small children.

ASSUMES Willingness to experience all major rides (including roller coasters) and shows.

Be forewarned that this plan requires a lot of walking and some backtracking; this is necessary to avoid long waits in line. A little extra walking coupled with some hustle in the morning will save you two to three hours of standing in line. Also be aware that you might not complete the tour. How far you get will depend on the size of your group, how quickly you move from ride to ride, how many times you pause for rest or food, how quickly the park fills, and what time the park closes.

Note: The success of this touring plan hinges on your entering the park when it first opens.

1. Arrive at the entrance turnstiles 40 minutes before official opening time with your admission in hand.
2 Head for Tomorrowland as soon as the park opens. Ride Space Mountain.
3. Also in Tomorrowland, ride the Buzz Lightyear Astro Blasters.

4. Proceed to the Matterhorn Bobsleds and ride.

5. Proceed to Splash Mountain in Critter Country. Ride Splash Mountain. Don't use FASTPASS unless the wait exceeds 30 minutes.

6. Also in Critter Country, experience The Many Adventures of Winnie the Pooh.

7. Exit Winnie the Pooh and backtrack to Adventureland. Ride Indiana Jones. Resist the urge to use FASTPASS. Your wait at this time of morning should be 35 minutes or less.

8. Exit Indiana Jones to the right and ride the Jungle Cruise, also in Adventureland. If you are a Disneyland Park veteran and have seen enough of the Jungle Cruise, or if the wait exceeds 20 minutes, skip to Step 9.

9. Cross the central hub entering Fantasyland on the left of Matterhorn Mountain. Ride Alice In Wonderland.

10. Turn left after Alice and proceed to the heart of Fantasyland. Ride Peter Pan's Flight.

11. Depart Fantasyland and enter Frontierland. Ride the Big Thunder Mountain Railroad. If the wait exceeds 25 minutes, obtain a FASTPASS.

12. Keeping the waterfront on your right, wind around through Frontierland to New Orleans Square.

13. In New Orleans Square, experience the Haunted Mansion.

14. Exit to the right and ride Pirates of the Caribbean, also in New Orleans Square.

15. Check your FASTPASS return time for Big Thunder Mountain and break off the Touring Plan when it's time to return and ride. Also, feel free at this time to grab a bite to eat if you're hungry.

16. Check your daily entertainment schedule for the next performance at the Golden Horseshoe Saloon (Frontierland) or the Fantasyland Theatre. Feel free to work a performance at any of the two into the Touring Plan. Be sure to arrive at the theater 20 minutes or so before show time.

17. In Adventureland, tour Tarzan's Treehouse. If you're up for something different, try the nearby *Enchanted Tiki Birds* show.

18. Return to the waterfront at New Orleans Square. Ride either the Sailing Ship *Columbia* or the *Mark Twain* Riverboat.

19. Go to Tomorrowland via the central hub. Obtain a FASTPASS for Star Tours. If the wait is less than 25 minutes, go ahead and ride.

20. In Tomorrowland, see *Honey, I Shrunk the Audience.*

21. From Tomorrowland, take the Disneyland Railroad for a round-trip ride.

22. Back in Tomorrowland, ride Star Tours.

23. Proceed to Fantasyland. Ride It's a Small World.

24. Passing under the railroad tracks, explore Mickey's Toontown. If you want to ride Roger Rabbit's Car Toon Spin, either get in line or obtain a FAST-PASS. Be aware that your FASTPASS return window might be several hours hence or all FASTPASSes may have been distributed.

25. Try any of the Fantasyland rides that you bypassed earlier in the day. Check for show times at the Fantasyland Theatre.

26. Check the daily entertainment schedule for parades, fireworks, and *Fantasmic!*. Work these shows into the remainder of your day as time and energy allow.

27. If you have any time left before closing, backtrack to pick up any attractions you may have missed or bypassed.

28. Continue to tour, saving Main Street for last. If you have any oomph left, see *Disneyland: The First 50 Years* on your way out of the park.

AUTHOR'S SELECT DISNEYLAND PARK ONE-DAY TOURING PLAN

FOR Adults touring without small children.

ASSUMES Willingness to experience all major rides (including roller coasters) and shows.

This touring plan is selective and includes only those attractions that, in the author's opinion, represent the best Disneyland Park has to offer.

Be forewarned that this plan requires a lot of walking and some backtracking; this is necessary to avoid long waits in line. A little extra walking coupled with some hustle in the morning will save you two to three hours standing in line. Note that you might not complete this tour. How far you get will depend on the size of your group, how quickly you move from ride to ride, how many times you pause for rest or food, how quickly the park fills, and what time the park closes. With a little zip and some luck, it is possible to complete the touring plan even on a busy day when the park closes early.

Note: The success of this touring plan hinges on your being among the first to enter the park when it opens.

1. Arrive at the entrance turnstiles 40 minutes before official opening time with your admission in hand.

2. Head for Tomorrowland as soon as the park opens. Ride Space Mountain.

3. Also in Tomorrowland, ride the Buzz Lightyear Astro Blasters.

4. Proceed to the Matterhorn Bobsleds and ride.

5. Proceed to Splash Mountain in Critter Country. Ride Splash Mountain. Don't use FASTPASS unless the wait exceeds 30 minutes.

6. Also in Critter Country, experience The Many Adventures of Winnie the Pooh.

7. Exit Winnie the Pooh and backtrack to Adventureland. Ride Indiana Jones. Resist the urge to use FASTPASS. Your wait at this time of morning should be 35 minutes or less.

8. Exit Indiana Jones to the right and ride the Jungle Cruise, also in Adventureland. If you are a Disneyland Park veteran and have seen enough of the Jungle Cruise, or if the wait exceeds 20 minutes, skip to Step 9.

9. Proceed via the central hub and the castle to Fantasyland. Ride Peter Pan's Flight.

10. Proceed to Frontierland via Fantasyland. Ride the Big Thunder Mountain Railroad. Don't use FASTPASS unless the wait exceeds 30 minutes.

11. Keeping the waterfront on your right, wind around through Frontierland to New Orleans Square. In New Orleans Square, experience the Haunted Mansion.

12. Exit to the right and ride Pirates of the Caribbean, also in New Orleans Square.

13. Feel free at this time to grab a bite to eat if you're hungry.

14. Return to the waterfront at New Orleans Square. Ride either the Sailing Ship *Columbia* or the *Mark Twain* Riverboat.

15. Check your daily entertainment schedule for the next performance at the Golden Horseshoe Saloon (Frontierland) or the Fantasyland Theatre. Feel free to work a performance at any of the two into the Touring Plan. Be sure to arrive at the theater 20 minutes or so before showtime. Likewise, try to work the afternoon parade into your itinerary.

16. Go to Tomorrowland via the central hub. Obtain a FASTPASS for Star Tours, if the wait exceeds 25 minutes. Otherwise, ride.

17. In Tomorrowland, see *Honey, I Shrunk the Audience.*

18. From Tomorrowland, take the Disneyland Railroad for a round-trip.

19. Back in Tomorrowland, ride Star Tours using your FASTPASS.

20. Returning to Fantasyland, ride It's a Small World.

21. Check the daily entertainment schedule for parades, fireworks, and *Fantasmic!* Work these shows into the remainder of your day as time and energy allow.

22. If you have any time left before closing, backtrack to pick up any attractions you may have missed or bypassed.

23. Continue to tour, saving Main Street for last. If you have any oomph left, see *Disneyland: The First 50 Years* on your way out of the park.

DUMBO-OR-DIE-IN-A-DAY TOURING PLAN FOR ADULTS WITH SMALL CHILDREN

FOR Parents with children under age 7 who feel compelled to devote every waking moment to the pleasure and entertainment of their small children, and rich people who are paying someone else to take their children to the theme park.

ASSUMES Periodic stops for rest, restrooms, and refreshment.

The name of this touring plan notwithstanding, this itinerary is not a joke. Regardless of whether you are loving, guilty, masochistic, truly selfless, insane, or saintly, this touring plan will provide a small child with about as perfect a day as is possible at Disneyland Park.

This touring plan represents a concession to those adults who are determined, even if it kills them, to give their small children the ultimate Disneyland Park experience. The plan addresses the preferences, needs, and desires of small children to the virtual exclusion of those of adults or older siblings. If you left the kids with a sitter yesterday, or wouldn't let little Marvin eat barbecue for breakfast, this is the perfect plan for expiating your guilt. This is also a wonderful plan if you are paying a sitter, nanny, or chauffeur to take your children to Disneyland Park.

If this description has intimidated you somewhat or if you have concluded that your day at Disneyland Park is as important as your childrens', use the One-Day Touring Plan for Adults, making use of the switching-off option (see page 107) at those attractions that impose height or age restrictions.

Because the children's attractions in Disneyland Park are the most poorly engineered in terms of handling large crowds, the following touring plan is the least efficient of the six plans we present. It represents the best way, however, to experience most of the child-oriented attractions in one day if that is what you are determined to do. We do not make recommendations in this plan for meals. If you can, try to hustle along as quickly as is comfortable until about noon. After noon, it won't make much difference if you stop to eat or take it a little easier.

Note: The success of this touring plan hinges on your being among the first to enter the park when it opens.

1. Arrive 30 to 40 minutes before the official opening time with your admission in hand.

2. Line up in front of gate 13 or 20.

3. When you are admitted to the park, move quickly to the far end of Main Street. If there is no rope barrier, continue to Fantasyland via the castle without stopping.

4. In Fantasyland, ride Dumbo, the Flying Elephant.

5. In Fantasyland, ride Peter Pan's Flight. Bear right on exiting; go past Mr. Toad's Wild Ride and around the corner to Alice in Wonderland.

6. Ride Alice in Wonderland.

7. Exit Alice in Wonderland to the left and ride the Mad Tea Party.

8. Next, head toward It's a Small World in the far corner of Fantasyland. Bypassing the ride for the moment, cross under the Disneyland Railroad tracks into Mickey's Toontown.

9. In Mickey's Toontown, try Roger Rabbit's Car Toon Spin if your children are plucky. Do not use FASTPASS unless the wait exceeds 30 minutes.

10. In Mickey's Toontown, ride Gadget's Go Coaster.

11. While in Mickey's Toontown, let off some steam in Goofy's Bounce House.

12. Tour Mickey's House and visit Mickey in his dressing room.

13. After seeing Mickey, turn right to enjoy the Chip 'n' Dale Treehouse.

14. Go to the far side of Mickey's House and tour Minnie's House.

15. Round out your visit to Mickey's Toontown with an inspection of Donalds boat tied up next to Goofy's Bounce House.

16. Depart Toontown. Take the Disneyland Railroad from the Fantasyland/Toontown station to New Orleans Square. Walk if you have a stroller that does not collapse.

17. Bear left on exiting the train station and follow the waterfront to Critter Country. Experience Winnie the Pooh.

18. Return to New Orleans Square and see Pirates of the Caribbean. If your children were frightened by Roger Rabbit's Car Toon Spin in Mickey's Toontown, skip ahead to Step 19.

19. Go left on leaving Pirates of the Caribbean to experience the Haunted Mansion. If your children were not frightened at Pirates of the Caribbean, they will do fine at the Haunted Mansion.

20. Go down to the waterfront and take a raft to Tom Sawyer Island. Allow the kids plenty of time to explore.

21. Catch the Disneyland Railroad at the New Orleans Square station and return to the Fantasyland/Toontown station.

22. In Fantasyland, ride It's a Small World.

23. Cross the Small World Mall and ride the Casey Jr. Circus Train or the Storybook Land Canal Boats, whichever has the shortest wait.

24. In Fantasyland, ride King Arthur Carousel.

25. In Fantasyland, also ride Pinocchio's Daring Journey if the wait does not exceed 15 minutes. Otherwise, skip ahead to Step 27.

26. Exit Pinocchio to your left and head to Frontierland.

27. In Frontierland, ride the *Mark Twain* Riverboat or the Sailing Ship *Columbia,* whichever departs first.

28. Leave Frontierland and go to Adventureland. Explore Tarzan's Treehouse if the wait is less than 15 minutes. Otherwise, skip ahead to Step 29.

29. In Adventureland, see the *Enchanted Tiki Birds* show.

30. Leave Adventureland, cross the central hub, and enter Tomorrowland via the path that runs along the right side (as you face it from the central hub) of the Matterhorn.

31. In Tomorrowland, obtain a FASTPASS for Autopia.

32. In Tomorrowland, take the Disneyland monorail for a round-trip ride.

33. After the monorail, walk across the plaza, keeping the Astro Orbiter on your left. Proceed to *Honey, I Shrunk the Audience.* Be aware that the 3-D effects and the high-volume level frighten some preschoolers. If your kids have been a little sensitive during the day, skip ahead to Step 35.

34. While in Tomorrowland, ride Autopia using your FASTPASS.

35. As soon as your return window for Autopia begins, obtain a FASTPASS for Buzz Lightyear. Your can do this either before or after riding Autopia.

36. This concludes the touring plan. Use any time remaining to revisit favorite attractions, see attractions that were not included in the touring

plan, or visit attractions you skipped because the lines were too long. Also, consult your daily entertainment schedule for parades, Fantasyland Theatre productions, or other live entertainment that might interest you. As you drag your battered and exhausted family out of the park at the end of the day, bear in mind that it was you who decided to cram all this stuff into one day. We just tried to help you get organized.

DISNEYLAND PARK TWO-DAY TOURING PLAN FOR ADULTS WITH SMALL CHILDREN

FOR Parents with children under age 7 who wish to spread their Disneyland Park visit over two days.

ASSUMES Frequent stops for rest, restrooms, and refreshments.

This touring plan represents a compromise between the observed tastes of adults and the observed tastes of younger children. Included in this touring plan are many of the midway-type rides that your children may have the opportunity to experience (although in less exotic surroundings) at local fairs and amusement parks. These rides at Disneyland Park often require long waits in line and consume valuable touring time that could be better spent experiencing the many rides and shows found only at a Disney theme park, and which best demonstrate the Disney genius. This touring plan is heavily weighted toward the tastes of younger children. If you want to balance it a bit, try working out a compromise with your kids to forgo some of the carnival-type rides (Mad Tea Party, Dumbo, King Arthur Carrousel, Gadget's Go Coaster) or such rides as the Tomorrowland Autopia.

Another alternative is to use one of the other two-day touring plans and take advantage of "switching off" (see page 107). This technique allows small children to be admitted to rides such as Space Mountain, Indiana Jones, Big Thunder Mountain Railroad, and Splash Mountain. The children wait in the loading area as their parents ride one at a time; the nonriding parent waits with the children.

TIMING The following Two-Day Touring Plan takes advantage of early morning touring. On each day you should complete the structured part of the plan by 3 p.m. or so. We highly recommend returning to your hotel by midafternoon for a nap and an early dinner. If the park is open in the evening, come back to the park by 7:30 or 8 p.m. for the evening parade, fireworks, and *Fantasmic!*.

Note: Because the needs of small children are so varied, we have not built specific instructions for eating into the touring plan. Simply stop for refreshments or a meal when you feel the urge. For best results, however, try to keep moving in the morning. In the afternoon, you can eat, rest often, and adjust the pace to your liking.

DAY ONE

1. Arrive 30 to 40 minutes before the official opening time with your admission in hand.

2. Line up in front of entrance gate 13 or 20.

3. When you are admitted to the park, move quickly to the far end of Main Street. If there is no rope barrier, continue without stopping to Critter Country and Splash Mountain.

4. Ride Splash Mountain, taking advantage of the switching-off option if your children are too young or too short to ride.

5. While in Critter Country, ride The Many Adventures of Winnie the Pooh.

6. Backtrack to New Orleans Square and experience the Haunted Mansion. If your children seem intimidated by the prospect of the Haunted Mansion, skip ahead to Step 8.

7. After the Haunted Mansion, turn right and try Pirates of the Caribbean.

8. Bear right into Adventureland. Ride the Jungle Cruise.

9. Exit to the left (back toward the Haunted Mansion) and go to the Frontierland/New Orleans Square Station. Take the Disneyland Railroad one stop to the Fantasyland/Toontown Station.

10. Cross under the Disneyland Railroad tracks into Mickey's Toontown.

11. In Mickey's Toontown, try Roger Rabbit's Car Toon Spin if your children are plucky and have strong stomachs. Obtain FASTPASSes if the wait exceeds 30 minutes.

12. In Mickey's Toontown, ride Gadget's Go Coaster.

13. While in Mickey's Toontown, let off some steam in Goofy's Bounce House.

14. Tour Mickey's House and visit Mickey in his dressing room.

15. After seeing Mickey, turn right to enjoy the Chip 'n' Dale Treehouse.

16. Go to the far side of Mickey's House and tour Minnie's House.

17. Round out your visit to Mickey's Toontown with an inspection of Donald's boat tied up next to Goofy's Bounce House.

18. Depart Mickey's Toontown the same way you entered, bearing left after you pass under the railroad tracks. Proceed to It's a Small World and ride.

19. Next, return to the Fantasyland/Toontown Station. Take the Disneyland Railroad all the way around the park (back to Toontown), then stay on for one more stop and disembark in Tomorrowland. If you have a stroller that cannot go on the train, make a complete circuit on the train without the stroller and then walk from Toontown to Tomorrowland.

20. In Tomorrowland, obtain a FASTPASS for Autopia.

21. Also in Tomorrowland, enjoy a performance of *Honey, I Shrunk the Audience.*

22. After the performance, take the monorail for a round-trip.

23. Return with your FASTPASS to ride Autopia.

24. This concludes the touring plan for Day One. Use any time remaining to revisit favorite attractions, see attractions that were not included in the touring plan, or visit attractions you skipped because the lines were too long. Also, consult your daily entertainment schedule for parades,

Fantasyland Theatre productions, or other live entertainment that might interest you. If the park is open in the evening, consider going back to your hotel for a nap and dinner and returning after 7 p.m. for a parade and *Fantasmic!*.

DAY TWO

1. Arrive 30 to 40 minutes before the official opening time with your admission in hand.

2. Line up in front of entrance gate 13 or 20.

3. When admitted to the park, move quickly to the far end of Main Street. If there is no rope barrier, continue on to Tomorrowland. If the adults and older children want to experience the Space Mountain, ride now, availing yourself of the switching-off option for the younger children.

4. Also in Tomorrowland, ride Buzz Lightyear.

5. Also in Tomorrowland, experience Star Tours.

6. Turn left on exiting Star Tours and proceed to the central hub. From there, enter Fantasyland through the castle.

7. In Fantasyland, ride Dumbo, the Flying Elephant.

8. Backtracking toward the castle, ride Peter Pan's Flight.

9 Exiting Peter Pan to the right, ride Mr. Toad's Wild Ride.

10. Exit Mr. Toad to the right and bear right around the corner to Alice in Wonderland. Ride.

11. After Alice in Wonderland, try the Mad Tea Party next door.

12. Next, ride the Storybook Land Canal Boats, across the walk from the Mad Tea Party.

13. Bear right after the Canal Boats and return to the center of Fantasyland by the castle. Ride the King Arthur Carousel.

14. Across from King Arthur Carousel, experience Pinocchio's Daring Journey (we recommend you skip the nearby Snow White's Scary Adventures).

15. Exit Pinocchio to your left, leave Fantasyland, and go into Frontierland.

16. If you want, ride Big Thunder Mountain, taking advantage of the switching-off option. Use FASTPASS if the wait exceeds 30 minutes.

17. Take a cruise on the *Mark Twain* Riverboat or the Sailing Ship *Columbia*, whichever departs first.

18. Keeping the waterfront on your right, proceed to the rafts for transportation to Tom Sawyer Island. Allow the children to explore the island.

19. Leave Critter Country and pass through New Orleans Square into Adventureland. Explore Tarzan's Treehouse.

20. See the *Enchanted Tiki Birds* show, also in Adventureland.

21. This concludes the touring plan for Day Two. Use any time remaining to revisit favorite attractions, see attractions that were not included in the touring plan, or visit attractions you skipped because the lines were

too long. Also, consult your daily entertainment schedule for parades, Fantasyland Theatre productions, or other live entertainment that might interest you. If the park is open in the evening, consider going back to your hotel for a nap and dinner and returning after 7 p.m. for a parade and *Fantasmic!*.

DISNEYLAND PARK TWO-DAY TOURING PLAN A
FOR DAYTIME TOURING OR FOR WHEN THE PARK CLOSES EARLY

FOR Parties wishing to spread their Disneyland Park visit over two days and parties preferring to tour in the morning.

ASSUMES Willingness to experience all major rides (including roller coasters) and shows.

TIMING The following Two-Day Touring Plan takes advantage of early-morning touring and is the most efficient of all the touring plans for comprehensive touring with the least time lost waiting in line. On each day you should complete the structured part of the plan by 3 p.m. or so. If you are visiting Disneyland Park during a period of the year when the park is open late (after 8 p.m.), you might prefer our Two-Day Touring Plan B, which offers morning touring on one day and late afternoon and evening touring on the other day. Another highly recommended option is to return to your hotel around midafternoon for a well-deserved nap and an early dinner, and to come back to the park by 7:30 or 8 p.m. for the evening parade, fireworks, and live entertainment.

DAY ONE

1. Arrive 30 to 40 minutes before the official opening time.
2. Line up in front of entrance gate 13 or 20.
3. When you are admitted to the park, move quickly to the far end of Main Street. If there is no rope barrier, continue without stopping to Tomorrowland and ride Space Mountain.
4. Ride Buzz Lightyear.
5. Also in Tomorrowland ride Star Tours.
6. Exit Star Tours to the right and then turn left toward the lagoon. Proceed to Fantasyland and ride the Matterhorn Bobsleds.
7. Exit the Bobsleds to your left and ride Alice in Wonderland in Fantasyland, next to the Matterhorn.
8. Continue to move to your left and ride Mr. Toad's Wild Ride.
9. Exit to the left and ride Peter Pan's Flight.
10. Across the street from Peter Pan, ride Snow White's Scary Adventures.
11. On exiting Snow White's Scary Adventures, go next door and ride Pinocchio's Daring Journey.
12. Continuing to your left, proceed to Frontierland and ride the Big Thunder Mountain Railroad. Get a FASTPASS and return later to ride if the wait exceeds 25 minutes.

13. If you are hungry, try Rancho del Zocalo, located across from the entrance to the Big Thunder Mountain Railroad.

14. While in Frontierland, ride the *Mark Twain* Riverboat or the Sailing Ship *Columbia* (whichever departs first).

    Note: At this point check your daily entertainment schedule to see if there are any parades, fireworks, or live performances that interest you. Make note of the times and alter the touring plan accordingly. Since you have already seen all of the attractions for Day One that cause bottlenecks and have big lines, an interruption of the touring plan here will not cause you any problems. Simply pick up where you left off before the parade or show.

15. While in Frontierland, take a raft to Tom Sawyer Island.

16. After you return to the mainland, proceed through New Orleans Square to Adventureland. Tour Tarzan's Treehouse.

17. Exit to your right and see the *Enchanted Tiki Birds* show.

18. Return to Main Street via the central hub. See *Disneyland: The First 50 Years.*

19. This concludes Day One of the touring plan. If you have any energy left, backtrack to pick up attractions you would like to ride again or may have missed or bypassed because the lines were too long. Check out any parades or live performances that interest you. Alternatively, return to your hotel and fall, exhausted, into bed.

DAY TWO

1. Arrive 30 to 40 minutes before the official opening time with your admission in hand.

2. Line up in front of entrance gate 13 or 20.

3. After passing through the turnstiles, continue to the end of Main Street. If there is no rope barrier, move as fast as you can to Adventureland and ride Indiana Jones.

4. Exit Indiana Jones to the left and pass through New Orleans Square to Critter Country. Ride Splash Mountain.

5. While in Critter Country, ride the Many Adventures of Winnie the Pooh.

6. After you ride Winnie the Pooh, leave Critter Country and return to Adventureland. Ride the Jungle Cruise.

7. Exit the Jungle Cruise to the left and go to New Orleans Square. Ride Pirates of the Caribbean.

8. While in New Orleans Square, experience the Haunted Mansion.

9. Returning to New Orleans Square, take the Disneyland Railroad to the Mickey's Toontown/Fantasyland Station, one stop down the line.

10. After you get off the train, bear to your left and cross under the railroad tracks to Mickey's Toontown.

11. In Mickey's Toontown, ride Roger Rabbit's Car Toon Spin. If the wait is prohibitive, obtain a FASTPASS and ride later.

12. If you have children in your party, tour Mickey's House and visit Mickey in his dressing room. Do the same at Minnie's House.

13. Leave Mickey's Toontown the same way you entered. Bear left after passing under the tracks and ride It's a Small World.

14. After It's a Small World, head toward the castle and the heart of Fantasyland. Ride the Storybook Land Canal Boats.

15. Passing between the lagoon and the Matterhorn, proceed to Tomorrowland and catch the Disneyland monorail for a complete round-trip. The loading platform for the monorail is built over the docks for the lagoon. An escalator takes you up to the monorail loading area. If you are hungry, consider getting off the monorail at Downtown Disney for lunch (don't forget to have your hand stamped for re-entry).

16. Return to Tomorrowland on the monorail. In Tomorrowland, see *Honey, I Shrunk the Audience.*

17. This concludes the touring plan. Revisit your favorite attractions, or try any rides and shows you may have missed. Check your daily entertainment schedule for parades or live performances that interest you.

DISNEYLAND PARK TWO-DAY TOURING PLAN B, FOR MORNING AND EVENING TOURING OR FOR WHEN THE PARK IS OPEN LATE

FOR Parties who want to enjoy Disneyland Park at different times of day, including evenings and early mornings.

ASSUMES Willingness to experience all major rides (including roller coasters) and shows.

TIMING This Two-Day Touring Plan is for those visiting Disneyland Park on days when the park is open late (after 8 p.m.). The plan offers morning touring on one day and late afternoon and evening touring on the other day. If the park closes early, or if you prefer to do all of your touring during the morning and early afternoon, use the Two-Day Touring Plan A, for Daytime Touring or for When the Park Closes Early.

DAY ONE

1. Arrive 30 to 40 minutes before the official opening time with your admission in hand.

2. Line up in front of entrance gate 13 or 20. Head directly to Tomorrowland as soon as the park opens and ride Space Mountain.

3. Also in Tomorrowland, experience Buzz Lightyear.

4. Cross into Fantasyland and ride the Matterhorn Bobsleds

5. Proceed to Splash Mountain in Critter Country. Do not use FASTPASS unless the wait exceeds 30 minutes.

6. Also in Critter Country, experience The Many Adventures of Winnie the Pooh.

7. Exit Winnie the Pooh and backtrack to Adventureland. Ride Indiana Jones. Resist the urge to use FASTPASS. Your wait at this time of morning should be 35 minutes or less.

8. Exit Indiana Jones to the right and ride Jungle Cruise, also in Adventureland. If you are a Disneyland veteran and have seen the Jungle Cruise, or if the wait exceeds 20 minutes, skip to Step 9.

9. Ride Alice in Wonderland.

10. Turn left after Alice and proceed to the heart of Fantasyland. Ride Peter Pan's Flight.

11. Depart Fantasyland and enter Frontierland. Ride the Big Thunder Mountain Railroad.

12. Backtrack to New Orleans Square and experience the Haunted Mansion.

13. Exit to the right and ride Pirates of the Caribbean, also in New Orleans Square.

14. Feel free at this time to grab a bite to eat if you're hungry.

15. Check your daily entertainment schedule for the next performance at the Golden Horseshoe Saloon (Frontierland) or the Fantasyland Theatre. Feel free to work a performance at any of the three into the Touring Plan. Be sure to arrive at the theater 20 minutes or so before show time.

16. In New Orleans Square, ride either the Sailing Ship *Columbia* or the *Mark Twain* Riverboat.

17. Return to Adventureland and tour Tarzan's Treehouse.

18. If you're up for something different, try the nearby *Enchanted Tiki Birds*.

19. Return to Main Street via the central hub. See *Disneyland: The First 50 Years*.

20. This concludes the Touring Plan for Day One.

DAY TWO

1. Eat an early dinner and arrive at the park about 5:30 p.m.

2. Go immediately to Tomorrowland and Star Tours. Ride if the wait is 30 minutes or less, otherwise obtain FASTPASSes.

3. Take the Disneyland Railroad from the Tomorrowland Station to the Fantasyland/Mickey's Toontown Station.

4. Pass under the railroad tracks into Mickey's Toontown. Ride Roger Rabbit's Car Toon Spin if the wait is not prohibitive.

5. After checking out Toontown, return to Fantasyland and ride It's A Small World.

   Note: At this point, check your daily entertainment schedule to see if there are any parades, fireworks, or live performances that interest you. Make note of the times and alter the touring plan accordingly. Since you have already seen all of the attractions for Day Two that cause bottlenecks and have big lines, an interruption of the touring plan here will not cause you any problems. Simply pick up where you left off before the parade or show. *Fantasmic!* is rated as not to be missed.

6. Also in Fantasyland, ride the Storybook Land Canal Boats.

7. Proceed to Tomorrowland. See *Honey, I Shrunk the Audience*.

8. Ride Star Tours using your FASTPASS.

9. This concludes Day Two of the touring plan. If you have some time left before closing, backtrack to pick up attractions you may have missed or bypassed because the lines were too long. Check out any parades, fireworks, or live performances that interest you. Grab a bite to eat. Save Main Street until last, since it remains open after the rest of the park closes.

PART FIVE

DISNEY'S CALIFORNIA ADVENTURE

A BRAVE NEW PARK

THE WALT DISNEY COMPANY'S newest American theme park, Disney's California Adventure, held its grand opening on February 8, 2001. Already known as "DCA" among Disneyphiles, the park is a bouquet of contradictions conceived in Fantasyland, starved in utero by corporate Disney, and born into a hostile environment of Disneyland loyalists who believe they've been handed a second-rate theme park. The park is new but full of old technology. Its parts are stunningly beautiful, yet come together awkwardly, failing to compose a handsome whole. And perhaps most lamentable of all, the California theme is impotent by virtue of being all-encompassing.

The history of the park is another of those convoluted tales found only in Robert Ludlum novels and corporate Disney. Southern California Disney fans began clamoring for a second theme park shortly after Epcot opened at Walt Disney World in 1982. Although there was some element of support within the Walt Disney Company, the Disney loyal had to content themselves with rumors and half-promises for two decades while they watched new Disney parks go up in Tokyo, Paris, and Florida. For years, Disney teasingly floated the "Westcot" concept, a California version of Epcot that was always just about to break ground. Whether a matter of procrastination or simply pursuing better opportunities elsewhere, the Walt Disney Company sat on the sidelines while the sleepy community of Anaheim became a sprawling city and property values skyrocketed. By the time Disney emerged from its Westcot fantasy and began to get serious about a second California park, the price tag—not to mention the complexity of integrating such a development into a mature city—was mind-boggling.

Westcot had been billed as a $2- to $3-billion, 100-plus-acre project, so that was what the Disney faithful were expecting when

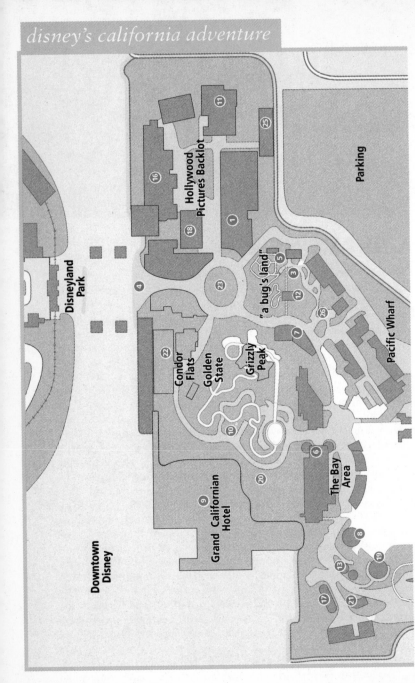

disney's california adventure

Disneyland Park

Hollywood Pictures Backlot

Parking

"a bug's land"

Pacific Wharf

Condor Flats

Golden State

Grizzly Peak

The Bay Area

Grand Californian Hotel

Downtown Disney

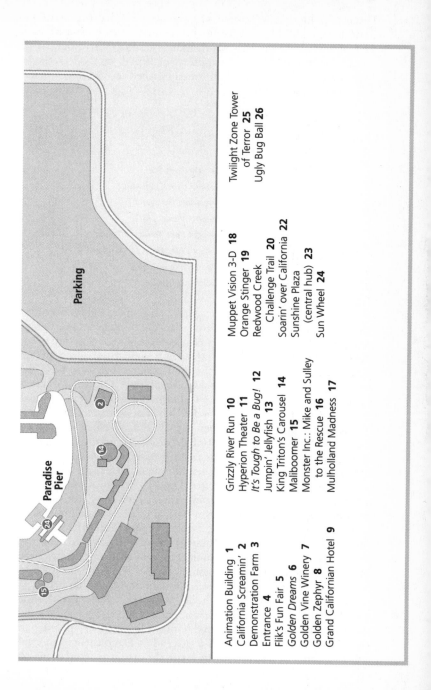

Parking

Paradise
Pier

Animation Building **1**
California Screamin' **2**
Demonstration Farm **3**
Entrance **4**
Flik's Fun Fair **5**
Golden Dreams **6**
Golden Vine Winery **7**
Golden Zephyr **8**
Grand Californian Hotel **9**

Grizzly River Run **10**
Hyperion Theater **11**
It's Tough to Be a Bug! **12**
Jumpin' Jellyfish **13**
King Triton's Carousel **14**
Maliboomer **15**
Monster Inc.: Mike and Sulley
    to the Rescue **16**
Mulholland Madness **17**

Muppet Vision 3-D **18**
Orange Stinger **19**
Redwood Creek
    Challenge Trail **20**
Soarin' over California **22**
Sunshine Plaza
    (central hub) **23**
Sun Wheel **24**

Twilight Zone Tower
    of Terror **25**
Ugly Bug Ball **26**

Disney's California Adventure was announced. What they got was a park that cost $1.4 billion (slashed from an original budget of about $2.1 billion), built on 55 acres including a sizable carve-out for the Grand Californian Hotel. It's quite a small park by modern theme-park standards, but $1.4 billion, when lavished on 55 acres, ought to buy a pretty good park.

Not to Be Missed at Disney's California Adventure

Golden State	**Grizzly River Run**
	Soarin' over California
Hollywood Studios Backlot	**Hyperion Theater**
	Muppet Vision 3-D
	Twilight Zone **Tower of Terror**
	Disney's Aladdin: A Musical Spectacular
Bug's Land	*It's Tough to Be a Bug!*
Paradise Pier	**California Screamin'**

Then there's the park's theme. Although flexible, California Adventure comes off like a default setting, lacking in imagination, weak in concept, and without intrinsic appeal, especially when you stop to consider that two-thirds of Disneyland guests come from Southern California. As further grist for the mill, there's precious little new technology at work in Disney's newest theme park. Of the headliner attractions, only one, Soarin' over California, a simulator ride, breaks new ground. All the rest are recycled, albeit popular, attractions from the Animal Kingdom and Disney-MGM Studios. When you move to the smaller-statured second half of the attraction batting order, it gets worse. Most of these attractions are little more than off-the-shelf midway rides spruced up with a Disney story line and facade.

From a competitive perspective, Disney's California Adventure is an underwhelming shot at Disney's three Southern California competitors. The Hollywood section of DCA takes a hopeful poke at Universal Studios Hollywood, while Paradise Pier offers midway rides à la Six Flags Magic Mountain. Finally, the whole California theme has for years been the eminent domain of Knott's Berry Farm. In short, there's not much originality in DCA, only Disney's now-redundant mantra that "whatever they can do, we can do better."

However, while the Disneyholics churn up cyberspace debating DCA's theme and lamenting what might have been, the rest of us will have some fun getting acquainted with the latest Disney theme park. Our guess is that the park will transcend its bland theme and establish an identity of its own. In any event, the operative word in the new park's name is "Disney," not "California" or "Adventure." Even if the park was called Disney's Slag Heap, the faithful would turn out en masse. Even so, Disney is working hard to placate their core market. The year 2002 saw the addition of Flik's Fun Fair, a modest complex of children's rides and play areas that incorporated the less than enthralling Bountiful Valley Farm. The year 2004, however, was the year the faithful had been waiting for. In the spring of 2004, DCA unveiled its own version of the *Twilight Zone* Tower of Terror, the most incredible attraction Disney has yet to produce. For the Disneyland anniversary celebration in 2005, Block Party Bash, a parade/street show hybrid, and a new dark ride, *Monsters, Inc.:* Mike and Sulley to the Rescue were introduced.

ARRIVING *and*
GETTING ORIENTED

THE ENTRANCE TO Disney's California Adventure faces the entrance to Disneyland Park across a palm-shaded pedestrian plaza called the Esplanade. If you arrive by tram from one of the Disney parking lots, you'll disembark at the Esplanade. Facing east toward Harbor Boulevard, Disneyland Park will be on your left and DCA will be on your right. In the Esplanade are ticket booths, the group sales office, and resort information.

Seen from overhead, Disney's California Adventure is roughly arrayed in a fan shape around the park's central visual icon, Grizzly Peak. At ground level, however, the park's layout is not so obvious. From the Esplanade you pass through huge block letters spelling "California," and through the turnstiles. To your left and right you'll find guest services, as well as some shops and eateries. Among the shops is **Greetings from California,** offering the park's largest selection of Disney trademark merchandise. A second shop of note, **Engine-Ears Toys,** selling upscale toys, creates the impression of stepping into a model train layout. To your right you'll find stroller and wheelchair rental, lockers, restrooms, an ATM machine, and phones.

After passing under a whimsical representation of the Golden Gate Bridge, you arrive at the park's central hub. The hub area is called Sunshine Plaza and is dominated by a fountain fronting an arresting metal sculpture of the sun. In addition to serving as a point of departure for the various theme areas, **Sunshine Plaza** is one of the best places in the park to encounter the Disney characters. With the fountain and golden sun in the background, it's a great photo op.

"Lands" at DCA are called "districts," and there are four of them. A left turn at the hub leads you to the **Hollywood Pictures Backlot** district of the park, celebrating California's history as the film capital of the world. The **Golden State** district of the park is to the right or straight. Golden State is a somewhat amorphous combination of separate theme areas that showcase California's architecture, agriculture, industry, history, and natural resources. Within the Golden State district, you'll find **Condor Flats** by taking the first right as you approach the hub. **Grizzly Peak** will likewise be to your right, though you must walk two-thirds of the way around the mountain to reach its attractions. The remaining two Golden State theme areas, **The Bay Area** and the **Pacific Wharf,** are situated along a kidney-shaped lake and can be accessed by following the walkway emanating from the hub at seven o'clock and winding around Grizzly Peak. A third district, **A Bug's Land,** is situated opposite the **Golden Vine Winery** and can be reached by taking the same route. The fourth district, **Paradise Pier,** recalls seaside amusement parks of the first half of the 20th century. It is situated in the southwest corner of the park, across the lake from The Bay Area.

Park-Opening Procedures

Guests are usually held at the turnstiles until official opening time. On especially busy days guests are admitted to Golden Gateway and Condor Flats 30 minutes before official opening time. Be aware that DCA usually opens at 10 a.m., one or two hours later than Disneyland Park.

HOLLYWOOD PICTURES BACKLOT

HOLLYWOOD PICTURES BACKLOT OFFERS attractions and shopping inspired by California's (and Disney's) contribution to television and the cinema. Visually, the district is themed as a studio backlot with sets, including an urban street scene, soundstages, and a central street with shops and restaurants that depict Hollywood's golden age.

Disney Animation

APPEAL BY AGE	PRESCHOOL ★★★	GRADE SCHOOL ★★★★	TEENS ★★★★
YOUNG ADULTS ★★★★		OVER 30 ★★★★	SENIORS ★★★★

What it is Behind-the-scenes look at Disney animation. **Scope and scale** Major attraction. **When to go** Anytime. **Author's rating** Quite amusing, though not very educational; ★★★★. **Duration of experience** 35–55 minutes. **Probable waiting time** 5 minutes.

DESCRIPTION AND COMMENTS The Disney Animation building houses a total of ten shows, galleries, and interactive exhibits that collectively provide a sort of crash course in animation. Moving from room to room and exhibit to exhibit, you follow the Disney animation process from concept to finished film, with a peek at each of the steps along the way. Throughout, you are surrounded by animation, and sometimes it's even projected above your head and under your feet!

Because DCA's Animation building is not an actual working studio, the attraction does not showcase artists at work on real features, and the interactive exhibits are more whimsical than educational. In one, for example, you can insert your voice into a cartoon character. You get the idea. It takes 40 to 55 minutes to do all the interactive stuff and see everything. Added to the Disney Animation lineup is Turtle Talk with Crush featuring the 152-year-old sea turtle from the Disney/Pixar film *Finding Nemo*. Originally developed for the Living Seas pavilion at Epcot, Turtle Talk with Crush is the first attraction incorporating the technology of real-time animation. Here Crush answers questions, jokes, and makes conversation with guests in real time. The animation is brilliant, and guests of all ages list Crush as their favorite Animation building feature.

TOURING TIPS On entering the Animation Building, you'll step into a lobby where signs mark the entrances of the various exhibits. Start with the Animation Screening Room, followed by Drawn to Animation. Both feature educational films and will provide a good foundation on the animation process that will enhance your appreciation of the other exhibits. Save Turtle Talk with Crush for last. You probably won't experience much waiting for the Disney Animation offerings except on weekends and holidays. Even then, the Animation Building clears out considerably by late afternoon.

Hyperion Theater

APPEAL BY AGE	PRESCHOOL ★★★	GRADE SCHOOL ★★★★	TEENS ★★★★
YOUNG ADULTS ★★★★		OVER 30 ★★★★	SENIORS ★★★★

What it is Venue for live shows. **Scope and scale** Major attraction. **When to go** After experiencing DCA's rides. **Author's rating** Great venue, not to be missed; ★★★★. **Duration of experience** 45 minutes. **Probable waiting time** 30 minutes.

DESCRIPTION AND COMMENTS This 2,000-seat theater is DCA's premiere venue for live productions, many of which are based on Disney-animated films and feature Disney characters. Shows exhibit Broadway quality in every sense, except duration of the presentation, and alone are arguably worth the price of theme-park admission. *Disney's Aladdin—A Musical Spectacular,* was the Hyperion Theater's feature show in 2005 and may well continue through 2006 or longer. A breezy stage version of the Aladdin story, it's by far Hyperion Theater's most accomplished production to date. We rate it not to be missed. In the evening, Hyperion Theater is often used as a separate-admission concert and special-events stage.

TOURING TIPS The lavish productions hosted by the Hyperion Theater are rightly very popular and commonly sell out on busier days. To reduce waiting time, the theater often gives out reserved show tickets at the entrance. The tickets, which work essentially like a FASTPASS, guarantee you a seat at any performance throughout the day as long as you show up 15 to 20 minutes prior to show time. The tickets differ from FAST-PASSes in that they operate separately from the FASTPASS system and do not affect your eligibility to obtain FASTPASSes for other attractions.

The tickets guarantee you a seat, but not an assigned seat. On busier days all of the tickets are distributed by noon or 1 p.m.

Presentations are described, and show times listed, in the park *Times Guide.* The theater is multilevel. Though all seats provide a good line of sight, we recommend sitting on the ground level relatively close to the entrance doors (if possible) to facilitate an easy exit after the performance. Finally, be forewarned that the sound volume for Hyperion Theater productions would give heavy-metal rock concerts a good run for the money.

Monsters, Inc.: Mike and Sulley to the Rescue (opens 2006)

APPEAL BY AGE　　NOT OPEN AT PRESS TIME

Type of attraction Dark ride. **Scope and scale** Major attraction. **When to go** Before 11 a.m. **Author's rating** Not open at press time. **Duration of ride** 3½ minutes. **Average wait in line per 100 people ahead of you** 4 minutes. **Loading speed** Moderate.

DESCRIPTION AND COMMENTS Based on characters and the story from the Disney/Pixar film *Monsters, Inc.,* the ride takes you through child-phobic Monstropolis as Mike and Sulley try to return baby Boo safely to her bedroom. If you haven't seen the film the story line won't make much sense. In a nutshell, a human baby gets loose in a sort of parallel universe populated largely by amusing monsters. Good monsters Mike and Sulley try to return Boo to her home before the bad monsters get their hands on her.

TOURING TIPS This attraction wasn't open when we went to press, but will undoubtedly draw good crowds simply because it's new. We recommend seeing it before 11 a.m. or late in the afternoon. Because it's near several theater attractions it is subject to experiencing a sudden deluge of guests when the theaters disgorge their audiences.

Muppet Vision 3-D

APPEAL BY AGE　PRESCHOOL ★★★★　GRADE SCHOOL ★★★★½　TEENS ★★★★
YOUNG ADULTS ★★★★½　OVER 30 ★★★★½　SENIORS ★★★★½

What it is 3-D movie featuring the Muppets. **Scope and scale** Major attraction. **When to go** Before noon or after 4 p.m. **Special comments** 3-D effects and loud noises frighten many preschoolers. **Author's rating** Must see; ★★★★½. **Duration of presentation** 17 minutes. **Probable waiting time** 20 minutes.

DESCRIPTION AND COMMENTS *Muppet Vision 3-D* provides a total sensory experience, with wild 3-D action augmented by auditory, visual, and tactile special effects. If you're tired and hot, this zany presentation will make you feel brand-new.

TOURING TIPS Although extremely popular, this attraction handles crowds exceedingly well. Your wait should not exceed 20 minutes except on days when the park is jam-packed. Special effects and loud noises may frighten some preschoolers.

Playhouse Disney: Live on Stage

APPEAL BY AGE	PRESCHOOL ★★★★★		GRADE SCHOOL ★★★	TEENS ★★
YOUNG ADULTS ★★★		OVER 30 ★★		SENIORS ★★★

What it is Live show for children. **Scope and scale** Minor attraction. **When to go** Per the daily entertainment schedule. **Author's rating** A must for families with preschoolers; ★★★★. **Duration of presentation** 20 minutes. **Special comments** Audience sits on the floor. **Probable waiting time** 10 minutes.

DESCRIPTION AND COMMENTS The show features characters from the Disney Channel's *Rolie Polie Olie, The Book of Pooh, Bear in the Big Blue House,* and *Stanley.* A simple plot serves as the platform for singing, dancing, some great puppetry, and a great deal of audience participation. The characters, who ooze love and goodness, rally throngs of tots and preschoolers to sing and dance along with them. All the jumping, squirming, and high-stepping is facilitated by having the audience sit on the floor so that kids can spontaneously erupt into motion when the mood strikes. Even for adults without children, it's a treat to watch the tykes rev up. If you have a younger child in your party, all the better: just stand back and let the video roll.

For preschoolers, *Playhouse Disney* will be the highlight of their day, as a Thomasville, North Carolina, mom attests:

Playhouse Disney at MGM was fantastic! My three-year-old loved it. The children danced, sang, and had a great time.

TOURING TIPS The show is headquartered in what was formerly the ABC Soap Opera Bistro restaurant to the right of the entrance to the Hollywood Studios District. Because the tykes just can't get enough, it has become a hot ticket. Show up at least 20 minutes before show time. Once inside, pick a spot on the floor and take a breather until the performance begins.

The Twilight Zone Tower of Terror (FASTPASS)

APPEAL BY AGE	PRESCHOOL ★★★	GRADE SCHOOL ★★★★★	TEENS ★★★★★
YOUNG ADULTS ★★★★★	OVER 30 ★★★★★		SENIORS ★★★★½

What it is Sci-fi-theme indoor thrill ride. **Scope and scale** Super headliner. **When to go** The first 30 minutes the park is open. **Special comments** Must be 40" tall to ride; switching-off option offered. **Author's rating** DCA's best attraction; not to be missed; ★★★★. **Duration of ride** About 4 minutes plus preshow. **Average wait in line per 100 people ahead of you** 4 minutes. **Assumes** All elevators operating. **Loading speed** Moderate.

DESCRIPTION AND COMMENTS The Tower of Terror, opened in the spring of 2004, is a new species of Disney thrill ride, though it borrows elements of The Haunted Mansion at Disneyland Park. The story is that you're touring a once-famous Hollywood hotel gone to ruin. As at Star Tours, the queuing area integrates guests into the adventure as they pass through the hotel's once-opulent public rooms. From the lobby, guests are escorted into the hotel's library, where Rod Serling, speaking on an old black-and-white television, greets the guests and introduces the plot.

The Tower of Terror is a whopper at 13-plus-stories tall. It breaks tradition in terms of visually isolating themed areas, and you can see the entire Studios from atop the tower, but you have to look quick.

The ride vehicle, one of the hotel's service elevators, takes guests to see the haunted hostelry. The tour begins innocuously, but at about the fifth floor things get pretty weird. You have entered the Twilight Zone. Guests are subjected to a full range of special effects as they encounter unexpected horrors and optical illusions. The climax of the adventure occurs when the elevator reaches the 13th floor and the cable snaps.

The big question before DCA's Tower of Terror opened was how will it compare to the Walt Disney World version. As it turns out, the attractions are very similar but definitely not clones. The adventure begins the same way—you pass through the hotel lobby and into the library for the preshow. Following the preshow, you enter the boarding area. Once you're on the elevator, however, the two attractions part company. In the Disney World version, the elevator stops at a couple of floors to reveal some eerie visuals, but then actually moves out of the shaft onto one of the floors. The effects during this brief sojourn are remarkable, and more remarkable still is that you don't know that you've reentered the shaft until the elevator speeds skyward. In the DCA Tower of Terror the elevator never leaves the shaft. The visuals and special effects are equally compelling, but there's never that feeling of disorientation that distinguishes the Florida attraction. The DCA Tower of Terror is more straightforward, therefore, and consequently a little less mysterious. Once the elevator-dropping ensues, both versions are about the same. Regardless which version you try, however, you won't be disappointed.

The Tower has great potential for terrifying young children and rattling more mature visitors. If you have teenagers in your party, use them as experimental probes—if they report back that they really, really liked it, run as fast as you can in the opposite direction. Seriously, avoid assuming this attraction isn't for you. A senior from the United Kingdom tried the Tower of Terror and liked it very much, writing:

I was thankful I read your review of the Tower of Terror, or I would certainly have avoided it. As you say, it is so full of magnificent detail that it is worth riding, even if you don't fancy the drops involved.

TOURING TIPS This one ride is worth your admission to DCA. Because of its height, the Tower is a veritable beacon, visible from outside the park and luring curious guests as soon as they enter. Because of its popularity with school kids, teens, and young adults, you can count on a footrace to the attraction when the park opens. For the foreseeable future, expect the Tower to be mobbed most of the day. If both the Tower of Terror and Soarin' Over California are on your must-see list, race to Soarin' the moment the park opens and ride. Yes, you'll burn a little shoe leather and a few calories too, but you'll save a bundle of time. Next, hoof over to the Tower of Terror and obtain a FASTPASS.

To access the Tower of Terror, bear left from the park entrance into the Hollywood Pictures Backlot. Continue straight to the Hyperion Theater and then turn right. To save time, when you enter the library waiting area, stand in the far back corner across from the door where you entered and at the opposite end of the room from the TV. When the doors to the loading area open, you'll be one of the first admitted.

GOLDEN STATE

THIS DISTRICT CELEBRATES California's cultural, musical, natural, and industrial diversity. The centerpiece of the district is Grizzly Peak—one of the sub-districts within Golden State, and yet another of Disney's famed "mountains" (with "Boulder Bear" at its summit). Surrounding Grizzly Peak are The Bay Area, Golden Vine Winery, Condor Flats, and Pacific Wharf. We've grouped those with attractions below.

THE BAY AREA

CURIOUSLY, IN DCA'S GOLDEN STATE the landmark chosen to represent the Bay Area is the Palace of Fine Arts built for the 1915 Panama Pacific International Expo. Inside you'll find artists and craftsmen busy at their trade, and, of course, ready to sell their creations. The theme area's only attraction is the film *Golden Dreams*.

Golden Dreams

APPEAL BY AGE	PRESCHOOL ★★½	GRADE SCHOOL ★★★★	TEENS ★★★
YOUNG ADULTS ★★★½	OVER 30 ★★★★		SENIORS ★★★★

What it is Film about the history of California. **Scope and scale** Major attraction. **When to go** After experiencing the rides, the *Muppets*, and *Bugs*. **Author's rating** Moving; ★★★½. **Duration of presentation** 17 minutes. **Probable waiting time** 15 minutes.

DESCRIPTION AND COMMENTS Narrated by Whoopi Goldberg, *Golden Dreams* is a nostalgic film about the history of California, recognizing the many different races, ethnicities, and people who contributed to the state's settlement and development. Originally designed to be a multimedia production with moving sets and animatronics similar to *American Adventure* at Epcot, the attraction was hammered by budget cuts and ultimately premiered with only a small (for Disney) arsenal of special effects.

A little heavy on schmaltz (which we *Unofficials* kinda like), *Golden Dreams* is a very sweet brotherhood-of-man flick. For once, Disney refrained from rewriting or overly sanitizing the historic content, and there's enough lightheartedness and humor to make the presentation fun. As a kaleidoscopic overview, it's debatable how much you'll learn about California's past, but you'll feel better (at least we did) for the film's uplifting message.

TOURING TIPS *Golden Dreams'* isolated location makes it a good choice for midday touring. Check it out after the rides, the *Muppets,* and *Bugs. Golden Dreams* was designed to run continuous back-to-back performances. On slow days, however, only a few shows a day are scheduled, and show times, unfortunately, are not listed in the park handout map. To determine performance times, it's necessary to actually go to the theater and eyeball an inconspicuous little sign.

CONDOR FLATS

SITUATED JUST TO THE RIGHT of the central hub, Condor Flats pays homage to California aviation. The pedestrian walkway is marked like a runway and all of the buildings look like airplane hangars. Condor Flats is the home of one of the park's super headliner attractions, Soarin' over California.

Soarin' over California (FASTPASS)

APPEAL BY AGE	PRESCHOOL —	GRADE SCHOOL ★★★★★	TEENS ★★★★½
YOUNG ADULTS ★★★★★		OVER 30 ★★★★★	SENIORS ★★★★

What it is Flight-simulation ride. **Scope and scale** Super headliner. **When to go** The first 30 minutes the park is open, or use FASTPASS. **Special comments** May induce motion sickness; 40" minimum-height requirement; switching off available (see page 107). **Author's rating** The park's best ride; ★★★★½. **Duration of ride** 4½ minutes. **Loading speed** Moderate.

DESCRIPTION AND COMMENTS Once you enter the main theater, you are secured in a seat not unlike those used on inverted roller coasters (where the coaster is suspended from above). Once everyone is in place, the floor drops away and you are suspended with your legs dangling. Thus hung out to dry, you embark on a hangglider tour of California with IMAX-quality images projected below you, and with the simulator moving  your seat in sync with the movie. The IMAX images are well chosen and slap-dab beautiful. Special effects include wind, sound, and even olfactory stimulation. The ride itself is thrilling but perfectly smooth, exciting, and relaxing simultaneously. We think Soarin' over California is a must-see for guests of any age who meet the 40" minimum-height requirement. And yes, seniors we interviewed were crazy about it.

TOURING TIPS Aside from being one of the two truly technologically innovative rides in the park, Soarin' over California also happens to be located near the entrance of the park, thus ensuring heavy traffic all day. It should be your very first attraction in the morning, or alternatively use FASTPASS. If you are among the first through the turnstiles at park opening, sprint to Soarin' over California as fast as your little feet can carry you. If you arrive later and elect to use FASTPASS, obtain your FASTPASS before noon. Later than noon you're likely to get a return period in the hour before the park closes, or worse, find that the day's supply of FASTPASSes is gone. If both Soarin' over California and the Tower of Terror are on your itinerary, sprint to Soarin' the moment the park opens and ride. Next, proceed to the Tower of Terror and obtain a FASTPASS (FASTPASS kiosks open the same time as the attraction). With Tower of Terror FASTPASS in hand, continue to the next attraction on your itinerary.

GOLDEN VINE WINERY

THIS DIMINUITIVE WINERY situated at the base of Grizzly Peak and across from A Bug's Land is the smallest of the Golden State theme areas. It would be a stretch to call it an attraction, much less a theme area.

Golden Vine Winery

APPEAL BY AGE	PRESCHOOL —	GRADE SCHOOL ★½	TEENS ★★½
YOUNG ADULTS ★★★	OVER 30 ★★★		SENIORS ★★★

What it is Infomercial and exhibit about California wines. **Scope and scale** Minor attraction/exhibit. **When to go** Anytime. **Author's rating** Quite informative; ★★★. **Duration of film** 7½ minutes. **Probable waiting time** 15 minutes for film.

DESCRIPTION AND COMMENTS This mission-style complex, squeezed into the side of Grizzly Peak, offers a demonstration vineyard and a short film that is basically an infomercial about wine-making. The rest of the facility, predictably, is occupied by shops, a tasting room, and a restaurant.

TOURING TIPS Save the winery for the end of the day. If there's much of a wait to see the film, leave it for another visit.

GRIZZLY PEAK

GRIZZLY PEAK, a huge mountain shaped like the head of a bear, is home to Grizzly River Run, a whitewater raft ride, and the Redwood Creek Challenge Trail, an outdoor playground for children that resembles an obstacle course.

Grizzly River Run (FASTPASS)

APPEAL BY AGE	PRESCHOOL —	GRADE SCHOOL ★★★★½	TEENS ★★★★½
YOUNG ADULTS ★★★★½	OVER 30 ★★★★½		SENIORS ★★★★½

What it is Whitewater raft ride. **Scope and scale** Super headliner. **When to go** First hour the park is open, or use FASTPASS. **Special comments** You are guaranteed to get wet, and possibly soaked; 42" minimum-height requirement. **Author's rating** Not to be missed; ★★★★½. **Duration of ride** 5½ minutes. **Average wait in line per 100 people ahead of you** 5 minutes. **Loading speed** Moderate.

DESCRIPTION AND COMMENTS Whitewater raft rides have been a hot-weather favorite of theme-park patrons for almost 20 years. The ride consists of an unguided trip down a man-made river in a circular rubber raft, with a platform mounted on top seating six to eight people. The raft essentially floats free in the current and is washed downstream through rapids and waves. Because the river is fairly wide with numerous currents, eddies, and obstacles, there is no telling exactly where the raft will go. Thus, each trip is different and unpredictable. The rafts are circular and a little smaller than those used on most rides of the genre. Because the current can buffet the smaller rafts more effectively, the ride is wilder and wetter.

What distinguishes Grizzly River Run from other theme-park raft rides is Disney's trademark attention to visual detail. Where many raft rides essentially plunge down a concrete ditch, Grizzly River Run winds around and through Grizzly Peak, the park's foremost visual icon, with the great rock bear at the summit. Featuring a 50-foot climb and two drops—including a 22-footer where the raft spins as it descends—the ride flows en route into dark caverns and along the mountain's precipitous side before looping over itself just prior to the final plunge. Although the mountain is visually arresting, Grizzly River Run is pretty much devoid of the animatronics and special effects that embellish Big Thunder Mountain and Splash Mountain.

When Disney opened the Kali River Rapids raft ride at the Animal Kingdom theme park at Walt Disney World, it was roundly criticized (and rightly so) for being a weenie ride. Well, we're here to tell you that Disney learned its lesson. Grizzly River Run is a heart-thumper, one of the best of its genre anywhere. And at five-and-a-half minutes from load to unload, it's also one of the longest. The visuals are outstanding, and the ride is about as good as it gets on a man-made river. While it's true that theme-park raft rides have been around a long time, Grizzly River Run has set a new standard, one we don't expect to be equaled for some time.

TOURING TIPS This attraction is hugely popular, especially on hot summer days. Ride the first hour the park is open, after 4:30 p.m., or use FASTPASS. Make no mistake, you will certainly get wet on this ride. Our recommendation is to wear shorts to the park and bring along a jumbo-sized trash bag, as well as a smaller plastic bag. Before boarding the raft, take off your socks and punch a hole in your jumbo bag for your head. Though you can also cut holes for your arms, you will probably stay drier with your arms inside the bag. Use the smaller plastic bag to wrap around your shoes. If you are worried about mussing your hairdo, bring a third bag for your head.

A Shaker Heights, Ohio, family who adopted our garbage-bag attire, however, discovered that staying dry on a similar attraction at Walt Disney World is not without social consequences:

I must tell you that the Disney cast members and the other people in our raft looked at us like we had just beamed down from Mars. Plus, we didn't cut arm holes in our trash bags because we thought we'd stay drier. Only problem was once we sat down we couldn't fasten our seat belts. The Disney person was quite put out and asked sarcastically whether we needed wetsuits and snorkels. After a lot of wiggling and adjusting and helping each other we finally got belted in and off we went looking like sacks of fertilizer with little heads perched on top. It was very embarrassing, but I must admit that we stayed nice and dry.

If you forgot your plastic bag, ponchos are available at the adjacent Rushin' River Outfitters.

Redwood Creek Challenge Trail and *Magic of Brother Bear* Show

APPEAL BY AGE	PRESCHOOL ★★★★		GRADE SCHOOL ★★★★★	TEENS ★★
YOUNG ADULTS ★★		OVER 30 ★★		SENIORS ★★

What it is Elaborate playground and obstacle course. **Scope and scale** Minor attraction. **When to go** Anytime. **Special comments** 42" minimum-height requirement. **Author's rating** Very well done; ★★★½. **Duration of experience** About 20 minutes, though some kids could stay all day.

DESCRIPTION AND COMMENTS An elaborate maze of rope bridges, log towers, and a cave, the Redwood Creek Challenge Trail is a scout-camp combination of elements from Tarzan's Treehouse and Tom Sawyer Island. Built into and around Grizzly Peak, the Challenge Trail has eye-popping appeal for young adventurers.

The *Magic of Brother Bear* is a sweet children's show about nature, starring the characters Koda and Kenai form the *Brother Bear* film. The show is pretty corny, but the kids eat it up. There's enough subtle humor to keep adults chuckling but the real attraction is watching the younger children interact with the characters. The signage to the tiny amphitheater is nonexistent. To get there, enter the Redwood Challenge Trail and descend the steps on the front left. At the bottom, turn left to the amphitheater.

TOURING TIPS The largest of several children's play areas in the park, and the only one that is both dry (mostly) and offers some shade, the Challenge Trail is the perfect place to let your kids cut loose for a while. Though the Challenge Trail will be crowded, you shouldn't have to wait to get in. Experience it after checking out the better rides and shows. Be aware, however, that the playground is quite large, and that you will not be able to keep your children in sight unless you tag along with them.

▌ A BUG'S LAND

THIS DISTRICT IS DISNEY'S RESPONSE to complaints that DCA lacked appeal for younger children. A Bug's Land incorporates the vestiges of Bountiful Valley Farm, celebrating California's agribusiness, into a bug's eye world of giant objects, children's rides, and the *It's Tough to Be a Bug!* attraction.

Bountiful Valley Demonstration Farm

APPEAL BY AGE	PRESCHOOL ★★★		GRADE SCHOOL ★★	TEENS ★½
YOUNG ADULTS ★★		OVER 30 ★★		SENIORS ★★½

What it is Farming exhibit and playground. **Scope and scale** Minor attraction/exhibit. **When to go** Anytime. **Author's rating** A bit anemic; ★★. **Touring time** About 10 minutes for a comprehensive look.

DESCRIPTION AND COMMENTS This area features demonstration crops, including an orange grove. Sponsored by Caterpillar, the farm includes an exhibit tracing the evolution of land cultivation from primitive methods to today's wonderful, large, Caterpillar tractors. Other features include the opportunity to sit on a Caterpillar tractor, to see a Caterpillar skid-steer loader, and, of course, to purchase "select Caterpillar merchandise and toys." Give me a break. There's also a kid's water-maze play area fashioned from leaking irrigation pipes and sprinklers (I promise I'm not making this up).

TOURING TIPS Check out the farm at your leisure and try not to step on the radishes. If you buy a tractor, have it sent to Package Pick-up to be retrieved when you leave the park.

Flik's Fun Fair

APPEAL BY AGE	PRESCHOOL ★★★★½		GRADE SCHOOL ★★★½	TEENS —
YOUNG ADULTS —		OVER 30 —		SENIORS —

What it is Children's rides and play areas. Scope and scale Minor attraction. When to go Before 11:30 a.m. for the rides; anytime for the play areas. Author's rating Preschool heaven: ★★★½. Touring time About 50 minutes for a comprehensive visit.

DESCRIPTION AND COMMENTS Flik's Fun Fair is a children's park as seen through the eyes of an insect. Children can wander among 20-foot-tall blades of grass, tunnel-sized garden hoses, an enormous anthill, and the like. Kiddie rides include: Flik's Flyers with a balloon-ride theme; a drive-it-yourself car ride called Tuck & Roll's Drive 'Em Buggies; Heimlich's Chew Chew Train, a miniature train ride; and a mini Mad Tea Party ride titled Francis's Ladybug Boogie, where you can spin your own "ladybug."

TOURING TIPS Though colorful and magnetically alluring to the under-eight crowd, all of the rides are low capacity, slow loading, and offer ridiculously brief rides. Our advice is to ride them sequentially before 11 a.m. if you visit on a weekend or during the summer. The play areas, of course, can be enjoyed anytime, but then you're faced with the prospect of the kids caterwauling to get on the rides.

Following is the relevant data on the kiddie rides (note that waiting times are per 50 people ahead of you as opposed to the usual 100 people):

HEIMLICH'S CHEW CHEW TRAIN (train ride)

Special Comments Adults as well as children can ride

Ride Time Almost 2 minutes

Average Wait in Line Per 50 People Ahead of You 5 minutes

TUCK AND ROLL'S DRIVE'EM BUGGIES (bumper cars)

Special Comments Adults as well as children can ride. Cars are much slower than on normal bumper-car rides.

Ride Time Almost 2 minutes

Average Wait in Line Per 50 People Ahead of You 12 minutes

FLIK'S FLYERS (suspended "baskets" swing around a central axis)

Ride Time Almost 1½ minutes

Average Wait in Line Per 50 People Ahead of You 6 minutes

FRANCIS' LADYBUG BOOGIE (children's version of the Mad Tea Party)

    Ride Time **1 minute**

    Average Wait in Line Per 50 People Ahead of You **8 minutes**

It's Tough to Be a Bug!

APPEAL BY AGE	PRESCHOOL ★★★★	GRADE SCHOOL ★★★★½	TEENS ★★★★½
YOUNG ADULTS ★★★★½		OVER 30 ★★★★½	SENIORS ★★★★½

What it is 3-D movie. **Scope and scale** Major attraction. **When to go** After experiencing DCA's better rides. **Special comments** 3-D effects and loud noises frighten many preschoolers. **Author's rating** ★★★★. **Duration of presentation** 8½ minutes. **Probable waiting time** 20 minutes.

DESCRIPTION AND COMMENTS *It's Tough to Be a Bug!* is an uproarious 3-D film about the difficulties of being a very small creature and features some of the characters from the Disney/Pixar film, *A Bug's Life. It's Tough to Be a Bug!* is similar to *Honey, I Shrunk the Audience* at Disneyland Park in that it combines a 3-D film with an arsenal of tactile and visual special effects. In our view, the special effects are a bit overdone and the film somewhat disjointed. Even so, we rate the *Bug* as not to be missed.

TOURING TIPS Because it's situated in one of the sleepier theme areas, *Bug* is not usually under attack from the hordes until late morning. This should make *It's Tough to Be a Bug!* the easiest of the park's top attractions to see.

    Be advised that *It's Tough to Be a Bug!* is very intense and that the special effects will do a number on young children as well as anyone who is squeamish about insects. Check out the following comments from readers who saw *It's Tough to Be a Bug!* at Walt Disney World. First, from a mother of two from Mobile, Alabama:

It's Tough to Be a Bug! was too intense for any kids. Our boys are five and seven and they were scared to death. They love bugs, and they hated this movie. All of the kids in the theater were screaming and crying. I felt like a terrible mother for taking them into this movie. It is billed as a bug movie for kids, but nothing about it is for kids.

But a Williamsville, New York, woman had it even worse:

We almost lost the girls to any further Disney magic due to the 3-D movie It's Tough to Be a Bug! *It was their first Disney experience, and almost their last. The story line was nebulous and difficult to follow—all they were aware of was the torture of sitting in a darkened theater being overrun with bugs. Total chaos, the likes of which I've never experienced, was breaking out around us. The 11-year-old refused to talk for 20 minutes after the fiasco, and the 3-½-year-old wanted to go home—not back to the hotel, but home.*

Most readers, however, loved the *Bugs,* including this mom from Brentwood, Tennessee:

Comments from your readers make It's Tough to Be a Bug! *sound worse than* Alien Encounter. *It's not. It's intense like* Honey, I Shrunk the Audience *but mostly funny. The bugs are cartoon-like instead of realistic and icky, so I can't understand what all the fuss is about. Disney has conditioned us to think of rodents as cute, so kids think nothing of walking up to a mouse the size of a port-a-john, but go nuts over some cartoon bugs. Get a grip!*

Ugly Bug Ball

APPEAL BY AGE	PRESCHOOL ★★★★	GRADE SCHOOL ★★★★	TEENS ★★
YOUNG ADULTS ★★★		OVER 30 ★★★	SENIORS ★★★

What it is Musical stage show about insects. **Scope and scale** Minor attraction. **When to go** Anytime as per the daily entertainment schedule. **Author's rating** A very pleasant surprise; ★★★½. **Duration of presentation** 17 minutes plus autographing session.

DESCRIPTION AND COMMENTS Madame Butterfly offers dancing lessons to prepare the insects and kids for the gala *Ugly Bug Ball* while a curmudgeonly spider gets in the way. Dances the kids learn include the Heimlich Maneuver and the Tarantula Tango. A very clever and witty show, the *Ugly Bug Ball* is as much fun for adults as for kids. In fact, we recommend it to adults without children in their party.

TOURING TIPS The tiny outdoor theater with bench seats is located between the demonstration gardens and Bountiful Valley Farmers Market counter-service restaurant. Shade is limited.

PARADISE PIER

WRAPPED AROUND THE SOUTHERN SHORE of the kidney-shaped lake, Paradise Pier is Disney's version of a seaside amusement park from the first five decades of the 20th century. It covers about one-third of Disney's California Adventure and contains around half of the attractions. Paradise Pier's presence at DCA is ironic, and in a perverse way brings the story of Walt Disney and Disneyland full circle. Walt, you see, created Disneyland Park as an alternative to parks such as this; parks with a carnival atmosphere, simple midway rides, carny games, and amply available wine, beer, and liquor. Amazingly, corporate Disney has made just such a place the centerpiece of Disneyland's sister park, slaughtering in effect one of the last of Walt's sacred cows. Fancy names and window dressing aside, what you'll find on Paradise Pier is a merry-go-round, a Ferris wheel, a roller coaster, a wild mouse, carny games (stacked against you), and beer.

California Screamin' (FASTPASS)

APPEAL BY AGE	PRESCHOOL —	GRADE SCHOOL ★★★★★	TEENS ★★★★½
YOUNG ADULTS ★★★★		OVER 30 ★★★★	SENIORS †

† The number of riding seniors surveyed was too small to derive a rating.

What it is Big, bad roller coaster. **Scope and scale** Super headliner. **When to go** Ride first thing in the morning, or use FASTPASS. **Special comments** May induce motion sickness; 48" minimum-height requirement; switching off available (see page 107). **Author's rating** Long and smooth; ★★★★. **Duration of ride** 2½ minutes. **Loading speed** Moderate to fast.

DESCRIPTION AND COMMENTS This apparently antiquated wooden monster is actually a modern steel coaster, and at 6,800 feet, the second longest in the U.S. California Screamin' gets off to a 0–55 mph start by launching you up the first hill like a jet fighter plane off the deck of a carrier (albeit with different technology). From here you will experience tight turns followed by a second launch sending you over the

crest of a 110-foot hill with a 107-foot drop on the far side. Next, you bank and complete an elliptical loop inside the giant Mickey head visible all over the park. A diving turn followed by a series of camelbacks brings you back to the station. Speakers play a synchronized soundtrack complete with recorded canned screaming.

We were impressed by the length of the course and the smoothness of the ride. From beginning to end, the ride is about 2½ minutes, with 2 minutes of actual ride time. En route the coaster slows enough on curves and on transition hills to let you take in the nice view. On the scary-o-meter, Screamin' is certainly worse than Space Mountain but doesn't really compare with some of the steel coasters at nearby Magic Mountain. What Screamin' loses in fright potential, however, it makes up in variety. Along its course, Disney has placed every known curve, hill, dip, and loop in roller-coaster design.

TOURING TIPS California Screamin' is a serious coaster, a coaster that makes Space Mountain look like Dumbo. Secure any hats, cameras, eyeglasses, or anything else that might be ripped from your person during the ride. Stay away completely if you're prone to motion sickness.

Engineered to run several trains at once, California Screamin' does a better job than any roller coaster we've seen at handling crowds, at least when the attraction is running at full capacity. Recently, presumably because of maintenance and staffing problems, several trains were sidetracked. This turned a well-designed coaster into a mammoth bottleneck. The coaster was sometimes shut down two or more times a day for technical problems. Early in the morning, however, it's usually easy to get two or three rides under your belt in about 15 minutes. Ride in the first hour the park is open or use FASTPASS.

Golden Zephyr

APPEAL BY AGE	PRESCHOOL ★★★½	GRADE SCHOOL ★★★½	TEENS ★★
YOUNG ADULTS ★½		OVER 30 ★½	SENIORS ★½

What it is Zephyrs spinning around a central tower. **Scope and scale** Minor attraction. **When to go** The first 90 minutes the park is open or just before closing. **Special comments** Can't operate on breezy days. **Author's rating** Totally redundant; ★★. **Duration of ride** About 2½ minutes. **Loading speed** Slow.

DESCRIPTION AND COMMENTS First, a zephyr is a term often associated with blimps. On this attraction, the zephyrs look like open-cockpit rockets. In any event, each zephyr holds about a dozen guests and spins around a central axis with enough centrifugal force to lay the zephyr partially on its side. As it turns out, the Golden Zephyrs are very touchy, as zephyrs go: they can't fly in a wind exceeding about 5 mph. Needless to say, the attraction is shut down much of the time.

TOURING TIPS A colorful, beautiful attraction, it is another slow-loading cycle ride. Go during the first hour-and-a-half the park is open or be prepared for a long wait.

Jumpin' Jellyfish

APPEAL BY AGE	PRESCHOOL ★★★	GRADE SCHOOL ★★★	TEENS ★½
YOUNG ADULTS ★★	OVER 30 ★★		SENIORS ★★

What it is Parachute ride. **Scope and scale** Minor attraction. **When to go** The first 90 minutes the park is open or just before closing. **Special comments** Can't operate on breezy days; 40" minimum-height requirement. **Author's rating** All sizzle, no meat; ★★. **Duration of ride** About 45 seconds. **Loading speed** Slow.

DESCRIPTION AND COMMENTS On this ride, you're raised on a cable to the top of the tower and then released to gently parachute back to earth. Mostly a children's ride, Jumpin' Jellyfish is paradoxically off-limits to those who would most enjoy it because of its 40" minimum-height restriction. For adults, the attraction is a real snore. Oops, make that a real bore. . . the paltry 45 seconds duration of the ride is not long enough to fall asleep.

TOURING TIPS The Jellyfish, so called because of a floating jellyfish's resemblance to an open parachute, is another slow-loading ride of very low capacity. Get on early in the morning or be prepared for a long wait.

King Triton's Carousel

APPEAL BY AGE	PRESCHOOL ★★★★	GRADE SCHOOL ★★★	TEENS —
YOUNG ADULTS —	OVER 30 —		SENIORS —

What it is Merry-go-round. **Scope and scale** Minor attraction. **When to go** Before noon. **Author's rating** Beautimus; ★★★. **Duration of ride** A little less than 2 minutes. **Loading speed** Slow.

DESCRIPTION AND COMMENTS On this elaborate and stunningly crafted carousel, dolphins, sea horses, seals, and the like replace the standard prancing horses.

TOURING TIPS Worth a look even if there are no children in your party. If you have kids who want to ride, try to get them on before noon.

Maliboomer

APPEAL BY AGE	PRESCHOOL —	GRADE SCHOOL ★★★½	TEENS ★★★★
YOUNG ADULTS ★★★½		OVER 30 ★★★	SENIORS †

† The number of riding seniors surveyed was too small to derive a rating.

What it is Vertical launch and free-fall thrill ride. **Scope and scale** Major attraction. **When to go** The first hour the park's open. **Special comments** May induce motion sickness; 52″ minimum-height requirement; switching off available (see page 107). **Author's rating** Overrated; ★★½. **Duration of ride** 50 seconds. **Loading speed** Slow.

Motion Sickness WARNING!

DESCRIPTION AND COMMENTS **Maliboomer** consists of three towers that are easy to recognize since they're the tallest structures in the park. It's themed to resemble a giant rendition of the midway test-of-strength booth where you try to ring a bell high atop a pole by hitting a plate on the ground with a sledge-hammer. When you hit the plate, a metal projectile is launched vertically up the shaft towards the bell. Well, on this attraction, you take the place of the metal projectile and are launched up the tower and allowed to free-fall during part of your trip back toward the ground. Naturally, this might leave you feeling like your own bell's been rung.

As it turns out, Maliboomer looks much scarier than it actually is. The launch speed is really quite civilized, though everyone screams for appearance's sake. In fact, there's so much high-decibel screaming on this attraction that Disney installed clear plastic "scream guards" to prevent all the hollering from being broadcast across Anaheim (I promise I'm not making this up). If the launch is so-so, the free fall wins the big-weenie award. The only real adrenalin rush comes from waiting anxiously to be launched. In short, there's not enough bite for a real thrill-ride enthusiast to justify the wait. If you've never experienced similar attractions at other parks, however, Maliboomer will provide a gentle introduction to the genre.

TOURING TIPS Though great fun for those with strong stomachs, this type of ride is an infamously slow loader. Try to ride during the first hour the park is open. Bins are provided to store purses, glasses, and other loose items while you ride. If the wait is long, split up your group and use the singles line.

Mulholland Madness (FASTPASS)

APPEAL BY AGE	PRESCHOOL †	GRADE SCHOOL ★★★½	TEENS ★★★½
YOUNG ADULTS ★★★		OVER 30 ★★★	SENIORS †

† The number of riding preschoolers and seniors surveyed was too small to derive a rating.

What it is Disney version of a wild (or mad) mouse ride. **Scope and scale** Major attraction. **When to go** During the first hour the park's open. **Special comments** May induce motion sickness; 42" minimum-height requirement; switching off available (see page 107). **Author's rating** Space Mountain with the lights on; ★★★. **Duration of ride** About 1½ minutes. **Loading speed** Slow to moderate.

DESCRIPTION AND COMMENTS Themed as a wild drive on the California freeways, Mulholland Madness is a designer wild mouse (sometimes also called "mad mouse"). If you're not familiar with the genre, it's a small, convoluted roller coaster where the track dips and turns unexpectedly, presumably reminding its inventor of a mouse tearing through a maze. To define it more in Disney terms, the ride is similar to Space Mountain, only outdoors and therefore in the light. Mulholland Madness is an off-the-shelf midway ride in which Disney has invested next to nothing in spiffing up. In other words, fun but nothing special.

TOURING TIPS A fun ride, but also a slow-loading one, and one that breaks down frequently. Ride during the first hour the park is open or use FASTPASS.

Orange Stinger

APPEAL BY AGE	PRESCHOOL ★★★	GRADE SCHOOL ★★★	TEENS ★½
YOUNG ADULTS ★★★		OVER 30 ★★	SENIORS ★★

What it is Swings rotating around a central tower. **Scope and scale** Minor attraction. **When to go** The first 90 minutes the park is open or just before closing. **Special comments** 48" minimum-height requirement. **Author's rating** Simple but fun; ★★★. **Duration of ride** Less than 1½ minutes. **Loading speed** Slow.

DESCRIPTION AND COMMENTS On the Orange Stinger you ride swings that look like giant bees. The bees swing in a circle around a central tower and inside of what looks like a partially peeled orange. Ride junkies state that the Orange Stinger has good "footchop," which essentially means that your feet come very close to the enclosing orange. In addition to the footchop, the ride is augmented by loud buzzing (really!). In the scary department, it's a wilder ride than Dumbo, but footchop and frenetic buzzing notwithstanding, the Orange Stinger is still just swings going in circles. Lamentably, the 48" minimum-height restriction precludes those who would most enjoy the attraction from riding.

TOURING TIPS This is a fun and visually appealing ride, but one that loads slowly and occasions long waits unless you wrangle your bee during the first hour or so the park is open. Be aware that it's possible for the swing chairs to collide when the ride comes to a stop. The author picked up a nice bruise when an empty swing smacked him during touchdown.

Sun Wheel

APPEAL BY AGE	PRESCHOOL ★★★	GRADE SCHOOL ★★★	TEENS ★★½
YOUNG ADULTS ★★½		OVER 30 ★★½	SENIORS ★★

What it is Ferris wheel. **Scope and scale** Major attraction. **When to go** The first 90 minutes the park is open or just before closing. **Special comments** May induce motion sickness. **Author's rating** The world's largest chicken coop; ★★. **Duration of ride** 2 minutes. **Loading speed** Slow.

Motion Sickness
WARNING!

DESCRIPTION AND COMMENTS Higher than the Matterhorn attraction at Disneyland Park, this whopper of a Ferris wheel tops out at 150 feet. Absolutely spectacular in appearance, with an enormous sun emblem in the middle of its wheel, the aptly named Sun Wheel offers stunning views in all directions. Unfortunately, however, the view is severely compromised by the steel mesh that completely encloses the passenger compartment. In essence, Disney has created the world's largest revolving chicken coop. As concerns the ride itself, some of the passenger buckets move laterally from side to side across the Sun Wheel in addition to rotating around with the wheel. Because it feels like your bucket has become unattached from the main structure, this lateral movement can be a little disconcerting if you aren't expecting it.

TOURING TIPS Ferris wheels are the most slow-loading of all cycle rides. Thus, we were very curious to see how the loading and unloading of the Sun Wheel is engineered. The Sun Wheel has a platform that allows three compartments to be loaded at once. The lateral sliding buckets are loaded from the two outside platforms, while the stationary compartments are loaded from the middle platform. Loading the entire wheel takes about 6½ minutes, following which the Sun Wheel rotates for a two-minute ride. And speaking of the ride, the Sun Wheel rotates so slowly that the wonderful rising and falling sensations of the garden-variety Ferris Wheel are completely absent. For our money, the Sun Wheel is beautiful to behold but terribly boring to ride. If you decide to give it a whirl, ride the first hour the park is open or in the hour before the park closes.

S. S. Rustworthy

APPEAL BY AGE	PRESCHOOL ★★★	GRADE SCHOOL ★★★	TEENS —
YOUNG ADULTS —	OVER 30 —		SENIORS —

What it is Wet play area. **Scope and scale** Minor attraction. **When to go** Anytime. **Special comments** Children will get drenched. **Author's rating** Small but effective; ★★★.

DESCRIPTION AND COMMENTS A rusty shipwreck (supposedly on the bottom of the sea) surrounded by giant starfish, clams, and other sea creatures, as well as by fountains that randomly erupt, squirt, and spray. Children pretend to avoid being squirted while contriving to get as wet as possible without drowning.

TOURING TIPS Your kids will want to cavort on the *S. S. Rustworthy* even if the weather is cool. Be prepared to set some limits or alternatively to carry some dry clothes.

PARADES *and* LIVE ENTERTAINMENT

AFTERNOON AND EVENING PARADES The afternoon parade has been usurped during the Disneyland anniversary celebration by the Block Party Bash described below. The evening parade is a reincarnation of the Main Street Electrical Parade from Disneyland Park.

The good news is that both the Block Party Bash and evening parades are good shows. The afternoon event makes up in color and enthusiasm what it lacks in coherence. And the evening Electrical Parade? Well, it's been a surefire winner for decades, featuring billions of itty-bitty lights, lots of floats, and a battalion of Disney characters. The parade route runs from a gate to the left of the Pizza Oom Mow Mow restaurant at Paradise Pier, through The Bay Area, around A Bug's Land side of Grizzly Peak, and on to Sunshine Plaza, where it takes a lap around the fountain and then disappears backstage near Playhouse Disney. On days when the crowds are light, any place along the parade route will suffice. On days of heavy attendance, try to score a viewing spot on the elevated courtyard or steps of the Golden Vine Winery.

The parade route jams pedestrian traffic throughout the park, essentially trapping you in place until the parade passes. If you don't intend to watch the parade, get situated wherever you want to be before it starts. Disney cast members will be able to tell you in which direction the parade will run.

BLOCK PARTY BASH This street festivity is DCA's main event in the Disneyland 50th anniversary celebration. The Bash consists of highly orchestrated "spontaneous" street parties that erupt around the park. Each party includes music (some live), dancing, and novel street entertainment. Featuring 26 characters from Disney/Pixar films *Toy*

Story, Monsters Inc., A Bug's Life, and *The Incredibles,* the Block Party Bash is three parts interactive shows and one part parade. Usually starting at Paradise Pier with the improbable gang of green army men, giant marching orange highway cones, alphabet blocks (the "block" party part), 60 dancers, 16 acrobats, 12 pairs of "jumping" stilts, three large floats, and the Pixar characters, the Bash stops for three 11-minute shows along its route. Each time it cranks up, pretty much everyone within 50 yards is sucked into the mayhem (when's the last time you danced with a highway cone?). Of the three performance stops, Golden State Park across from Paradise Pier and Sunshine Plaza near the park's entrance offer the best viewing and most elbow room. The third stop is at the entrance to A Bug's Land.

HYPERION THEATER A state-of the-art theater that is the venue for the best of DCA's live shows, as well as for special concerts and events. Check the daily entertainment schedule in the handout park map to see what's playing and for show times.

HOLLYWOOD BACKLOT STAGE This open-air stage features top-notch improv comedy. It's one of our favorite venues in the park.

PACIFIC WHARF STAGE A small outdoor stage that features live rock, country, and pop music. Check the daily entertainment schedule to see who's playing.

"THE MAGIC OF BROTHER BEAR" TOTEM CEREMONY Storytelling at the Redwood Creek Challenge Trail across from Grizzly Mountain.

STREET ENTERTAINMENT Mobile rock bands (on flatbed trailers and woody wagons), acrobats, and comedy sketches on the Hollywood Pictures Backlot are part of the scheduled street entertainment. Unlike at Disneyland Park where street entertainers appear on a more or less impromptu basis, most of DCA's street acts operate according to a specific performance schedule listed on the back of the park handout map.

DISNEY CHARACTERS Character appearances are listed in the daily entertainment schedule. In addition, Flik and Atta can usually be found at A Bug's Land, Chip 'n' Dale hang out around the Redwood Challenge Trail, Cruella De Vil makes appearances in the Hollywood Pictures Backlot, and Ariel's Grotto restaurant at Paradise Pier offers character dining featuring Captain Mickey and friends.

TRAFFIC PATTERNS AT DISNEY'S CALIFORNIA ADVENTURE

ONE OF THE PROBLEMS Disney had at DCA early on was that there was no traffic to create patterns. Attendance figures were far less than projected, though guests on hand did stack up daily at Soarin' over California and Grizzly River Run. On the relatively few crowded days (mostly weekends), the park didn't handle crowds particularly well. If Disney's gate projections had panned out, the park would have been in gridlock much of the time. The year 2005 was better, thanks primarily to the new *Twilight Zone* Tower of Terror.

If you happen to hit DCA on a day of high attendance, here's what to expect. A high percentage of the early morning arrivals will beat feet directly to the Tower of Terror and/or Soarin' over California and then continue (on warmer days) to Grizzly River Run. When the Tower of Terror opened in 2004 it instantly became the park's biggest draw and relieved much of the pressure on Soarin' over California and Grizzly River Run. Other than the Tower of Terror, the Hollywood Pictures Backlot is deserted, as are Golden State Winery, Pacific Wharf, A Bug's Land, and The Bay Area until midmorning. As the lines build at Tower, Soarin', and Grizzly, and as guests begin opting for FASTPASSes at these attractions, the crowd begins working its way into Paradise Pier. California Screamin' sees its share of traffic as locals in the know arrive to beat the crowd at the coaster and at the slow-loading cycle rides at Paradise Pier. By late morning on a busy day, you'll find sizable lines at most of DCA's rides. By noon or earlier, the ride queues are substantial and the crowds redistribute to the park's shows. Playhouse Disney, *Muppet Vision,* and the Hyperion Theater draw good-sized crowds. By 2 p.m. the whole park is fairly socked in with guests, and even minor attractions and displays like the sourdough-bread and tortilla-baking demonstrations build lines. Park departures increase significantly after 3 p.m., with lots of Park Hopper and Annual Pass holders heading over to Disneyland Park. By the dinner hour, crowds at DCA have thinned appreciably. As closing time approaches, long lines are found only at the park's premier attractions. During our research visits there was no daily capstone event at DCA comparable to *Fantasmic!* and the fireworks at Disneyland Park. When DCA offers a capstone event, the bulk of the evening crowd will depart at the conclusion of the show. During our visits, the largest wave of departing guests occurred following the Electrical Parade. Just before closing, crowd levels are thin except, of course, at Soarin' over California and the Tower of Terror.

DISNEY'S CALIFORNIA ADVENTURE ONE-DAY TOURING PLAN

Before You Go

1. Buy your admission in advance (see page 17).
2. Call ☎ 714-781-7290 the day before your visit for the park's official opening time.

At the Park

This touring plan assumes a willingness to experience all rides and shows. If the plan calls for you to experience an attraction that does not interest you, simply skip it and proceed with the plan. Height and age requirements apply to many attractions. If you have children who are not eligible to ride, avail yourself of the switching-off option. This touring plan includes most of the amusement park rides on Paradise Pier. If you're short on time or wish to allocate more of the day to DCA's theater attractions, consider foregoing a few of the slow-loading rides

1. Arrive at the entrance turnstiles with admission in hand 30 minutes before official opening time.

2. Bear right after entering the park to Condor Flats. Ride Soarin'. Do not use FASTPASS.

3. Retracing your steps toward the park entrance, enter the Hollywood Studios Backlot and proceed to the Tower of Terror. Obtain FAST-PASSes. The FASTPASSes will be honored from the beginning of the return window until park closing.

4. In the Hollywood Studios Backlot, ride *Monsters, Inc.: Mike and Sulley to the Rescue* (opens 2006).

5. Proceed back through Condor Flats and beyond to the Grizzly River Run. Either ride or obtain a FASTPASS. Usually Grizzly River Run's FASTPASS machines are not hooked up to the park's FASTPASS system. This means that you will be issued a FASTPASS even though you're currently holding one for the Tower of Terror.

6. Continue on to the California Screamin' roller coaster on the far side of the lake in the Paradise Pier section of the park. Ride. Feel free to ride the coaster a second or third time if the waiting times are short.

7. Bear left on exiting and continue around the lake to Mulholland Madness. Do not use FASTPASS.

8. Across the plaza from Mulholland Madness, ride the Sun Wheel.

9. Backtracking with the lake on your right, proceed next to the Orange Stinger and ride.

10. Continuing back toward the roller coaster, ride the Golden Zephyr.

11. If your party includes small children, ride King Triton's Carousel.

12. Departing Paradise Pier, stop in the San Francisco area and check out the show times for *Golden Dreams* starring Whoopi Goldberg. Interrupt the touring plan to return and see the show if it's on your do-list.

13. You may remember from our coverage of FASTPASS that you can obtain a second FASTPASS anytime after the return window on your first FAST-PASS begins. So head back to Grizzly River Run if you elected to skip it earlier. Go ahead and ride if the wait is 30 minutes or less. Otherwise obtain FASTPASSes.

14. Head back toward the lake and turn left keeping Grizzly Peak on your left side. Proceed to A Bug's Land. See *It's Tough To Be A Bug*.

15. Also in A Bug's Land, try the kiddie rides at Flik's Fun Fair, if there are small children in your party. Check the *Times Guide* for scheduled performances of *Ugly Bug Ball*.

16. Turn right on exiting A Bug's Land and return to the Hollywood Studios Backlot. Ride *Monsters, Inc.* From this point on, feel free to interrupt the touring plan for lunch or a snack.

17. There are three excellent shows in the Hollywood Pictures Backlot district: *Playhouse Disney: Live on Stage,* whatever the current show is at the Hyperion Theater, and *Muppet Vision 3-D. Muppet Vision 3-D* runs back-to-back shows all day, but the other presentations offer a limited number of performances with show times listed in the park *Times Guide.* The Hyperion Theater should be on everyone's itinerary. *Playhouse Disney: Live on Stage* is an absolute must for families with children seven years and younger, but is expendable for groups of adults or older children.

    What you want to do at this point, using the entertainment schedule in the *Times Guide,* is to work out a plan for seeing the shows that interest you. We suggest making the excellent Hyperion Theater production your top priority. Find the next scheduled performance and plan to be there, arriving 20 to 30 minutes prior to show time. Between arriving early, getting seated, seeing the 40-minute show, and exiting, allocate about an hour and 15 minutes altogether for this activity.

    Once you determine the specific Hyperion Theater performance you'll attend (and know what time you have to be there and when you'll be done), you can develop a schedule for seeing the other presentations. As concerns the other shows, allocate 30 to 35 minutes for *Muppet Vision* and 45 to 55 minutes for *Playhouse Disney.* You don't have to worry about arriving early for the *Muppets* because the show runs continuously back-to-back.

    If you have time gaps in your schedule (once you've got everything sorted out), you can use the gaps to tour the Animation Building. If you have a big gap, say 45 minutes, you can use it to ride Tower of Terror and Grizzly River Run utilizing the FASTPASSes you obtained earlier. Remember that the return window printed on the FASTPASS is only a preferred time. The FASTPASS is good from the beginning of the time window until park closing.

18. Return to Golden State and visit any of the minor attractions, including the film about winemaking at the winery, and tortilla- and bread-making demonstrations on Pacific Wharf. See *Golden Dreams* in the San Francisco area if you missed it earlier.

19. If you have children, let them take a crack at the Redwood Creek Challenge Trail near Grizzly River Run and the fountain playground nearby in Paradise Pier.

20. This concludes the touring plan. Check your daily entertainment schedule for parades, live performances, fireworks, and special events. Adjust the remainder of your visit accordingly. Drop by the Animation Building in Hollywood on your way out of the park if you missed some of the exhibits earlier in the day.

PART SIX

UNIVERSAL STUDIOS HOLLYWOOD

UNIVERSAL STUDIOS HOLLYWOOD WAS THE FIRST film and television studio to turn part of its facility into a modern theme park. By integrating shows and rides with behind-the-scenes presentations on movie-making, Universal Studios Hollywood created a new genre of theme park, stimulating in the process a number of clone and competitor parks. First came the Disney-MGM Studios at Walt Disney World, followed shortly by Universal Studios Florida, also near Orlando. Where Universal Studios Hollywood, however, evolved from an established film and television venue, its cross-country imitators were launched primarily as theme parks, albeit with some production capability on the side. Disney is also challenging Universal in California with Disney's California Adventure. The new park, adjacent to Disneyland Park, does not have production facilities, but one of its theme areas focuses on Hollywood and the movies.

Located just off US 101 north of Hollywood, Universal Studios operates on a scale and with a quality standard rivaled only by Disney, SeaWorld, and Busch parks. Unique among American theme parks for its topography, Universal Studios Hollywood is tucked on top of, below, and around a tall hill that in many states would pass for a mountain. The studios are divided into an open-access area and a controlled-access area. The controlled-access area contains the working soundstages, backlot, wardrobe, scenery, prop shops, postproduction, and administration. Guests can visit the controlled-access area only by taking the Studio Tour. The open-access area, which contains the park's rides, shows, restaurants, and services, is divided into two sections. The main entrance provides access to the upper section, the Upper Lot, on top of the hill. Seven theater shows and one ride, as well as the loading area for the Studio Tour, are located in the Upper Lot. The Lower Lot, at the northeastern base of the hill, is accessible from the Upper Lot via escalators. There are two rides, two shows, and walk-through exhibits in the Lower Lot. All attractions, including rides, shows, tours, and exhibits, are fully profiled in the section "Universal Studios Hollywood Attractions."

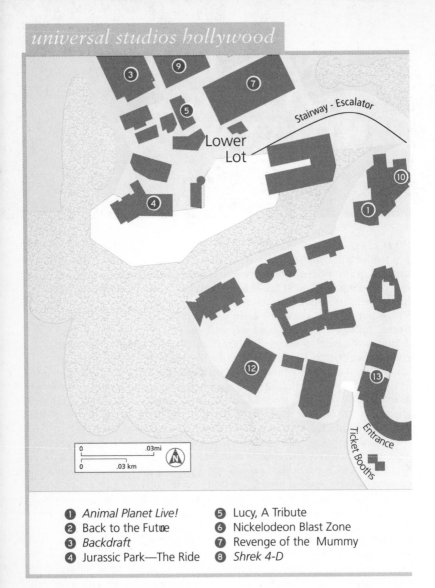

universal studios hollywood

Stairway - Escalator

Lower Lot

Entrance

Ticket Booths

0   .03mi
0   .03 km
N

❶ *Animal Planet Live!*   ❺ Lucy, A Tribute
❷ Back to the Future   ❻ Nickelodeon Blast Zone
❸ *Backdraft*   ❼ Revenge of the Mummy
❹ Jurassic Park—The Ride   ❽ *Shrek 4-D*

The park offers all standard services and amenities, including stroller and wheelchair rental, lockers, diaper-changing and infant-nursing facilities, car assistance, and foreign language assistance. Most of the park is accessible to disabled guests, and TDDs are available for the hearing-impaired. Almost all services are in the Upper Lot, just inside the main entrance.

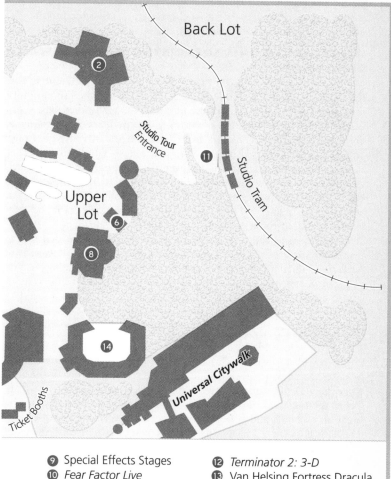

⑨ Special Effects Stages
⑩ *Fear Factor Live*
⑪ Studio Tour

⑫ *Terminator 2: 3-D*
⑬ Van Helsing Fortress Dracula
⑭ *Waterworld*

GATHERING INFORMATION

THE MAIN UNIVERSAL STUDIOS information number is ☎ 818-622-3801. Calling this number, however, often results in up to 20 minutes of holding time or about 7 minutes on hold followed by a disconnect. If you have problems, try calling ☎ 818-622-3735 or 818-622-3750. While Universal Studios' Web site at **www.universalstudioshollywood.**

com is easy to navigate, obtaining information over the phone would try the patience of Buddha. For all three numbers listed, a recording recites the park's operating hours for every day of the month (!!!) before you're offered a menu to choose from. To short circuit the interminable operating-hours litany, dial 4.

WHAT MAKES UNIVERSAL STUDIOS HOLLYWOOD DIFFERENT

WHAT MAKES UNIVERSAL STUDIOS HOLLYWOOD different is that the attractions, with a couple of exceptions, are designed to minimize long waits in line. The centerpiece of the Universal Studios experience is the Studio Tour. While on the tram, you experience an earthquake, are attacked by the killer shark from *Jaws,* are grabbed by King Kong, and endure a simulated rain shower and a flash flood, among other things. In other parks, including Universal's sister park in Florida, each of these spectacles is presented as an individual attraction, and each has its own long queue. At Universal Studios Hollywood, by contrast, you suffer only one very manageable wait to board the tram and then experience all of these events as part of the tour.

In addition to the time savings and convenience provided by the tram tour, most of the live shows at Universal Studios Hollywood are performed in large theaters or stadiums. Instead of standing in line outside, guests are usually invited to enter the theater and wait in seated comfort for the production to begin.

TIMING *your* VISIT

CROWDS ARE LARGEST IN THE SUMMER (Memorial Day through Labor Day) and during specific holiday periods during the rest of the year. Christmas Day through New Year's Day is extremely busy, as are Thanksgiving weekend, the week of Washington's Birthday, spring break for schools and colleges, and the two weeks bracketing Easter. The least busy time is from after Thanksgiving weekend until the week before Christmas. The next slowest times are September through the weekend preceding Thanksgiving, January 4th through the first week of March, and the week following Easter to Memorial Day weekend.

SELECTING THE DAY OF THE WEEK FOR YOUR VISIT

WEEKENDS ARE MORE CROWDED than weekdays year-round. Saturday is the busiest day. Sunday, particularly Sunday morning, is the best bet if you have to go on a weekend, but it is still extremely busy. During the summer, Friday is very busy; Monday, Wednesday, and Thursday are usually less so; Tuesday is normally the slowest of all. During the off-season (September through May, holidays excepted), Tuesday is usually the least-crowded day, followed by Thursday.

HOW MUCH TIME TO ALLOCATE

ALTHOUGH THERE'S A LOT TO SEE and do at Universal Studios Hollywood, you can (unlike at Disneyland) complete a comprehensive tour in one day. If you follow our touring plan, which calls for being on hand at park opening, you should be able to check out everything by mid- to late afternoon, even on a crowded day.

ENDURANCE LEVELS

NEVER MIND that Universal Studios Hollywood claims to cover 400 acres; the area you will have to traverse on foot is considerably smaller. In fact, you will do much less walking and, miracle of miracles, much less standing in line at Universal Studios Hollywood than at Disneyland.

COST

ONE-DAY TICKETS ARE AVAILABLE for about $53 for adults, about $43 for children ages 3 to 9, and about $50 for seniors age 60 and over. For $99 (adults and children) you can obtain a Front of Line Pass that allows you to skip right to the front of the line at all attractions. Discounts in the neighborhood of 11% are often available if you buy your passes on the Universal Web site. Moreover, you can print tickets purchased on the Universal Web site and thereby eliminate any waiting associated with buying your admission at the park ticket kiosks. In 2005 Universal ran a special where you could upgrade your one-day admission to a pass that would be good for the remainder of the calendar year. The cost of the upgrade was $36 with no blackout dates or $10 with about 25 blackout dates. The cut-off date for purchasing the upgrade was July 31st. Universal was unsure at press time whether they'd repeat the offer in 2006.

You can count on being able to see all you want in a single day, even during the busier times of year. In addition to the Web site discounts, admission discounts are sometimes offered in area freebie publications available in hotels. Admission discounts are also periodically offered to AAA members. Vacation packages including lodging and park admission are available from Hilton and Sheraton hotels, both of which offer accommodations close to the studios.

For avid fans, Universal offers several annual passes. Ranging in cost from around $79 to $129 the main differences are free parking and no blackout dates with the pricier passes. For more information see the Universal Web site of call ☎ 808-309-9625.

In a groundbreaking initiative, Universal Studios Hollywood became the first major theme park to offer a guaranteed rain check. If it rains more than one-eighth of an inch, Universal will issue you a rain check good for 30 days.

ARRIVING *and*
GETTING ORIENTED

MOST FOLKS ACCESS UNIVERSAL STUDIOS by taking US 101, also called the Hollywood Freeway, and following the signs to the park. If the freeway is gridlocked, you can also get to the Studios by taking Cahuenga Boulevard and then turning north toward Lankershim Boulevard. If you are coming from Burbank, take Barham Boulevard toward US 101, and then follow the signs.

Universal Studios has a big, multilevel parking garage at the top of the hill. Signs directing you to the garage are a bit confusing, so pay attention and stay to the far right when you come up the hill. Even after you have made it to the pay booth and shelled out $10 to park (and that's $15 if your RV is over 15 feet long), it is still not exactly clear where you go next. Drive slowly, follow other cars proceeding from the pay booths, and avoid turns onto ramps marked "Exit." You may become a bit disoriented, but ultimately you will blunder into the garage. Once parked, make a note of your parking level and the location of your space.

Walk toward the opposite end of the garage from where you entered and exit into Universal CityWalk, a shopping, dining, and entertainment complex (no admission required) situated between the parking structure and the main entrance of the park. As an aside, CityWalk is much like Downtown Disney at Disneyland. Some of Universal's better restaurants and more interesting shops are at City-Walk, and it's so close to the theme-park entrance that you can conveniently pop out of the park to grab a bite (don't forget to have your hand stamped for re-entry).

The Universal Studios ticket booths and turnstiles are about 100 yards from the main parking garage. If you need cash, an ATM is located outside and to the right of the main entrance. Nearby is a guest services window. As you enter the park be sure to pick up a park map and a daily entertainment schedule.

THE UPPER LOT

THE UPPER LOT IS ESSENTIALLY a large, amorphous pedestrian plaza. The freebie park map shows a number of street names such as New York Street and Baker Street, and place names like Cape Cod and Moulin Rouge, but on foot these theme distinctions are largely lost and placement of buildings appears almost random. In other words, do not expect the sort of thematic integrity that you find at Disneyland.

Inside the main entrance, stroller and wheelchair rentals are on the right, as are rental lockers. Straight ahead is a TV Audience Ticket Booth, where you can obtain free tickets to join the audience for any TV shows that are taping during your visit (subject to availability).

Attractions in the Upper Lot are situated around the perimeter of the plaza. If you picture an imaginary clock with the main entrance at 6 o'clock, then *Animal Planet Live!* is at 10 o'clock, *Fear Factor Live* at 11 o'clock, Back to the Future: The Ride at 12 o'clock, the Studio Tour at 1 o'clock, *Shrek 4-D* at 3 o'clock, and *Waterworld* at 5 o'clock. Between *Fear Factor Live* and Back to the Future (11 and 12 o'clock) are the escalators and stairs that lead to the Lower Lot. The Upper Lot attractions are described in detail below.

THE LOWER LOT

THE LOWER LOT IS ONLY accessible via the escalators and stairs descending from the back left section of the Upper Lot. Configured roughly in the shape of the letter T, the Lower Lot is home to Jurassic Park: The Ride, currently one of the headliner attractions at Universal Studios Hollywood. Stepping off the escalator, Jurassic Park is straight ahead. A hard right brings you to The Revenge of the Mummy; moving down the stem of the T, Lucy: A Tribute is on your left—both are walk-through, interactive exhibits. At the base of the T are two theater attractions. To your left is *Backdraft,* and to your right, the Special Effects Stages. The Lower Lot attractions are described below, following the Upper Lot attractions.

UNIVERSAL STUDIOS HOLLYWOOD ATTRACTIONS

UPPER LOT ATTRACTIONS

Animal Planet Live!

What it is Trained-animals stadium performance. **Scope and scale** Major attraction. **When to go** After you have experienced all rides. **Author's rating** Warm and delightful; ★★★½. **Duration of presentation** 20 minutes. **Probable waiting time** 15 minutes.

DESCRIPTION AND COMMENTS   *Animal Planet Live!* features various animals, including some rescued from shelters, demonstrating behaviors that animals often perform in the making of motion pictures. The live presentation is punctuated by clips from Animal Planet television shows. Of course, the animals often exhibit an independence that frustrates their trainers while delighting the audience.

TOURING TIPS   Presented five or more times daily, the program's schedule is in the daily entertainment guide. Go when it's convenient for you; queue about 15 minutes before show time.

Back to the Future: The Ride

APPEAL BY AGE	PRESCHOOL —	GRADE SCHOOL ★★★★★	TEENS ★★★★★
YOUNG ADULTS ★★★★		OVER 30 ★★★★	SENIORS ★★½

What it is Flight-simulator thrill ride. **Scope and scale** Super headliner. **When to go** First thing in the morning. **Special comments** Very rough ride; may induce motion sickness; must be 40" tall to ride; switching off available (page 107). **Author's rating** Not to be missed, if you have a strong stomach; ★★★★★. **Duration of ride** 4½ minutes. **Loading speed** Moderate.

Motion Sickness

WARNING!

DESCRIPTION AND COMMENTS Guests in Doc Brown's lab get caught up in a high-speed chase through time that spans a million years. An extremely intense simulator ride, Back to the Future is similar to Star Tours at Disneyland Park, but it is much rougher and jerkier. Though the story doesn't make much sense, the visual effects are wild and powerful. The vehicles (Delorean time machines) in Back to the Future are much smaller than those of Star Tours, so the ride feels more personal and less like a group experience.

In a survey of tourists who had experienced simulator rides in Universal Studios and Disneyland Park, riders age 34 and under preferred Back to the Future to the Disney attraction by a 7:5 margin. Older riders, however, stated a 2:1 preference for Star Tours over Back to the Future. The remarks of a woman from Mount Holly, New Jersey, are typical:

Our favorite [overall] attraction was Back to the Future at Universal. Comparing it to Star Tours, it was more realistic because the screen surrounds you.

Most guests also find Back to the Future wilder than its Disney cousins. A Michigan woman writes:

Back to the Future was off the charts on the scary-o-meter. It made Splash and Big Thunder Mountains seem like carnival kiddie rides.

An English woman from Fleet Hants, who was tired of being jerked around, finally got mad:

The simulators were fun, but they do seem to go out of their way to jerk you about, and the Back to the Future one was SO jerky that it made me quite angry.

A man from Evansville, Indiana, reminds us that Back to the Future can humble even the most intrepid:

The Back to the Future ride at Universal was very rough, and we are members of a roller-coaster club. We have seldom experienced such a rough ride and have ridden over 300 coasters. If it was too strong for us, we shudder to think about mere mortals.

Because the height requirement on Back to the Future has been lowered from 46" to 40", younger children are riding. Many of them require preparation. A Virginia mother suggests:

The five-year-old was apprehensive about the ride, but he liked it a lot. We assured him ahead of time that 1) it's only a movie, and 2) the car doesn't actually go anywhere, just shakes around. This seemed to increase his ability to enjoy that ride (rather than taking all the fun out of it).

TOURING TIPS As soon as the park opens, ride Revenge of the Mummy and Jurassic Park in the Lower Lot and then return to the Upper Lot for Back to the Future. *Note:* Sitting in the rear seat of the car makes the ride more realistic.

Fear Factor Live

APPEAL BY AGE	PRESCHOOL ★	GRADE SCHOOL ★★★★	TEENS ★★★★
YOUNG ADULTS ★★★½		OVER 30 ★★★½	SENIORS ★★★

What it is Live version of the gross-out stunt television show on NBC. **Scope and scale** Headliner. **When to go** Six to eight shows daily; crowds are smallest at the first and second-to-last shows. **Author's rating** Great fun if you love the TV show; ★★★.

DESCRIPTION AND COMMENTS In each show, park guests compete against each other in several extreme stunts. The stunts—like drinking bug smoothies, scaling tall walls, and swimming in a tank full of eels—were developed with help from the brains (?) behind the NBC television show *Fear Factor,* and are no less creepy than the ones you see on TV.

The primary contestants, screened and chosen in advance, compete for prizes by performing three different elimination stunts. In between these stunts are two mini-stunts with contestants chosen from the audience.

If you don't want to be onstage, you can still play an interactive role in the audience by controlling cannons that blast contestants with water, air and other such things (like hard rubber balls. . . ouch!). Prepare to be grossed out—parts of this show are not for the faint of heart or anyone with a weak stomach. Many of the stunts may be too intense for kids younger than eight.

TOURING TIPS Apparently, the odds are more in your favor for getting into Harvard than being chosen to appear on the TV version of *Fear Factor,* so if you've ever wanted a chance to test your mettle, the theme park version may be your big chance. Participants for the physical stunts are chosen early in the morning outside the theater. The victims—er, contestants—for the ick-factor stunts, like the bug smoothie drinking, are chosen directly from the audience. Sit close to the front and wave your hands like crazy when it comes time for selection.

Nickelodeon Blast Zone

APPEAL BY AGE	PRESCHOOL ★★★★	GRADE SCHOOL ★★★★	TEENS ★★★★
YOUNG ADULTS ★★★½		OVER 30 ★★★½	SENIORS ★★★½

What it is Elaborate interactive playground. **Scope and scale** Major attraction. **When to go** Anytime. **Author's rating** Almost overwhelming; ★★★★. **Duration of experience** Either set limits up front or plan to stay all day.

DESCRIPTION AND COMMENTS The Nickelodeon Blast Zone is a Wal-Mart–sized themed area based on various Nickelodeon channel television shows. Within the Blast Zone are three interactive play areas.

The first play area, Wild Thornberry's Adventure Temple, is a jungle-themed, two-story enclosure containing some 25,000 foam balls. Children (of all ages) can throw or (using air cannons) shoot the balls at each other. To add to the mayhem, there's an orangutan statue that spits balls in all directions when irritated (not hard to do). The second area, Nickelodeon Splash, is also a two-story affair where the idea is to come as close as possible to drowning on dry land while fully clothed. There are geysers, water cannons, a rocket blasting water, and the periodic dumping of two 500-gallon water buckets (in case you're wondering, that's enough water to fill a 20-by-30-foot swimming pool). Some of the spewing, squirting, and dousing you can control yourself. Other soggy manifestations erupt periodically with little warning. Finally, there's the Nick Jr. Backyard, a playground for ages 6 and under, featuring slides, cargo nets, a climbing pole, and assorted other equipment.

TOURING TIPS Wild Thornberry's foam-ball extravaganza and the splash zone can be enjoyed by mischievous guests of any age. The balls neither hurt when they hit nor get you wet. As for the water playground, it's hard to participate without getting pretty soaked. Stay away on colder days, and bring a change of clothes on warmer ones. Be forewarned that even the Nick Jr. Backyard toddler playground comes equipped with a set of little water jets.

The foam-ball palace and the drowning factory are both big places where you can lose sight of your kids in a hurry (or until they nail you with a foam ball or water cannon). Keeping an eye on your children at Nick Jr.'s, by contrast, is easy.

Shrek 4-D

| APPEAL BY AGE | PRESCHOOL ★★★★ | GRADE SCHOOL ★★★★½ | TEENS ★★★★½ |
| YOUNG ADULTS ★★★★½ | | OVER 30 ★★★★½ | SENIORS ★★★★ |

What it is 3-D theater show. Scope and scale Headliner. When to go The first hour the park is open or after 4 p.m. Author's rating ★★★★. Duration of show About 20 minutes.

DESCRIPTION AND COMMENTS Shrek 4-D is based on characters from the hit movie Shrek. A preshow presents the villain from the movie, Lord Farquaad, as he appears on various screens to describe his posthumous plan to reclaim his lost bride, Princess Fiona, who married Shrek. The plan is posthumous since Lord Farquaad ostensibly died in the movie, and it's his ghost making the plans, but never mind. Guests then move into the main theater, don their 3-D glasses, and recline in seats equipped with "tactile transducers" and "pneumatic air propulsion and water spray nodules capable of both vertical and horizontal motion." As the 3-D film plays, guests are also subjected to smells relevant to the on-screen action (oh boy).

Technicalities aside, *Shrek* is a real winner. It's irreverent, frantic, laugh-out-loud funny, and iconoclastic. Concerning the latter, the film takes a good poke at Disney with Pinocchio, the Three Little Pigs, and Tinker Bell (among others) all sucked into the mayhem. The film quality and 3-D effects are great, and like the feature film, it's sweet without being sappy. Plus, in contrast to Disney's *Honey, I Shrunk the Audience* or *It's Tough to Be a Bug!*, *Shrek* 4-D doesn't generally frighten children under seven years of age.

TOURING TIPS   Universal claims they can move 2,400 guests an hour through *Shrek* 4-D. If true, that should keep things moving efficiently. Still, expect big crowds. Try to see *Shrek* before 11 a.m.

Studio Tour

APPEAL BY AGE	PRESCHOOL ★★★	GRADE SCHOOL ★★★★	TEENS ★★★★
YOUNG ADULTS ★★★★		OVER 30 ★★★★	SENIORS ★★★★

What it is Indoor-outdoor tram tour of soundstages and backlot. **Scope and scale** Headliner. **When to go** After experiencing the other rides. **Author's rating** ★★★★½. **Duration of ride** About 42 minutes. **Loading speed** Fast.

DESCRIPTION AND COMMENTS   The Studio Tour is the centerpiece of Universal Studios Hollywood, and at 42 minutes, it is one of the longest attractions in American theme parks. The tour departs from the tram tour boarding facility to the *right* of *Back to the Future* and down the escalator. (Please note that there is also an escalator to the left of Back to the Future, so don't get confused.)

The tram circulates through the various street scenes, lagoons, special-effects venues, and storage areas of Universal's backlot. Recognizable scenery includes the house from *Psycho,* the town square from *Back to the Future,* and the Amity waterfront from *Jaws.* The tram passes several soundstages where current television shows and movies are in production and actually enters three soundstages where action inspired by *Earthquake, The Mummy,* and *King Kong* is presented. As a great enhancement, all trams are equipped with video monitors showing clips from actual movies that demonstrate how the various sets and soundstages were used in creating the films.

The great thing about the Studio Tour is that you see everything without leaving the tram—essentially experiencing four or five major attractions with only one wait.

TOURING TIPS   Though the wait to board might appear long, do not be discouraged. Each tram carries several hundred people and departures are frequent, so the line moves quickly. We recommend taking the tram tour after experiencing the other rides plus the two theater/soundstage presentations on the Lower Lot.

Including your wait to board and the duration of the tour, you will easily invest an hour or more at this attraction. Remember to take a restroom break before queuing up. Though the ride as a whole is gentle, some segments may induce vertigo or motion sickness—especially "The Curse of the Mummy's Tomb," inspired by *The Mummy* and adapted from the old avalanche-effect section of the tour. Finally, be aware that several of the scenes may frighten small children.

Terminator 2: 3-D

APPEAL BY AGE	PRESCHOOL ★★★	GRADE SCHOOL ★★★★★	TEENS ★★★★★
YOUNG ADULTS ★★★★★		OVER 30 ★★★★★	SENIORS ★★★★

What it is 3-D thriller mixed-media presentation. **Scope and scale** Super headliner. **When to go** Just after opening or after 4:30 p.m. **Special comments** Our favorite California attraction; very intense for some preschoolers and grade-schoolers. **Author's rating** Furiously paced high-tech experience; not to be missed; ★★★★★. **Duration of presentation** 20 minutes, including an 8-minute preshow. **Probable waiting time** 20–40 minutes.

DESCRIPTION AND COMMENTS The Terminator "cop" from *Terminator 2* morphs to life and battles Arnold Schwarzenegger's T-100 cyborg character. For those who missed the *Terminator* flicks, here's the plot: A bad robot arrives from the future to kill a nice boy. Another bad robot (who has been reprogrammed to be good) pops up at the same time to save the boy. The bad robot chases the boy and the rehabilitated robot while menacing the audience in the process.

The attraction, like the films, is all action, and you really don't need to understand much. What's interesting is that it uses 3-D film and a theater full of sophisticated technology to integrate the real with the imaginary. Images seem to move in and out of the film, not only in the manner of traditional 3-D, but also in actuality. Remove your 3-D glasses momentarily and you'll see that the guy on the motorcycle is actually on stage.

We've watched this type of presentation evolve, pioneered by Disney's *Captain EO, Honey, I Shrunk the Audience,* and *MuppetVision 3-D. Terminator 2: 3-D,* however, goes way beyond lasers, with moving theater seats, blasts of hot air, and spraying mist. It creates a multidimensional space that blurs the boundary between entertainment and reality. Is it seamless? Not quite, but it's close. We rank *Terminator 2: 3-D* as not to be missed and consider it the absolute best theme-park theater attraction in the United States. If *Terminator 2: 3-D* is the only attraction you see at Universal Studios Hollywood, you'll have received your money's worth.

TOURING TIPS The 700-seat theater changes audiences about every 19 minutes. Even so, because the show is very popular, expect to wait about 25 to 40 minutes. The attraction, opposite the Hollywood Globe Theater and behind Van Helsing Fortress Dracula, receives much traffic during the morning and early afternoon. By about 4 p.m., however, lines diminish somewhat. We recommend seeing the show first thing after the park opens or holding off until afternoon. If you can't stay until late afternoon, see the show first thing in the morning. Families with young children should know that the violence characteristic of the *Terminator* movies is largely absent from the attraction. It has suspense and action but not much blood and guts.

Van Helsing Fortress Dracula

APPEAL BY AGE	PRESCHOOL —	GRADE SCHOOL ★★★	TEENS ★★★½
YOUNG ADULTS ★★★½		OVER 30 ★★★	SENIORS ★★½

What it is A funhouse-style walk-through of scenes based on the film *Van Helsing,* incorporating robotics, hydraulics, real people, smoke, and mirrors. **Scope and scale** Minor attraction. **When to go** Anytime. **Special comments** Not suitable for ages 10 and under. **Author's rating** ★★★. **Duration of presentation** Varies. **Probable waiting time** 3–5 minutes.

DESCRIPTION AND COMMENTS This attraction is an extremely elaborate horror maze. It's quite similar to the walk-through "haunted houses" that spring up all over the country for Halloween. Basically you walk in near darkness through the tight winding corridors of Dracula's castle, occasionally coming upon a large set from the Van Helsing vampire-killing film (including a 50-foot bridge overlooking Frankenstein's monster while he enjoys a little electroshock therapy). As you pick your way through the dark, there are lots of gruesome sights, disorienting devices like mirrors, and worst of all, live people springing out of dark corners and cubby holes to startle you. This last factor makes Van Helsing Fortress Dracula a bad bet for kids under ten years of age. If you don't like being startled, but really want to see the attraction, follow some teenage or college girls through. The leaping, growling, menacing ghouls will expend lots of extra energy on the girls and be in a state of relative depletion when you pass through.

TOURING TIPS Van Helsing Fortress Dracula is located very near the main entrance to the park. It doesn't last long (as the length of the experience depends on how badly you want out), and it can be gotten out of the way quickly. The only time things slow down is when a herd of guests clogs the entrance right after the adjacent *Terminator 2: 3-D* show lets out.

Waterworld

APPEAL BY AGE	PRESCHOOL ★★★	GRADE SCHOOL ★★★★	TEENS ★★★★
YOUNG ADULTS ★★★★		OVER 30 ★★★½	SENIORS ★★★½

What it is Arena show featuring simulated stunt-scene filming. **Scope and scale** Major attraction. **When to go** After experiencing all of the rides and the tram tour. **Author's rating** Well done; ★★★★. **Duration of presentation** 15 minutes. **Probable waiting time** 15 minutes.

DESCRIPTION AND COMMENTS Drawn from the film *Waterworld,* this outdoor theater presentation features stunts and special effects performed on and around a small man-made lagoon. The action involves jet skis and various other craft, and of course, a lot of explosions and falling from high places into the water. Fast-paced and well-adapted to the theater, the production is in many ways more compelling than the film that inspired it.

TOURING TIPS Wait until you have experienced all of the rides and the tram tour before checking out *Waterworld.* Because it is located near the main entrance, most performances are sold out. Arrive at the theater at least

15 minutes before the show time listed in the daily entertainment schedule.

LOWER LOT ATTRACTIONS

Backdraft

APPEAL BY AGE PRESCHOOL ★★★½ GRADE SCHOOL ★★★★ TEENS ★★★★
YOUNG ADULTS ★★★★ OVER 30 ★★★★ SENIORS ★★★★

What it is A multisequence minicourse on special effects. **Scope and scale** Major attraction. **When to go** After you have experienced all of the rides. **Author's rating** Sugar-coated education; ★★★★. **Duration of presentation** About 14 minutes. **Probable waiting time** 20 minutes.

DESCRIPTION AND COMMENTS Guests move from theater to theater in this minicourse attraction. The presentation draws its inspiration from the movie *Backdraft,* which is about firefighters. Segments show the use of miniatures, demonstrate blue matte filming techniques, and discuss the precautions necessary for filming explosions and fire. The finale involves a "hot set" where a *Backdraft* scene involving a fire in a chemical warehouse is re-created. Consistently high-tech, the entire presentation is nicely organized, well paced, and unexpectedly informative. In addition to learning something about how movies are made, you will gain some insight into the origin of fires and how firefighters extinguish them.

TOURING TIPS See *Backdraft* after you've ridden all the rides on your must-see list.

Jurassic Park: The Ride

APPEAL BY AGE PRESCHOOL ★★★ GRADE SCHOOL ★★★★½ TEENS ★★★★½
YOUNG ADULTS ★★★★ OVER 30 ★★★★ SENIORS ★★★★

What it is Indoor-outdoor adventure ride based on the movie *Jurassic Park.* **Scope and scale** Super headliner. **When to go** Before 10:30 a.m. **Special comments** 46" minimum-height requirement. **Author's rating** ★★★★. **Duration of ride** 6 minutes. **Loading speed** Fast.

DESCRIPTION AND COMMENTS Guests board boats for a water tour of Jurassic Park. Everything is tranquil as the tour begins; the boat floats among large herbivorous dinosaurs such as brontosaurus and stegosaurus. Then word is received that some of the carnivores have escaped their enclosure, and the tour boat is accidentally diverted into Jurassic Park's water treatment facility. Here the boat and its riders are menaced by an assortment of hungry meateaters led by the ubiquitous T. Rex. At the climactic moment, the boat and its passengers escape by dropping over a waterfall.

Jurassic Park is impressive in its scale, but the number of dinosaurs is a little disappointing. The big herbivores are given short shrift to set up the plot for the carnivore encounter, which leads to floating around in what looks like a brewery. When the carnivores make their appearance, however, they definitely get your attention. The final drop down a three-story flume to safety is a dandy.

TOURING TIPS You can get very wet on this ride. Even before the boat leaves the dock you must sit in the puddles left by previous riders. Once the boat is underway there's a little splashing, but nothing major until the big drop at the end of the ride. When you hit the bottom, enough water will cascade into the boat to extinguish a three-alarm fire. Our recommendation is to bring along an extra-large plastic garbage bag and (cutting holes for your head and arms) wear it like a sack dress. If you forget to bring a garbage bag, you can purchase a Universal Studios poncho for about $8.

Young children must endure a double whammy on this ride. First, they are stalked by giant, salivating (sometimes spitting) reptiles, and then they are catapulted over the falls. Wait until your kids are fairly stalwart before you spring Jurassic Park on them.

Jurassic Park stays jammed most of the day. Ride early in the morning after Revenge of the Mummy.

Lucy, A Tribute

APPEAL BY AGE	PRESCHOOL ★	GRADE SCHOOL ★	TEENS ★★
YOUNG ADULTS ★★★		OVER 30 ★★★	SENIORS ★★★

What it is Walk-through tribute to Lucille Ball. **Scope and scale** Diversion. **When to go** Anytime. **Author's rating** A touching remembrance; ★★★. **Duration of experience** About 10 minutes. **Probable waiting time** None.

DESCRIPTION AND COMMENTS The life and career of comedienne Lucille Ball are spotlighted, with emphasis on her role as Lucy Ricardo in the long-running television series *I Love Lucy*. Well-designed and informative, the exhibit succeeds admirably in recalling the talent and temperament of the beloved redhead.

TOURING TIPS See Lucy during the hot, crowded midafternoon, or after you have seen all of the other Lower Lot attractions. Adults could easily stay 15 to 30 minutes. Children, however, get restless after a few minutes.

Revenge of the Mummy

APPEAL BY AGE	PRESCHOOL —	GRADE SCHOOL ★★★½	TEENS ★★★★½
YOUNG ADULTS ★★★★½		OVER 30 ★★★★	SENIORS ★★★½

What it is High-tech dark ride. **Scope and scale** Super headliner. **When to go** The first hour the park is open or after 4 p.m. **Author's rating** Wear your asbestos: hot! ★★★★. **Duration of ride** About 2½ minutes.

DESCRIPTION AND COMMENTS The Revenge of the Mummy replaced the now-closed E.T. attraction in spring 2004. It's kinda hard to wrap your mind around the actual attraction, but it pretty much lives up to the Universal press release, though the press release is generally incomprehensible. Here, quoting that press release, are some of the things you can look forward to: "authentic Egyptian catacombs; high-velocity show immersion system [we think this has something to do with very fast baptism]; magnet-propulsion launch wave system; a "Brain Fire" [!] that hovers [over you] with temperatures soaring to 2,000 degrees Fahrenheit; and canoptic jars containing grisly remains."

Of course the art of the press release is to create allure and excitement without actually spilling the beans. Actually, Revenge of the Mummy is an indoor dark ride based on the *Mummy* flicks, where guests fight off "deadly curses and vengeful creatures" while flying through Egyptian tombs and other spooky places on a high-tech roller coaster. The special effects are cutting-edge, integrating the best technology from such attractions as *Terminator 2: 3-D, Fear Factor,* and Back to the Future, with a propulsion system and visuals that are way cool.

The queuing area serves to establish the story line: You're in a group touring a set from the *Mummy* films when you enter a tomb where the fantasy world of film gives way to the real thing. Along the way you are warned about a possible curse. The visuals are rich and compelling as the queue makes its way to the loading area where you board a sort of clunky, jeep-looking vehicle. The ride begins as a slow, very elaborate dark ride, passing through various chambers including one where flesh-eating scarab beetles descend on you. Suddenly your vehicle stops, then drops backwards and rotates. Here's where the aforementioned "magnet-propulsion launch wave system" comes in. In more ordinary language, this means you're shot at high speed up the first hill of the roller-coaster part of the ride. We don't want to ruin your experience by divulging too much, but the coaster part of the ride offers its own panoply of surprises. We will tell you this, however: there are no barrel rolls or any upside-down stuff. And though it's a wild ride by anyone's definition, the emphasis remains as much on the visuals, robotics, and special effects as on the ride itself.

TOURING TIPS Revenge of the Mummy has a very low riders-per-hour capacity for a super-headliner attraction, and especially for the park's top draw. Waits will run longer than an Academy Awards show. Your only prayer for a tolerable wait is to be on hand when the park opens and sprint immediately to the Mummy. Concerning motion sickness, if you can ride Space Mountain without ill effect, you should be fine on Revenge of the Mummy. Switching off is available.

Special Effects Stages

APPEAL BY AGE	PRESCHOOL ★★½		GRADE SCHOOL ★★★	TEENS ★★★½
YOUNG ADULTS ★★★½		OVER 30 ★★★		SENIORS ★★★½

What it is A three-part minicourse on special effects, filming action sequences, and sound effects. **Scope and scale** Major attraction. **When to go** Anytime. **Special comments** May frighten young children. **Author's rating** Predictable, but still interesting; ★★★. **Duration of presentation** 30 minutes. **Probable waiting time** 15 minutes.

DESCRIPTION AND COMMENTS Formerly known as The World of CineMagic, the basic structure of this attraction is unchanged. Guests view a presentation on special effects, and audience members participate in a demonstration showing how actors are filmed against a blue or green screen in the studio, then superimposed onto film shot on location. Next, the audience is ushered to an adjoining stage to view a presentation on makeup and movie monsters. The final destination is a sound-stage, in which the audience views and participates in a presentation on Foley art—a.k.a. sound effects—culminating in a movie scene based on the film *Shrek*.

TOURING TIPS This high-capacity attraction is in the most remote corner of the park. Its capacity for handling crowds combined with its isolated location usually add up to short waits. The daily entertainment schedule lists the Special Effects Stages show as running continuously: it does not. It operates on a fixed performance schedule that is posted (as of this writing) nowhere except at the attraction.

UNIVERSAL STUDIOS HOLLYWOOD FOR YOUNG CHILDREN

WE DO NOT RECOMMEND Universal Studios Hollywood for preschoolers. Of 11 major attractions, all but 2 (*Animal Planet Live!* and *Shrek 4-D*) have the potential for flipping out sensitive little ones. See the Young-Child Fright-Potential Chart below.

Universal Studios Hollywood Young-Child Fright-Potential Chart

Animal Planet Live! Not frightening in any way.

Backdraft Intense re-creation of fire terrifies many preschoolers.

Back to the Future Intense, rough thrill ride. Potentially terrifying for people of any age. Switching off available.

Fear Factor Live Gross, loud, and frenetic, the show can freak out guests of any age.

Jurassic Park: The Ride Intense water-flume ride. Potentially terrifying for people of any age. Switching off available.

Nickelodeon Blast Zone Nature of the attraction encourages aggressive play. Getting soaked is a definite possibility at the Nickelodeon Splash section of the Zone.

Revenge of the Mummy Scares guests of all ages.

Shrek 4-D Special effects may frighten preschoolers.

Special Effects Stage Some intense special effects. Shows the murder scene in the shower from *Psycho*.

Studio Tour Certain parts of the tour are too frightening and too intense for many preschoolers.

Terminator 2: 3-D Extremely intense and potentially frightening for visitors of any age.

Van Helsing Fortress Dracula Frightens guests of all ages.

Waterworld Fighting, gunplay, and explosions may frighten children ages 4 and under.

LIVE ENTERTAINMENT AT UNIVERSAL STUDIOS HOLLYWOOD

THE THEATER AND AMPHITHEATER ATTRACTIONS operate according to the entertainment schedule available with handout park maps. The number of daily performances of each show varies from as few as three a day during less busy times of year to as many as ten a day during the summer and holiday periods. Blues Brothers impersonators offer a high-energy show in the Upper Lot near the front entrance. The instrumental track is unfortunately prerecorded, but the show is a spirit lifter nonetheless. Also in the Upper Lot, look for the Doo Wop Singers belting out 1950s and 1960s harmonies near Mel's Diner.

In addition to scheduled presentations, a number of street performers randomly work the park. These include Marvel Comics characters such as Spider-Man, cartoon characters such as Woody Woodpecker, and various film-star impersonators.

DINING AT UNIVERSAL STUDIOS HOLLYWOOD

THE COUNTER-SERVICE FOOD at Universal Studios runs the gamut from burgers and hot dogs to pizza, fried chicken, crêpes, and Mexican specialties. We rank most selections marginally better than fast food. Prices are comparable to those at Disneyland, and on average the quality of the food is similar.

If you are looking for full-service dining, try **Wolfgang Puck's Cafe, Cafe TuTu Tango,** or the **Hard Rock Café** in the Universal CityWalk just outside the park entrance. Our favorite in the park is the **Hollywood Grill** burger joint across from *Waterworld*. If you leave the park for lunch, be sure to have your hand stamped for re-entry.

UNIVERSAL STUDIOS HOLLYWOOD ONE-DAY TOURING PLAN

This plan is for groups of all sizes and ages and includes thrill rides that may induce motion sickness or get you wet. If the plan calls for you to experience an attraction that does not interest you, simply skip that attraction and proceed to the next step. Be aware that the plan calls for minimal backtracking.

Before You Go

1. Call ☎ 818-622-3801 the day before your visit for the official opening time. If you can't get through, call ☎ 818-622-3735 or 818-622-3750.

2. If you have young children in your party, consult the Universal Studios Hollywood Small-Child Fright-Potential Chart (page 235).

At the Park

1. On the day of your visit, eat breakfast and arrive at Universal Studios Hollywood 20 minutes before opening time. Park, buy your admission, and wait at the turnstiles. If you drive, you will save some time by drop-

ping a member of your party off at the front entrance to purchase tickets while you park.

2. At the turnstile, ask an attendant whether any rides or shows are closed that day. Adjust the touring plan accordingly.

3. When the park opens, head for the back left section of the Upper Lot. Take the escalators to the Lower Lot and make a hard right to Revenge of the Mummy.

4. Exiting the Mummy, experience Jurassic Park across the plaza.

5. Skip the other Lower Lot attractions for now. Return to the Upper Lot, bearing left to Back To the Future. Ride.

6. Next see *Shrek 4-D,* also in the Upper Lot.

7. Head toward the park entrance bearing right before the turnstile to *Terminator 2: 3-D.* Note that *Terminator* sometimes runs back-to-back shows and at other times schedules shows at specific times as detailed in the daily entertainment schedule.

8. Our apologies for all the walking, but the walking saves a lot of time standing in line. Return to the Lower Lot and see Backdraft and the Special Effects Stages. Ask a Universal cast member about performance times before you make the long trek.

9. If you are a Lucille Ball fan, check out the tribute to Lucy before you depart the Lower Lot. Return to the Upper Lot.

10. Check your daily entertainment schedule for *Fear Factor Live, Waterworld,* and *Animal Planet Live!* show times. Plan the rest of your schedule around seeing these shows. Note that you should arrive at the theater 30 minutes before show time for *Fear Factor* and *Waterworld* and 20 minutes prior to *Animal Planet Live!*

11. With your show schedule in mind, decide when you'd like to eat lunch and when you'd like to take the Studio Tour. Allocate an hour and 10 minutes for the tour (counting the 45-minute tour, coming and going, and waiting to load).

12. If you have time to kill between stage shows, check out Van Helsing Fortress Dracula and the *Blue Brothers* Show. If you have children 12 years and younger, try the Nickelodeon Blast Zone play area.

13. This concludes the touring plan. Spend the remainder of your day revisiting your favorite attractions or inspecting sets and street scenes you may have missed. Also, check your daily entertainment schedule for live performances that interest you.

PART SEVEN

DINING *and* SHOPPING *in and around* DISNEYLAND

DINING

THE DISNEYLAND RESTAURANT selection exploded with the opening of Disney's California Adventure theme park, the Grand Californian Hotel, and the Downtown Disney dining, shopping, and entertainment complex.

DINING AT DISNEY'S CALIFORNIA ADVENTURE

DINING AT DISNEY'S CALIFORNIA ADVENTURE (DCA) reflects the immense diversity of California's robust culinary scene. DCA has three full-service restaurants. The very upscale **Vineyard Room** at the Golden Vine Winery serves California cuisine—multi-course meals on the upper level accompanied by wines selected specifically to go with each course. The mission-style design of the restaurant and the relative tranquility of the setting transport you, at least mentally, out of the theme park for the duration of your meal. On the lower level of the winery is **Wine Country Trattoria** serving sandwiches, pastas, and salad. The Vineyard Room is open evenings, and dinners are fixed price, with or without accompanying wines. Main courses at the Trattoria range from $10 to $14. **Ariel's Grotto** is the park's other upscale restaurant. Specializing in local seafood preparations, Ariel's Grotto overlooks Paradise Bay and the midway rides of Paradise Pier on the opposite shore. In addition to the restaurant, there's a cozy bar that also offers a knockout view of Paradise Pier. Though we are not particularly high on the Paradise Pier attractions, we must admit that they create a stunning nighttime vista as seen from the Ariel's Grotto restaurant or bar. Weather permitting, both the Vineyard Room and Ariel's Grotto offer alfresco dining.

Both lunch and dinner at Ariel's Grotto are fixed-price character meals with Ariel, Goofy, and Minnie in attendance. The menu is the same at both lunch and dinner. Lunch runs $15 for adults and $11 for kids. Dinner is $20 and $13 respectively, but, unlike lunch, includes dessert and a nonalcoholic drink.

All three full-service restaurants accept priority seatings. For additional information or to make a priority seating, call ☎ 714-781-3463.

Counter-service dining abounds at DCA and while you won't have any problem finding a burger, pizza, or hot dog, there's a wide range of more interesting fare. Our picks of the litter are **Cochina Cucamonga** at Pacific Wharf serving carne asada, carnitas, and tacos, and **Pacific Wharf Café** specializing in clam chowder and corn chowder as well as designer salads. A fast-food trend at both DCA and Disneyland Park is the mandatory combo. No longer can you simply purchase a sandwich. Now everything comes with fries, potato chips, or whatever, like it or not. Throughout the park, combos run in the $6–$9 range and, unlike McDonald's combos, do not include your drink.

DINING AT DISNEYLAND PARK

THE FOOD AT DISNEYLAND PARK has improved substantially over the past couple of years. True, the fare is still overpriced and there are plenty of culinary landmines to avoid, but on average the food is much better. Expanded menu selections provide more choice and variety and lend authenticity and an ethnic touch to the various theme areas. It is fun, for example, to at last be able to enjoy jambalaya in New Orleans Square. If, however, you prefer simpler, more traditional fare, don't worry: there is no chance that hamburgers or hot dogs will become endangered species at Disneyland Park. As for our personal favorites, we like **Rancho del Zocalo** in Frontierland, the **Hungry Bear Restaurant** (burgers) in Critter Country, and the German wursts at the **Enchanted Cottage** in Fantasyland.

Finally, be aware that, like DCA, Disneyland Park has gone the combo route. In other words, you're going to get (and pay for) fries with that burger, like it or not.

A Word about Fast Food at Disneyland Park and DCA

To give you some sense of what fast food and snacks in the parks will cost, we provide the following list:

Coffee: $2–$4	Salads: $4–$9
Bottled water: $2.59–$2.75	Fries: $2.69–$3
Potato chips: $2.50	Pizza: $6 per slice
Ice cream: $3–$5	Popcorn: $3–$5
Sandwiches, burgers, hot dogs: $6–$9	Pretzel: $2.99–$3.29
Sandwich combos: $7–$11	Children's meals: $5–$6
Soft drinks, iced tea, lemonade: $2.49–$2.70	

Alternatives and Suggestions for Eating in the Parks:

1. Eat a good breakfast before arriving. You do not want to waste early morning touring time eating breakfast at the park.

2. Having eaten a good breakfast, keep your tummy happy with snacks from your fanny pack or purchases from vendors.

3. Disneyland Park's premiere full-service restaurant is the **Blue Bayou** in New Orleans Square. The restaurant serves palatable though rarely outstanding food in an arresting bayou setting that overlooks the Pirates of the Caribbean boat ride.

   For full-service dining at Disney's California Adventure, try **The Vineyard Room** in the winery or **Ariel's Grotto** across from Paradise Pier.

   Reservations for full-service restaurants can be made at the door of the restaurant any time after park opening. Theme-park full-service restaurants also accept priority seatings 60 days in advance (☎ 714-781-DINE). All park restaurants are accustomed to dealing with small children, both well-behaved and otherwise.

4. Park restaurants are most crowded between 11:30 a.m. and 2:30 p.m. Good counter-service restaurants frequently overlooked at Disneyland Park include the **Rancho del Zocalo** on the front side of Big Thunder, the **Enchanted Cottage** at the Fantasyland Theater, and the **Plaza Inn** buffet on Main Street.

   Disney's California Adventure counter-service restaurants in the Pacific Wharf and Bountiful Valley Farm theme areas of the Golden State district are our picks for good food and tolerable lines.

   If you are on a tight schedule and the parks close early, stay until closing and eat dinner outside the parks before returning to your hotel. If the park stays open late, eat an early dinner about 4 to 4:30 p.m. in the eatery of your choice. You should miss the last wave of lunch diners and sneak in just ahead of the dinner crowd. However, if you wish to wait and have a late dinner, you can eat without much hassle after 8:30 p.m., but you will miss the evening parades, fireworks, and other live entertainment.

5. If you are tired of fighting crowds and eating at odd times, exit the park for lunch or dinner at one of many Downtown Disney restaurants, or for a little relaxation and decompression at one of its watering holes. The coming and going isn't nearly as time-consuming as it appears, and you will probably be able to get a better meal with faster service in a more relaxed atmosphere. The trip over and back takes very little time, and the restaurants are often slack, particularly at lunch.

6. Several park eateries serve cold deli sandwiches. It is possible to buy a cold lunch (except for the drinks) before 11 a.m. and then carry your food until you are ready to eat. We met a family that does this routinely, with Mom always remembering to bring several small plastic bags for packing the food. Drinks can be purchased at the appropriate time from any convenient vendor.

7. Most fast-food eateries in the parks have more than one service window. Regardless of the time of day, check out the lines at all of the windows before queuing up. Sometimes a manned but out-of-the-way window will have a much shorter line or no line at all. Be forewarned that most patrons in the food lines are buying for their whole family or

group, and that the ten people in line ahead of you will require the serving of 30 to 40 meals, not just 10.

8. After years of prodding, Disney has reconfigured several fast-food eateries as self-serve food courts. You simply go around and pick up whatever you want in the way of food and drink and then head for the checkout counter. This eliminates standing in line once to order and pay and then again to pick up your food. Restaurants adopting this format, all in Disneyland Park, are **Redd Rocket's Pizza Port** in Tomorrowland, the **Plaza Inn** buffet on Main Street, and the **French Market** in New Orleans Square.

9. For your general information, the Disney people have a park rule (that they don't enforce) against bringing your own food and drink. We interviewed one woman who, ignoring the rule, brought a huge picnic lunch for her family of five, packed into a large diaper/baby paraphernalia bag. Upon entering the park, she secured the bag in a locker and retrieved it later when the family was hungry. A San Diego family returned to their van in the parking lot for lunch. There they had a cooler, lawn chairs, and plenty of food, in the college-football tailgating tradition.

Because dining in restaurants (particularly Disney restaurants) is so expensive, we get a lot of suggestions from readers on how to cut costs. Representative are these notes passed along by a mom from Bridgeton, Missouri:

We shopped [in advance] and arrived with our steel Coleman cooler well stocked with milk and sandwich fixings. I froze a block of ice in a milk bottle, and we replenished with ice from the resort ice machine daily. I also froze small packages of deli-type meats for later in the week. We ate cereal, milk, and fruit each morning, with boxed juices. I also had a hot pot to boil water for instant coffee, oatmeal, and soup.

Each child had a belt bag of his own, which he filled from a special box of "goodies" each day. I made a great mystery of filling that box in the weeks before the trip. Some things were actual food, like packages of crackers and cheese, packets of peanuts and raisins. Some were worthless junk, like candy and gum. They grazed from their belt bags at will throughout the day, with no interference from Mom and Dad. Each also had a small, rectangular, plastic water bottle that could hang on the belt. We filled these at water fountains before getting into lines and were the envy of many.

We left the park before noon, ate sandwiches, chips, and sodas in the room, and napped. We purchased our evening meal in the park, at a counter-service eatery. We budgeted for both morning and evening snacks from a vendor, but often did not need them. It made the occasional treat all the more special.

In case you're wondering, the security people checking purses, packs, and the like at the park entrances won't hassle you or confiscate your goodies if they discover you're bringing in food. They've got bigger fish to fry.

Incidentally, if you are looking for quiet, intimate dining, your chances of finding it are directly proportional to your distance from Disneyland: that is, the farther the better. A honeymooner from Slidell, Louisiana, learned this lesson the hard way, writing:

> We made dinner reservations at some of the nicer Disney restaurants. We made sure our reservations were past the dinner hours, and we tried to stress that we were on our honeymoon. [At] every restaurant we went to, we were seated next to large families. The kids were usually tired and cranky and, after a long day in the park, were not excited about sitting through a [lengthy] meal. It's very difficult to enjoy a romantic dinner when there are small children crawling around under your table. We looked around the restaurant and always noticed lots of non-children couples. Our suggestion is this: Seat couples without children together and families with kids elsewhere. If Disney is such a popular honeymoon destination, then some attempt should be made to keep romantic restaurants romantic.

DINING OUTSIDE THE PARKS

THE PREMIERE RESTAURANT at the Grand Californian Hotel is **Napa Rose** featuring California cuisine and premium California wines. The restaurant seats 237 and overlooks Grizzly Peak in Disney's California Adventure. The **Storyteller's Café** serves as the Grand Californian's informal restaurant and character-meal venue.

In Downtown Disney, you can choose from among six restaurants, including the **Rainforest Café, ESPN Zone** sports bar, and the **House of Blues**—all serving American fare. **Ralph Brennan's Jazz Kitchen** offers Louisiana specialties, **Naples Ristorante e Pizzeria** features Italian dishes and pizza, and **Tortilla Jo's** serves Mexican specialties. **Catal Restaurant** serves Mediterranean fare and tapas. Many of the Downtown Disney restaurants accept real reservations (that is, not priority seatings). Call the restaurants direct: Rainforest Café ☎ 714-772-0413; Ralph Brennan's ☎ 714-776-5200; Catal ☎ 714-774-4442; House of Blues ☎ 714-778-BLUE.

Granville's Steak House at the Disneyland Hotel, though expensive, is one of the best Disney restaurants in or out of the parks. You can arrange dinner priority seatings via phone at City Hall at the Town Square end of Main Street, or call ☎ 714-781-3463. Your waiter will tout the porterhouse, but the filet mignon and the New York strip are better. For feed-trough dining at the Disneyland Hotel, try **Goofy's Kitchen,** which serves brunch and dinner character buffets (you eat *with* the characters). Goofy's offers an excellent spread for adults and a separate, kid-sized serving line for the little guys. The children's buffet features a veritable hit parade of kids' favorites, including hot dogs, fried fish, spaghetti, and macaroni and cheese.

If none of the restaurants at the Disneyland Hotel appeal to you, there's **Yamabuki,** a Japanese restaurant and sushi bar, and the **P.C.H.**

Grill, serving Pacific fusion cuisine, at the Paradise Pier Hotel next door. If none of these suit you, or are too pricey, it is easy to take a taxi to a nearby non-Disney restaurant.

SHOPPING

SHOPS ADD REALISM AND ATMOSPHERE to the various theme settings and make available an extensive inventory of souvenirs, clothing, novelties, jewelry, decorator items, and more. Much of the merchandise displayed (with the exception of Disney trademark souvenir items) is available back home and elsewhere. In our opinion, shopping is not one of the main reasons for visiting Disneyland Resort. We recommend bypassing the shops on a one-day visit. If you have two or more days to spend at Disneyland Resort, browse the shops during the early afternoon when many of the attractions are crowded.

Our recommendations notwithstanding, we realize that for many guests Disney souvenirs and memorabilia are irresistible. If you have decided that you would look good in a Goofy hat with shoulder-length floppy ears, you are in the right place. What's more, you have plenty of company. One of our readers writes:

I've discovered that people have a compelling need to buy Disney stuff when they are at Disneyland. When you get home you wonder why you ever got a cashmere sweater with Mickey Mouse embroidered on the breast, or a tie with tiny Goofys all over it. Maybe it's something they put in the food.

If you don't want to lug your packages around you can leave them at the information stand just inside the front gate and pick them up as you exit the park. Be mindful that retrieving your purchases might take a while if you depart after a parade, fireworks, or at closing when guests head for exits en masse. If you are a guest at a Disneyland Resort hotel, your purchases will be delivered on request directly to your room.

If you have a problem with your purchases, need to make a return, or simply forgot to pick up something for Uncle Ned, you can call Disneyland Exclusive Merchandise at ☎ 800-760-3566, Monday through Friday, from 8 a.m. to 5 p.m. PST, and Saturday from 8 a.m. to 4 p.m PST, and get it all worked out over the phone. Uncle Ned's gift plus anything else you buy will be shipped via UPS standard delivery.

DOWNTOWN DISNEY

DOWNTOWN DISNEY, verdant and landscaped by day, pops alive with neon and glitter at night. The complex offers more than 300,000 square feet of specialty shopping, clubs, restaurants, and movie theaters. Many of the restaurants offer entertainment in addition to dining, including **House of Blues** and **Ralph Brennan's Jazz Kitchen** (specializing in New Orleans jazz). The **ESPN Zone** is a sports bar and

downtown disney

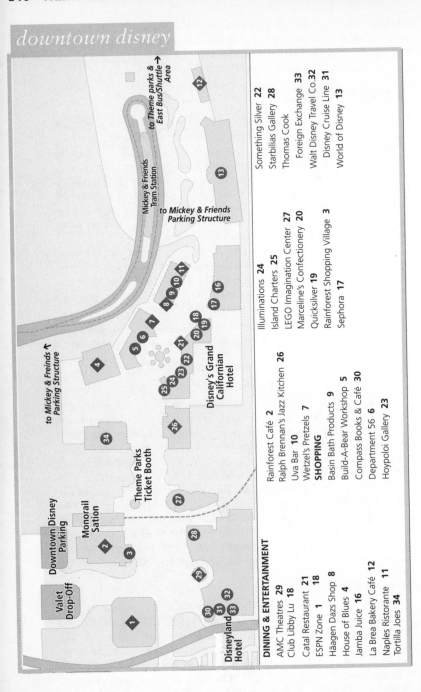

DINING & ENTERTAINMENT

AMC Theatres **29**
Club Libby Lu **18**
Catal Restaurant **21**
ESPN Zone **1**
Häagen Dazs Shop **8**
House of Blues **4**
Jamba Juice **16**
La Brea Bakery Café **12**
Naples Ristorante **11**
Tortilla Joes **34**

Rainforest Café **2**
Ralph Brennan's Jazz Kitchen **26**
Uva Bar **10**
Wetzel's Pretzels **7**

SHOPPING

Basin Bath Products **9**
Build-A-Bear Workshop **5**
Compass Books & Café **30**
Department 56 **6**
Hoypoloi Gallery **23**

Illuminations **24**
Island Charters **25**
LEGO Imagination Center **27**
Marceline's Confectionery **20**
Quicksilver **19**
Rainforest Shopping Village **3**
Sephora **17**

Something Silver **22**
Starbilias Gallery **28**
Thomas Cook
Foreign Exchange **33**
Walt Disney Travel Co. **32**
Disney Cruise Line **31**
World of Disney **13**

restaurant with dozens of giant screens for viewing sporting events. Other restaurant options include the **Naples Ristorante e Pizzeria, Tortilla Jo's** Mexican restaurant, and jungle-themed dining at the **Rainforest Café.**

If you're not hungry, there's always shopping and a 12-theater, AMC Movieplex to keep you occupied. A 40,000-square-foot World of Disney Store, the second largest on the planet, anchors the shopping scene. Other retailers include **Compass Books; Basin,** a bath store; **Starabilias** for antiques, memorabilia, and gifts; **Department 56** for handcrafted collectibles; cosmetics at **Sephora; Something Silver** specializing in jewelry; and **Hoypoloi** for one-of-a-kind stuff. A combination store, exhibit, and activity center describes the **LEGO Imagination Center.** On display is a 25-foot LEGO giraffe that took 5 people 600 hours to build. The center also features interactive play tables where children build whatever their imagination conjures up with LEGO bricks. Once the kids get hooked at the play tables, there's enough LEGO stuff available for sale to build an addition to your house.

Though most of the Downtown Disney shops are pretty interesting, the **Build-a-Bear Workshop** is a must visit. Here you choose from among a couple dozen, unstuffed bearskins ranging in price from $12 to $25. Types of bears vary from pandas to old-fashioned teddy bears and everything in between. Once you have a bear, you have the option of choosing a sound box to be implanted when the bear gets stuffed. Activated when you handle the bear, the sound box (depending on which one you choose) can say hello, sing a song, recite a poem, giggle, or growl (nicely, of course). Next you proceed to the stuffing machine. This contraption is a big transparent box with stuffing whirling around inside on air currents. When the stuffer depresses a foot pedal, the stuffing is sucked out of the machine into a hose with a sharpish stainless-steel nozzle on the end. This last is inserted into the flaccid bearskin until the skin is appropriately plumped. Stuffing the bear requires much reaming of the aforementioned nozzle throughout the bear's head and innards. Because this is somewhat disquieting to witness, you must think sweet thoughts about how your finished bear will look as opposed to what he's going through at the moment. Before sewing the bear up, you insert a little red heart and make a wish (probably that you don't ever have to witness such a process again). When your bear is stuffed, hearted, and sewn, you have the option to accessorize, choosing from a veritable Macy's of bear clothes, hats, shoes, jewelry, sunglasses, roller skates, and myriad other even more unlikely items. After all your bear has been through, it's only natural to want to buy him a present or two, but watch out—you can easily blow a hundred bucks getting your bear outfitted.

Our map of Downtown Disney, listing storefronts and restaurants, appears on the opposite page.

PART EIGHT

APPENDIX

 READERS' QUESTIONS *to* *the* **AUTHOR**

QUESTION:

When you do your research, are you admitted to the park for free? Do the Disney people know you are there?

ANSWER:

We pay the regular admission and usually the Disney people do not know we are on site. Both in and out of Disneyland, we pay for our own meals and lodging.

QUESTION:

How often is the Unofficial Guide *revised?*

ANSWER:

We publish a new edition once a year, but make minor corrections every time we go to press.

QUESTION:

I have an older edition of the Unofficial Guide. *How much of the information in it is still correct?*

ANSWER:

Veteran travel writers will acknowledge that 5 to 8% of the information in a guidebook is out of date by the time it comes off the press! Disneyland is always changing. If you are using an old edition of the *Unofficial Guide,* the descriptions of attractions existing when the guide was published should still be generally accurate. Many other things, however, particularly the touring plans and the hotel and restaurant reviews, change with every edition. Finally, and obviously, older editions of the *Unofficial Guide* do not include new attractions or developments.

QUESTION:

Do you write each new edition from scratch?

ANSWER:

We do not. With a destination the size of Disneyland, it's hard enough keeping up with what is new. Moreover, we put great effort into communicating the most salient and useful information in the clearest possible language. If an attraction or hotel has not changed, we are very reluctant to tinker with its coverage for the sake of freshening up the writing.

QUESTION:

Do you stay at Disneyland hotels? If not, where do you stay?

ANSWER:

We do stay at Disneyland-area hotels from time to time, usually after a renovation or management change. Since we began writing about Disneyland in 1984 we have stayed in more than 31 different properties in various locations around Anaheim.

QUESTION:

How many people have you interviewed or surveyed for your age-group ratings on the attractions?

ANSWER:

Since the publication of the first edition of the *Unofficial Guide* in 1985, we have interviewed or surveyed just over 12,000 Disneyland patrons. Even with such a large sample, however, we continue to have difficulty with certain age groups. Specifically, we love to hear from seniors concerning their experiences with Splash Mountain, Big Thunder Mountain Railroad, Space Mountain, the Matterhorn Bobsleds, Star Tours, Indiana Jones, and Disney's California Adventure attractions.

QUESTION:

How are your age-group ratings determined? I am 42 years old. During Star Tours, I was quite worried about hurting my back. If the senior citizens rating is determined only by those brave enough to ride, it will skew the results.

ANSWER:

The reader makes a good point. Unfortunately, it's impossible to develop a rating unless the guest (of any age group) has actually experienced the attraction. So yes, all age group ratings are derived exclusively from members of that age group who have experienced the attraction. Health problems, such as a bad back, however, can affect guests of any age, and Disney provides more than ample warnings on attractions that warrant such admonitions. But if you are in good health, our ratings will give you a sense of how much others your age enjoyed the attraction. Our hope is two-fold: First, that you will be stimulated to be adventurous, and second, that a positive experience will help you to be more open-minded.

QUESTION:

I laughed at the "When to go" suggestions [for the attractions]. Too many were before 10 a.m. and after 5 p.m. What are we supposed to do between 10 a.m. and 5 p.m. ?

ANSWER:

Our best advice is to go back to your hotel and take a nice nap. More in keeping with the spirit of your question, however, the attractions with the shortest waits between 10 a.m. and 5 p.m. are as follows:

DISNEYLAND PARK	DISNEY'S CALIFORNIA ADVENTURE
Enchanted Tiki Birds	Boudin Bakery
Fantasyland Theater	Bountiful Valley Farm
Innoventions	Disney Animation
It's a Small World	*Golden Dreams*
Mark Twain Riverboat	*It's Tough to Be a Bug!*
Sailing Ship *Columbia*	Mission Tortilla Factory
Tom Sawyer Island	Redwood Creek Challenge Trail
Disneyland: The First 50 Years	

QUESTION:

I have heard that when there are two lines to an attraction, the left line is faster. Is this true?

ANSWER:

In general, no. We have tested this theory many times and usually have not gained an advantage of even 90 seconds by getting in one line versus another. What *does* occasionally occur, however, is after a second line has *just been opened*, guests ignore the new line and persist in standing in the established line. As a rule of thumb, if you encounter a two-line waiting configuration with no barrier to entry for either and one of the lines is conspicuously less populated than the other, get in it.

In closing we leave you with a poem/song submitted by Alan Beckley of Rock Hill, South Carolina. It can be sung to the tune of Simon and Garfunkel's "Homeward Bound."

MOUSEWARD BOUND

I'm sittin' here trying to be patient
Got tickets for my destination, m-mmm
On a tour of four theme lands
My suitcase and swimsuit in hand
And every day is neatly planned
For attractions, rides, and marching bands

Mouseward bound, I wish I was
Mouseward bound
Mouse, where my sleep's escaping
Mouse, where my kids are playing
Mouse, where my wallet's deflating
Poverty for me

Every day's an endless stream
Of movie skits and dance routines
And each line looks the same to me
For trips through space and fantasy
And every stranger turns to see
That FASTPASS is the way to be

Mouseward bound, I wish I was
Mouseward bound
Mouse, where my sleep's escaping
Mouse, where my kids are playing
Mouse, where my wallet's deflating
Poverty for me

Tonight I'll stay 'til closing again
I'll shop for souvenirs and pretend
But all my pockets are empty
Still wet from the River of Kali
Like Snow White, Dumbo, and Bambi
I need someone to comfort me

Mouseward bound, I wish I was
Mouseward bound
Mouse, where my sleep's escaping
Mouse, where my kids are playing
Mouse, where my wallet's deflating
Poverty for me
Poverty for me

HOTEL INDEX

SUBJECT INDEX

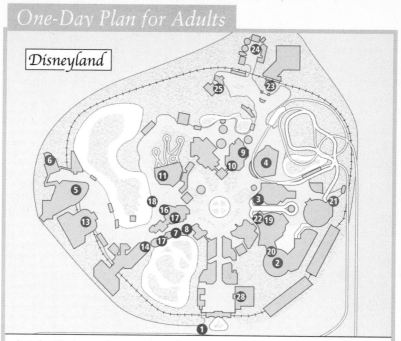

Disneyland

1. Arrive 40 minutes prior to opening.
2. Go to Tomorrowland. Ride Space Mountain.
3. In Tomorrowland, ride the Buzz Lightyear.
4. Go to Fantasyland. Ride the Matterhorn Bobsleds.
5. Go to Critter Country and ride Splash Mountain. Use FASTPASS if the wait exceeds 35 minutes.
6. Ride Winnie the Pooh.
7. In Adventureland ride Indiana Jones. Use FASTPASS if the wait exceeds 30 minutes.
8. Ride the Jungle Cruise.
9. In Fantasyland ride Alice in Wonderland.
10. In Fantasyland ride Peter Pan.
11. In Frontierland ride Big Thunder Railroad. If the wait exceeds 20 minutes use FASTPASS.
12. Go to New Orleans Square.
13. Experience the Haunted Mansion.
14. Ride Pirates of the Caribbean.
15. Check the return time of FASTPASSes. Eat if you're hungry.
16. Work in a show at the Golden Horseshoe Saloon.
17. In Adventureland tour Tarzan's Treehouse and see the *Tiki Birds*.
18. In New Orleans Square ride the riverboat.
19. In Tomorrowland ride Star Tours. Use FASTPASS if the wait exceeds 30 minutes.
20. In Tomorrowland see *Honey, I Shrunk the Audience*.
21. From Tomorrowland, take a round trip on the Disney Railroad.
22. Back in Tomorrowland ride Star Tours
23. Go to Fantasyland. Ride It's A Small World.
24. Explore Mickey's Toontown.
25. Check show times for the Fantasyland Theater.
26. Check for parades, fireworks, and *Fantasmic!* and work them into your schedule.
27. See attractions you missed.
28. On Main Street see *Disneyland: The First 50 Years*.

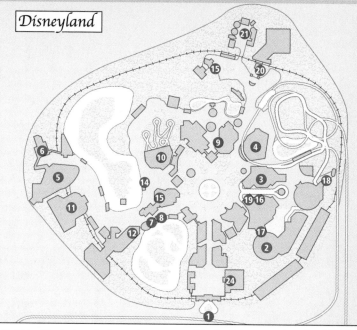

Disneyland

1. Arrive 40 minutes prior to opening.
2. Go to Tomorrowland. Ride Space Mountain.
3. In Tomorrowland, ride the Buzz Lightyear.
4. Go to Fantasyland. Ride the Matterhorn Bobsleds.
5. Go to Critter Country and ride Splash Mountain. Use FASTPASS if the wait exceeds 35 minutes.
6. Ride Winnie the Pooh.
7. In Adventureland ride Indiana Jones. Use FASTPASS if the wait exceeds 30 minutes.
8. Ride the Jungle Cruise.
9. In Fantasyland ride Peter Pan.
10. In Frontierland ride Big Thunder Railroad. If the wait exceeds 20 minutes use FASTPASS.
11. Go to New Orleans Square. Experience the Haunted Mansion.
12. Ride Pirates of the Caribbean.
13. Check the return time of FASTPASSes. Eat if you're hungry.
14. In New Orleans Square ride the riverboat.
15. Check for shows at the Golden Horseshoe and the Fantasyland Theater.
16. In Tomorrowland ride Star Tours. Use FASTPASS if the wait exceeds 30 minutes.
17. In Tomorrowland see *Honey, I Shrunk the Audience.*
18. From Tomorrowland, take a round trip on the Disney Railroad.
19. Back in Tomorowland ride Star Tours.
20. Go to Fantasyland. Ride It's A Small World.
21. Explore Mickey's Toontown.
22. Check for parades, fireworks, and *Fantasmic!* and work them into your schedule.
23. See attractions you missed.
24. On Main Street see Disneyland: *The First 50 Years.*

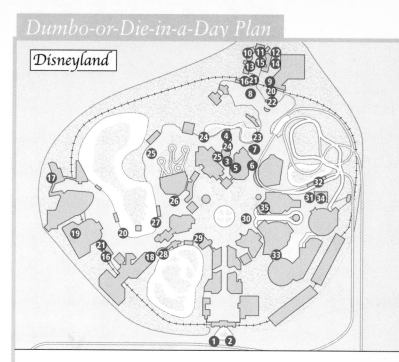

Disneyland

1. Arrive 30–40 min. prior to opening.
2. Line up at any gate with a short line.
3. Go to Fantasyland via the castle.
4. Ride Dumbo, the Flying Elephant.
5. Ride Peter Pan's Flight.
6. Ride Alice in Wonderland.
7. Ride the Mad Tea Party.
8. Go to Mickey's Toontown.
9. Ride Roger Rabbit's Car Toon Spin (FASTPASS).
10. Ride Gadget's Go Coaster.
11. Try Goofy's Bounce House.
12. Tour Mickey's House.
13. Tour Chip 'n' Dale Treehouse.
14. Tour Minnie's House.
15. See *Miss Daisy,* Donald's Blast.
16. Take the train to New Orleans Square.
17. Walk to Critter Country, see Winnie the Pooh.
18. Ride Pirates of the Caribbean.
19. See the Haunted Mansion.
20. Take a raft to Tom Sawyer Island.
21. Take the train from New Orleans Square to Fantasyland/Toontown.
22. Ride It's a Small World.
23. Ride the Casey Jr. Circus Train or the Storybook Land Canal Boats.
24. Ride the King Arthur Carousel.
25. Ride Pinocchio's Daring Journey if the wait is less than 15 minutes.
26. Go to Frontierland.
27. Ride the *Mark Twain* Riverboat or the Sailing Ship *Columbia.*
28. Explore Tarzan's Treehouse.
29. See the *Enchanted Tiki Birds* show.
30. Go to Tomorrowland.
31. Obtain a FASTPASS for Autopia.
32. Take a round-trip monorail ride.
33. See *Honey, I Shrunk the Audience.*
34. Ride the Tomorrowland Autopia.
35. Ride Buzz Lightyear using FastPass.
36. See parades and live shows.

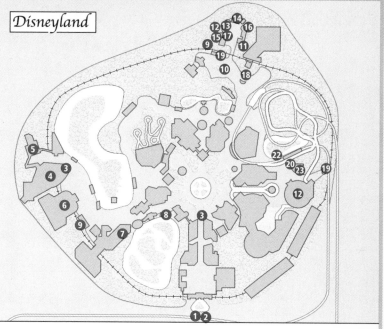

Disneyland

1. Arrive 30–40 min. prior to opening.
2. Line up at any gate 13 ot 20.
3. Go to Critter Country.
4. Ride Splash Mountain.
5. Experience Winnie the Pooh.
6. See the Haunted Mansion.
7. Ride Pirates of the Caribbean.
8. Take the Jungle Cruise.
9. Take the train from New Orleans Square to Fantasyland/Toontown.
10. Go to Mickey's Toontown.
11. Ride Roger Rabbit's Car Toon Spin.
12. Ride Gadget's Go Coaster.
13. Try Goofy's Bounce House.
14. Tour Mickey's House.
15. Tour Chip 'n' Dale Treehouse.
16. Tour Minnie's House.
17. See the *Miss Daisy*, Donald's boat, Next to Goofy's Bounce House.
18. Ride It's a Small World.
19. Take the train from Fantasyland/ Toontown around the park once, then get off at Tomorrowland.
20. Obtain a FASTPASS for Autopia.
21. See *Honey, I Shrunk the Audience*.
22. Take a round-trip monorail ride.
23. Ride Autopia.
24. See parades and live shows.

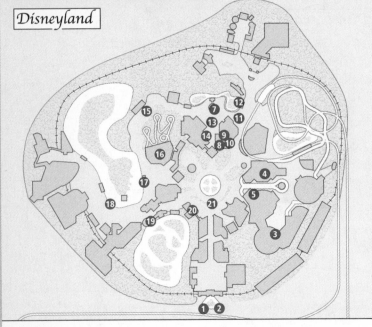

Disneyland

1. Arrive 30–40 min. prior to opening. If
2. Line up at gate 13 or 20.
3. Ride Space Mountain.
4. Ride Buzz Ligtyear.
5. Ride Star Wars.
6. Go to Fantasyland.
7 Ride Dumbo, the Flying Elephant.
8. Ride Peter Pan's Flight.
9. Ride Mr. Toad's Wild Ride.
10. Ride Alice inWonderland.
11. Ride the Mad Tea Party.
12. Ride the Storybook Land Canal
    Boats.
13. Ride the King Arthur Carousel.
14. Ride Pinocchio's Daring Journey.
15. Go to Frontierland.
16. Ride Big Thunder Mountain.
17. Ride the *Mark Twain* Riverboat or
    the Sailing Ship *Columbia*.
18. Take a raft to Tom Sawyer Island.
19. Explore Tarzan's Treehouse.
20. See the show at the Enchanted Tiki
    Room.
21. See parades and live shows.

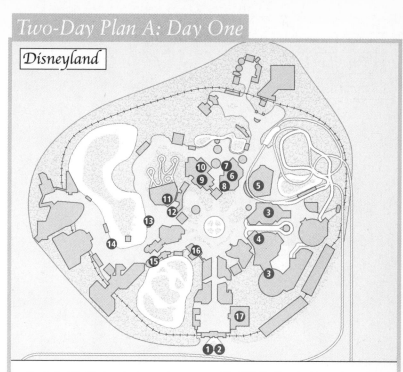

1. Arrive 30–40 min. prior to opening.	**11.** Ride Big Thunder Mountain.
2. Line up at gate 13 or 20.	**12.** Eat lunch.
3. Ride Space Mountain and Buzz Lightyear.	**13.** Ride the *Mark Twain* Riverboat or the Sailing Ship *Columbia*. (Work live shows and parades into the Touring Plan.)
4. Ride Star Tours.	
5. Ride the Matterhorn Bobsleds.	
6. Ride Alice in Wonderland.	**14.** Take a raft to Tom Sawyer Island.
7. Ride Mr. Toad's Wild Ride.	**15.** Tour Tarzan's Treehouse.
8. Ride Peter Pan's Flight.	**16.** See the *Enchanted Tiki Birds* show.
9. Ride Snow White's Scary Adventures.	**17.** See *Disneyland: The First 50 Years*.
10. Ride Pinocchio's Daring Journey.	**18.** See parades and live shows.

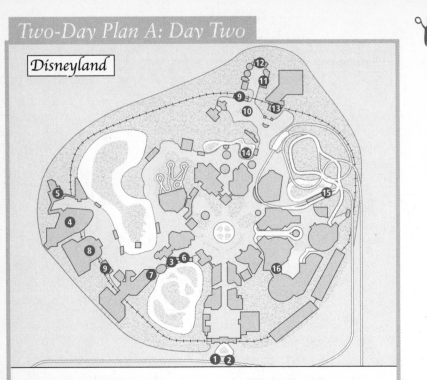

Disneyland

1. Arrive 30–40 min. prior to opening.
2. Line up at gate 13 or 20.
3. Ride Indiana Jones.
4. Ride Splash Mountain.
5. Experience Winnie the Pooh.
6. Ride the Jungle Cruise.
7. Ride Pirates of the Caribbean.
8. See the Haunted Mansion.
9. Take the train from New Orleans Square to the Fantasyland/Toontown Station.
10. Go to Mickey's Toontown.
11. Ride Roger Rabbit's Car Toon Spin (FASTPASS).
12. Tour Mickey's and Minnie's houses.
13. Ride It's a Small World.
14. Ride the Storybook Land Canal Boats.
15. Take a round-trip on the monorail.
16. Return to Tomorrowland on the monorail. See *Honey, I Shrunk the Audience*.
17. See parades and live shows.

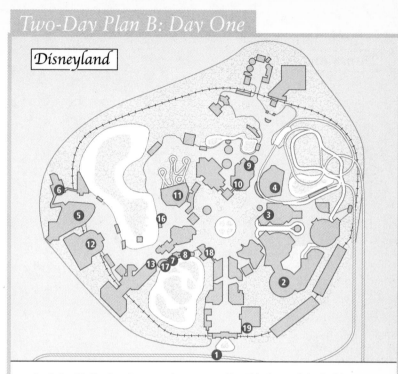

Disneyland

1. Arrive 30–40 min. prior to opening.
2. Ride Space Mountain
3. Ride Buzz Lightyear.
4. Ride the Matterhorn Bobsleds.
5. Ride Splash Mountain.
6. Experience Winnie the Pooh.
7. Ride Indiana Jones.
8. Ride the Jungle Cruise.
9. Ride Alice in Wonderland.
10. Ride Peter Pan's Flight.
11. Ride Big Thunder Mountain.
12. See the Haunted Mansion.

13. Ride Pirates of the Caribbean.
14. Eat lunch.
15. Check daily schedule for live performances.
16. Ride the *Mark Twain Riverboat* or the Sailing Ship *Columbia*. (Work live shows and parades into the Touring Plan.)
17. Tour Tarzan's Treehouse.
18. See the *Enchanted Tiki Birds* show.
19. See *Disneyland: The First 50 Years*.

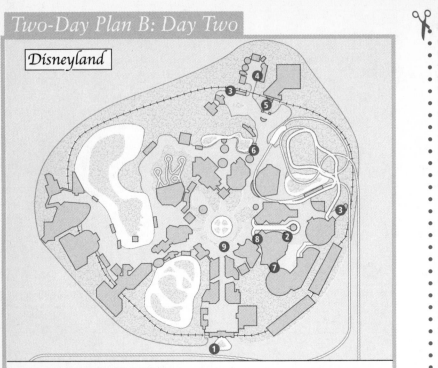

Disneyland

1. Arrive at the park about 5:30 p.m.
2. Ride Star Tours or obtain a FASTPASS.
3. Take the Disneyland Railroad from Tomorrowland to Mickey's Toontown.
4. In Toontown, ride Roger Rabbit's Car Toon Spin.
5. Ride It's a Small World. (Work live shows and parades into Touring Plan.)
6. Ride the Storybook Land Canal Boats.
7. See Honey, *I Shrunk the Audience* in Tomorrowland.
8. Ride Star Tours using your FASTPASS.
9. See parades and live shows.

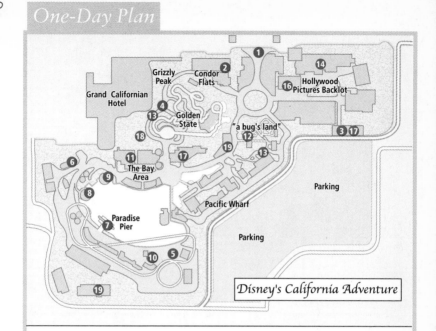

Disney's California Adventure

1. Arrive 30 min. prior to opening.
2. Ride Soarin' over California.
3. Go to the Tower of Terror and obtain FASTPASS.
4. Ride Grizzly River Run or get FASTPASS.
5. Ride California Screamin'.
6. Ride Mulholland Madness.
7. Ride the Sun Wheel.
8. Ride the Orange Stinger.
9. Ride the Golden Zephyr.
10. If your party includes small children, ride King Triton's Carousel.
11. See *Golden Dreams* as your schedule permits.
12. See *It's Tough to Be a Bug*.
13. Try the kiddie rides at Flik's Fun Fair if there are small children in your party.

14. Ride Monsters, Inc.
15. Eat lunch if you like.
16. See any of the three shows in the Hollywood Pictures Backlot: *Playhouse Disney: Live on Stage,* the current show at the Hyperion Theater, and *Muppet Vision 3-D.*
17. Ride Tower of Terror, using FASTPASS.
18. If you have children, visit the Redwood Creek Challenge Trail.
19. Visit the winery and tortilla and bread–making demonstrations in Golden State.
20. Check the entertainment schedule for parades, live performances, fireworks, and special events.

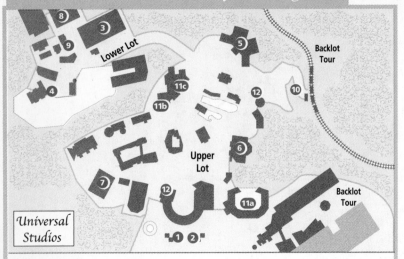

1. Arrive 20 minutes prior to opening, buy your admission, and wait at the turnstiles.
2. Ask if any rides or shows are closed. Adjust your plan accordingly.
3. Go to Lower Lot and ride Revenge of the Mummy.
4. Experience Jurassic Park: The Ride.
5. In the Upper Lot ride Back to the Future: The Ride.
6. See *Shrek 4-D*.
7. See *Terminator 2: 3-D*.
8. See *Backdraft* and the Special Effects stages.
9. Visit Lucy, A Tribute.
10. Eat lunch and take the Studio Tour if you wish.
11. See (in any order) *Waterworld* **(11a)**, *Animal Planet Live!* **(11b)**, and *Fear Factor Live* **(11c)**.
12. Check out Van Helsing Fortress Dracula, the *Blues Brothers Show,* or the Nickelodeon Blast Zone.
13. Check the daily schedule for live performances.